Embodied Music Cognition and Mediation Technology

# Embodied Music Cognition and Mediation Technology

Marc Leman

The MIT Press
Cambridge, Massachusetts
London, England

MIT Press books may be purchased at special quantity discounts for business or sales promotional use. For information, please email special_sales@mitpress.mit .edu or write to Special Sales Department, The MIT Press, 55 Hayward Street, Cambridge, MA 02142.

This book was set in Sabon on 3B2 by Asco Typesetters, Hong Kong. Printed and bound in the United States of America.

Library of Congress Cataloging-in-Publication Data

Leman, Marc, 1958–
Embodied music cognition and mediation technology / Marc Leman.
  p.  cm.
Includes bibliographical references and index.
ISBN 978-0-262-12293-1 (hardcover : alk. paper)
1. Music—Psychological aspects. 2. Music—Physiological aspects. 3. Musical perception. I. Title.
ML3800.L57  2007
781′.11—dc22                                             2006035169

10  9  8  7  6  5  4  3  2  1

# Contents

# Preface

The idea to write a book about embodied music cognition was inspired by traveling. Visits to the postgraduate school of the Music Technology Group of Pompeu Fabra University in Barcelona (June 2003), the Kulturwissenschaftliches Forschungskolleg Media und Kulturelle Kommunikation (December 2003) of the University of Cologne, and the Max Planck Institute for Cognitive Neuroscience in Leipzig (May 2005) introduced me to research groups that specialized in different methodologies. These groups were all working on music, but their diversity in approaching the matter was quite striking and was largely determined by the research discipline. Attending the Conference on Interdisciplinary Musicology (CIM 2004), the Computer Music Modeling and Retrieval Conference (CMMR 2004), the Rhythm Perception and Production Workshop (RPPW 2005), the International Conference on Music Information Retrieval (ISMIR 2004), and participating in national and international research projects (e.g., MAMI, MEGA, ConGAS, S2S²) convinced me that there was a need for an approach that would unify music research, thereby focusing on what music is about and what it does to people.

I thought that such a unifying approach could be of value to a broad range of scholars and students with backgrounds in musicology, philosophy, engineering, physics, psychology, and neuroscience. However, I realize that my ambition is a very tall order and that this book is just the starting point of that idea. In that sense, this book is more a philosophical essay about the foundations of music research and a journey into possibilities rather than a survey of all empirical research results that would support my viewpoint. I hope that the viewpoints presented here can be elaborated and expanded in the near future.

My viewpoints were discussed with colleagues with whom I was involved in several scientific and educational activities. In particular, I thank my colleagues and friends A. Camurri (Genoa), R. I. Godøy (Oslo), J. Louhivuori and P. Toiviainen (Jyväskylä), A. Schneider (Hamburg), and U. Seifert (Cologne), who have been very close to me for many years, and with whom I organized three summer schools in systematic musicology (1999, 2001, 2006). It was in 2001, on a terrace in Jyväskylä, that the need for such a book was first expressed, and I am pleased to offer here my part of the work.

Basic ideas of this book have been explored at my institute (IPEM, Department of Musicology) at Ghent University, and I thank my students, collaborators, and colleagues O. Cornelis, L. De Bruyn, F. Desmet, L. De Voogdt, J. Dierickx, A. Ganzevoort, E. Heylen, M. Lesaffre, H. Li, G. Martens, J.-P. Martens, D. Moelants, I. Schepers, F. Styns, K. Tanghe, L. van Noorden, and V. Vermeulen for their contributions, which include their participation in the lively IPEM think tank meetings. Thanks also to the many colleagues abroad who contributed to my viewpoint in discussions and during project meetings, workshops, lectures, collaborations, and summer schools. I thank F. Carreras (Pisa) and H. Sabbe (Bruges) for critical comments on the first draft of this book. They supported me to continue and clarify my topic. I owe much to the late J. L. Broeckx (Ghent), great musicologist and humanist, for his friendship. Finally, this book could never have been written without the help of my family. My last words of thanks go to my wife, Magda, and son, Batist, for their patience with a husband and father who was too often mentally absent, even if corporeally present.

# Introduction

Modern digital media tend to handle music as encoded physical energy, while the human way of dealing with music is based on beliefs, intentions, interpretations, experiences, evaluations, and significations. How can this gap be closed? What kind of mediation is needed to bridge the gap? And how can engineers, psychologists, brain scientists, and musicologists contribute to this? What would be a good approach in handling these questions?

This book offers a framework for dealing with the above questions. It is based on a hypothesis about the nature of musical communication, which is supposed to be rooted in a particular relationship between musical experience (mind) and sound energy (matter). In this mind/matter relationship, the human body can be seen as a biologically designed mediator that transfers physical energy up to a level of action-oriented meanings, to a mental level in which experiences, values, and intentions form the basic components of music signification. The reverse process is also possible: that the human body transfers an idea, or mental representation, into a material or energetic form. This two-way mediation process is largely constrained by body movements, which are assumed to play a central role in all musical activities. The embodied music cognition approach assumes that the (musical) mind results from this embodied interaction with music. The approach can be considered an extension of, or perhaps an alternative to, the classical (disembodied) music cognition approach.

The first chapter introduces the main theme of the book by considering the practice of musical signification. This practice is fundamentally based on musical experience, but it also involves music description, in particular when these experiences are communicated. I argue in favor of a musical signification practice that is based on action, action measurement, and action-based descriptors of music. This approach holds the promise that the natural mediator for music (which is the human body) can be extended with (artificial) mediation technologies so that mental activity can cross the traditional boundaries into environments (digital or virtual) that cannot otherwise be accessed by the natural mediator. The rest of the book can be seen as an unfolding and an application of this idea. Broadly speaking, the theory of embodied music cognition is developed in chapters 3–5, and the applications are discussed in chapters 6–7.

The second chapter gives a historical and philosophical overview of the major music research paradigms that are important as background for this book. Starting from Greek philosophy, attention is focused on the difference between disembodied and embodied approaches to music, and on the role of empirical approaches and technology in modern music research.

In the third chapter, I start constructing the framework by looking at the relationship between a human subject and its environment. This chapter introduces a dynamic ecological model for understanding how subjects can realize the transformation from physical energy to cultural abstractions, and vice versa. The next chapter goes deeper into the central mechanism of embodied cognition: the coupling of action and perception. It investigates how music can be understood as having an action-based and goal-directed character. The fifth chapter explores the idea that action-based understanding of music may be stratified, involving different degrees of corporeal engagement from synchronization to attuning and to empathy, and from observation to imitation and to emotional engagement.

In chapters 6 and 7, the feasibility of the embodied music cognition approach is studied in two core areas of modern music mediation research: interaction with musical instruments (how to build mediation tools that allow flexible and spontaneous expression of artistic ideas), and music search and retrieval (how to build mediation tools that allow search for and retrieval of music in a database or digital music library). The enormous reservoir of musical information on the Internet, for example, calls for flexible access based on the connection between human communication, and machine search-and-retrieval technology. Can we find a way of searching for music on the Internet which does justice to human perception, human cognition, motor interaction, and emotive involvement with music? Can we find a way of interacting with machines so that artistic expression can be fully integrated with contemporary technologies? What tools should be developed in order to achieve these goals, and what are the human ways of acting in these contexts? In these two domains, I show how an embodied music cognition approach, based on corporeal articulations and semantic descriptions, can contribute to the development of a mediation technology.

Embodied Music Cognition and Mediation Technology

# 1 Musical Experience and Signification

During the twentieth century, there was a dramatic change in the way people had access to music. Originally, music was accessible only in an environment where it was played. There needed to be a direct transfer of sound energy from musician to listener. However, since the late nineteenth century, music recording technology has made it possible to encode the sound energy on a material substrate. As a result, access to music has become mediated by technologies. The encoded energy can be purchased in a shop and reproduced as audible music at home, using an appropriate player.

Since the mid-1990s, with the advent of electronic media and communication networks, the economic chain involving music has developed to a level where access to the production, distribution, and consumption of music has become fast, individualized, and, above all, mediated by electronic technology. The major outcome of one century of technological development is that music is available in huge amounts, just a few computer mouse clicks away from our ears.

Yet, while music may be available in large quantities just a few mouse clicks away, it is far from evident which mouse clicks should be used in order to find and retrieve the music one really wants to purchase. Music is still accessed in terms of metadata such as the name of a composer or the title of a song, but not in terms of how it sounds or how it feels. Technologies for content-based access to music—that is, for access to the inside of music, as exists for texts—are still in development. Access to music from a personal, experience-based point of view is in the research phase. At this moment, there is a media technology which can provide a stream of musical information in just a few seconds, but there is no mature mediation technology based on content and experience. Nor is the technology always very transparent. In many cases, the technology is an obstacle that makes access to music difficult for many users.

Hence the paradoxical situation that music is available in abundance, but it is barely accessible by using existing descriptions and obtrusive technologies. Similar problems occur in relation to interactive music systems. These systems are equipped with sensors and sound synthesizers, and they allow the transformation of all possible gestural controls into sounds. Yet musicians often have the feeling that a fine-grained control over the music performance is missing, and that mediation technology stands between what they want and what they get.

What is needed is a transparent mediation technology that relates musical involvement directly to sound energy. Transparent technology should thereby give a feeling of non-mediation, a feeling that the mediation technology "disappears" when it is used. Such a technology would then act as a natural mediator for search-and-retrieval purposes as well as for interactive music-making.

I believe that the apparent non-mediation of mediation technology is a very challenging problem that cannot be solved by technology alone. It calls for a more general solution in which an overall theory of the human mind, body, and sound is needed.

How such a theory and technology of music mediation should look, and how an intermediary relationship between encoded musical information and the intentional use of that information should be worked out, is the major topic of this book. Given the challenge and interdisciplinary grounding of the problem, technological aspects should be sorted out in collaboration with engineering specialists. Note that what I am going to offer in this book is just a theory, or perhaps just a viewpoint, not techniques or technical specifications related to technology. My focus will be on mind/body/matter relationships rather than on the tools that implement their connections.

However, as always, a good understanding of the problem is halfway to the solution. Therefore, the first thing needed in order to build the theory is an understanding of the practice of music signification: of how humans engage themselves with music and why they do so. From there, it will be possible to outline the main themes that should be taken into account. Accordingly, this chapter introduces the problem of music signification and aims at analyzing the main themes of a theory of music mediation. Section 1.1 introduces the distinction between direct involvement with music and description of this involvement. In both cases, it seems that subjective engagement with music is important. The section 1.2 considers to what extent a subjectivist approach can contribute to a technology of music mediation. In section 1.3 it will be argued that the position of subjectivism is difficult to maintain because of its weak philosophical foundation in skepticism, but an alternative subject-oriented account, based on human action, can be proposed. In section 1.4, this action-oriented alternative is considered in terms of three foundations: linguistic descriptions, corporeal descriptions, and the call for a transparent, technology-mediated access to music. These three foundations will form the framework for the chapters that follow.

## 1.1    Experience and Description

Musical sound can have a large impact on a human being, and this impact may be beneficial or, in some cases, harmful. For example, music can be beneficial for personal development, such as the forming of a personal self or identity, or for social bonding, such as the forming of a group identity (Hargreaves and North, 1999). Music may enhance sports activities and consumption (Wilson, 2003), and it can have healing effects (Thaut, 2005). On the other hand, there is evidence that certain types of music can have a harmful effect, even driving people to self-destruction and suicide (e.g., Maguire and Snipes, 1994; Wintersgill, 1994; Gowensmith and Bloom, 1997; Scheel and Westefeld, 1999; Stack, 2000; Lacourse et al., 2001; Rustad et al., 2003).

In this book, I take it for granted that music can have a powerful effect on humans, and I focus on a better understanding of this effect. This is necessary for two reasons: first, for the development of technologies for music mediation, and second, for improving our involvement with music and our use of music. Obviously, technologies for music mediation may facilitate access to music and, therefore, contribute to a better involvement with music. Technologies will be treated in the last two chapters of this book. Before that, we need to know what is meant by "being involved with music."

Involvement assumes a relationship between a person (henceforth also called a subject) and music. This relationship may be either direct or indirect. Figure 1.1 provides a schematic view of the subject/music relationship in terms of direct and indirect involvement.

First consider the notion of direct involvement with music. Many people try to get in direct contact with music. Why do they do so? Why do people make great efforts to attend a concert? Why do they invest so much time in learning to play a musical instrument? What is so attractive about music that all cultures have music, and that people want to repeat the musical experience many times?

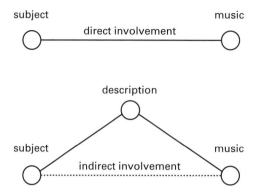

**Figure 1.1**
Schematic representation of the relationship between a subject and music in terms of access.

One plausible answer is that people try to be involved with music because this involvement permits an experience of behavioral resonance with physical energy. People seek such an experience with sound energy (among other types of energy) because they are moved by it and get absorbed by it, thereby attaining a particular feeling of unification with reality (Jourdain, 1997; Lowis, 2002). It may be assumed that this behavioral resonance gives a feeling of self-reward which is beneficial for their self-identity, interpersonal relationships, and mood (Hargreaves and North, 1999). Being involved with music may take the mind away from the routines of everyday life. It may contribute to mental order, and the general effect is happiness, consolation, and well-being. The effort is likely to be based on self-motivation, and the reason people try to reach this level of direct involvement may be largely for its own sake (Csikszentmihalyi, 1990).

This type of involvement is direct in the sense that it is a matter of corporeal immersion in sound energy, which is a direct way of feeling musical reality.[1] It is less concerned with cognitive reflection, evaluation, interpretation, and description. This involvement is a purely subjective activity based on personal opinions and feelings and on social musical activities such as being part of an audience listening to music at a concert or being part of an ensemble playing music. In essence, the feeling of being directly involved is something personal, experienced only by the subject. It does not require great skills to have direct involvement with musical reality, but if they are desired, great skills can be developed. In fact, the skills needed to deal with musical reality may vary largely—depending, for example, on whether it is just listening to music or playing it.

Next, consider the indirect way of being involved with music. This way proceeds by means of a mediator, such as a linguistic description of music, a score, or an audio player. The score and the linguistic description are examples of symbolic mediators. They mediate access to music as mental representation, but not access to music as sound energy. In contrast, the audio player is an example of a physical mediator. It mediates access to music as sound (or physical) energy, and via this way it is possible to form a mental representation of the music that is heard.[2]

### 1.1.1   Behavioral Resonance, Awareness, and Description

The relationship between direct involvement and indirect involvement, or between behavioral resonance and description, is peculiar in that the one does not exclude the other. In fact, it often happens that direct and indirect involvement reinforce one another. In this relationship, awareness (or consciousness) plays a central role.

Awareness can be seen as the subject's knowledge of the state of the environment in which music occurs. This knowledge may be a key factor in establishing behavioral resonance with music. In a concert hall, it may involve a process of mutual adaptive behavioral resonances (called entrainment; see Clayton et al., 2004) between musicians and the audience in the concert hall. The shared focal point, the attention of the audience directed toward the performers, the movements of other people: all may contribute to the "magic" atmosphere that facilitates direct involvement with what happens on the scene.

Yet, being too much aware, being too conscious of the musicians and the audience, may engage the mind in thinking and reasoning about the others. Activities such as reasoning, interpretation, and evaluation may disturb the feeling of being directly involved because the mind gets involved in a representation of the state of the environment, which distracts the focus and, as a result, may break the "magic spell" of being entrained. That is why the measurement of musical involvement by introspection is so difficult. Asking a subject to move a slider according to the self-evaluated degree of resonance with music engages the subject's mind in a process that may break direct involvement. As soon as direct involvement is self-evaluated and mentally represented in a conscious way, it seems to disappear. Verbal description is even worse because it requires that the situation first be mentally interpreted and then made explicit in verbal terms.

It is a likely assumption that awareness and immersion have to be balanced in order to be effective. As soon as awareness becomes too dominant and turns into a mental activity involved in representation and description, it may disturb behavioral resonance and entrainment.

### 1.1.2   The Need for Description

It would seem that direct involvement is what most people are looking for in music, whereas description is a disturbing factor in our relationship with music. Yet descriptions of music have a strong appeal to human communication needs as well. After all, the sharing of experiences by means of descriptions, shapes social bonding and is self-rewarding.

Information from other persons can establish the cognitive apparatus required to be able to make sense of music and thus to be involved with it. For example, modern music can be difficult to understand, but a proper description of the cultural context in which the music has been created may help greatly in appreciating it. Thus, description can open the ears to unknown aspects of the music. That is why talk about music is a daily occurrence. Even when the descriptions are incomplete, vague, and even partly incorrect, talk is often the only vehicle by which we can communicate about musical experiences, share our experiences, and make sense of them. While description of music may be secondary to the real world of music, it may serve as a tool to get involved with it. Description may set the resonance filters, deepen the involvement, and provide a signification. Therefore, it would be very useful to integrate that property into a music mediation technology.

The fascinating issue here is that a description may be of interest even if it is largely incomplete. For example, most descriptions of music are fairly general and abstract, such as "a melody which goes right to the heart," "wonderful colors," or "energetic rhythms." Yet these descriptions may be sufficient for other people to want that music, to purchase it, and to get involved with it.

In talking about descriptions it is important to note that what most people hear in music is often determined largely by the cultural context in which the music is heard. Often, the cultural context is rarely mentioned. Nevertheless, incomplete description works because the users of this description share common experiences and probably a common cultural context as well. This common cultural background is often known tacitly and, therefore, it need not be made explicit in the description. If the shared cultural context is an experienced context, then only a few words may be needed for people to understand each other. It can be assumed that descriptions work rather well with music, because, as humans, we share the experience of music, and often we also share the context in which music is happening.

Another important observation is that most descriptions of music are normally not directly observable in the sound energy that makes up the musical signal. Even if properties of sound energy are visualized, descriptions often cannot be directly associated with them. Indeed, how could we relate the term *beautiful* to some pattern in the sound energy? Many descriptions of music stem from subjective experiences which involve personal memories and interpretations of the cultural environment and social functions in which music appears. This tension between music and its linguistic description is well known in musicology. It has led to the widespread belief (in musicology) that description of music is all about this subjective involvement. People communicate about music because it is an essential aspect of life, giving meaning to the surrounding world, and because of shared musical experiences and musical contexts. Description forms part of a signification practice in which it helps people to get access to music. Therefore, it has been suggested that musicology should address signification practice. Musicology would be most useful for setting the cognitive resonance filters necessary for having access to music.

Yet, the type of description discussed so far is mainly based on abstraction, conceptualization, and verbalization. One may question whether this so-called linguistic description is the only possible form of music description, and whether alternative forms of description—nonlinguistic—should be considered which involve different levels of awareness and different perspectives of observation and signification. For example, a graphical description based on body movements of subjects involved in direct experiences with music could become an item for nonlinguistic description and further use in technology. In this book, I intend to show that embodied involvement with music may offer new possibilities for music description that challenge the role of linguistic description in music signification practice. The sections that follow explore the difference between linguistic descriptions and nonlinguistic descriptions of music in more detail.

## 1.2   Description as Subjective Interpretation

Musicology is traditionally concerned with musical signification practices in which linguistic-based description plays a central role. Musicologists tend to assume that direct involvement with music has an
individual and subjective bias which can be given a meaningful interpretation in relation to a cultural and historical context. The nature of this
interpretation process is worth considering in more detail. To what extent does this musical signification practice (and derived hermeneutic
methodology) provide access to music? And how can it be linked with
technology?

### 1.2.1   Signification Practice

The basic rationale of signification practice is that interpretations of
music can be turned into verbal descriptions that help people to get in
contact with the meaning of music. Descriptions reveal hidden meanings.
They provide access to signification, and hence may enhance the level of
direct involvement with music.

   The task of musicology is to reveal the meaning of music by linking
the subjective experiences with a broader historical and cultural context.
The method for doing this consists of a speculative pursuit of potential
interpretations (Hatten, 1994).

**Description as Subjective Interpretation**
According to Tarasti (2002, p. 117), "Music has always a content, and
this content has a conventional, arbitrary relationship with its signifier,
i.e. the aural and physical embodiment of the musical sign." In similar
words, Hatten (1994, p. 275) says, "Meanings are not the equivalent
of sounding forms. The linkage between sound and meaning, though
mediated by forms, is also mediated by habits of association that, when
stylistically encoded, produce correlations, and when strategically earned
(inferred through a stylistically constrained interpretive process) produce
interpretations." Monelle (2000), for example, speaks about cultural
temporalities and themes whose functions we can understand in particular contexts.

   However, reference to a broader historical and cultural context
does not necessarily imply that the clarification of musical meaning is
just a discourse about something outside music. Rather, what counts
is the interaction between the experience of involvement and the cul-

tural context (Scruton, 1997). This dynamic interaction draws on subjective grounds. It means that the interpretation, and hence the description, may change, depending on the subjective bias of the moment. Indeed, the cultural context is an extramusical reality which is shaped through arbitrary conventions that form part of our background and through which we have direct access to music. We use context to experience music, and we give significance to experienced music with reference to that context. A proper musicological interpretation, and associated description therefore should be based on a well-informed cultural and historical background.

### 1.2.2   Hermeneutic Methodology

A description of the fourth movement of Beethoven's Piano Sonata in A (op. 101) (Hatten, 2003; based on Hatten, 1994) makes it easier to understand the methodology of cultural musical signification (and its associated approach to music description) in more detail. The example aims at clarifying the way in which music may create figurative meanings (metaphors) in the eight-bar theme of the opening of the fourth movement (figure 1.2):

The fanfare-like allusion to victory in the first four bars is made authoritative by the *simultaneous* use of a 2–3 suspension chain from the learned style. The *successive* use of musette-like sixteenth-note swirls over a pedal in the next four bars evokes the pastoral, tropologically elevated by the juxtaposed learned style to a "high" pastoral emblematic of the spiritual or sublimely serene. The pastoral is

**Figure 1.2**
Beethoven, Piano Sonata in A (op. 101), beginning of the fourth movement.

contiguous with the fanfare and learned style in the narrow confines of a thematic period, and the result of their implied interaction is a fresh, emergent meaning that draws upon elements of each of the topics—something along the lines of "authoritative inner victory of the spirit," as opposed to the more familiar "heroic outer victory of the will." (Hatten, 2003, p. 82)

Hatten's description involves correlations of elements of musical structure with stylistic categories, all embedded in semantic interpretations that are driven by subjective experience. Hatten distinguishes no fewer than three stylistic categories: in the first four bars, the heroic style which is fanfare-like, based on a diatonic scale, played forte; the learned style, which uses imitation and implied 2–3 suspensions; and, in the last four bars, the pastoral style based on a soft, musette-like syncopated pedal point, flowing sixteenths in simple stepwise motion. According to Hatten, a first metaphor, or figurative meaning, emerges through the synchronic interaction of the heroic style with the learned style, such that the learned style enhances the heroic style to become authoritative. A second metaphor then is formed by the diachronic interaction of the learned-heroic (first four bars) and the pastoral style (second four bars). The learned-heroic style has an effect on the interpretation of the pastoral in that it becomes an inward spiritual victory instead of an outward heroic triumph.

The methodology thus becomes visible: particular musical configurations, made up of melodic, rhythmic, harmonic, durational, and textural elements, are related to knowledge of stylistic categories (called topics or themes). This forms the reference framework for the creation of stylistic opposition whose markedness gives rise to figurative meanings that are called musical metaphors or tropes. A narrative is thus constructed which relates musical structure to cultural meanings. In this method, subjective experience forms the basis of selecting the proper correlations and interpretations.

The method is known as the hermeneutic method. It is a speculative method because it is hard to prove that an interpretation (and its description) may be true. Several interpretations of a single musical fragment are possible. At best, an interpretation can be argued to be relevant given the cultural and historical context.

### 1.2.3 Dealing with Intentionality

In this approach, a description is conceived as a description of the music's intentionality, that is, a description of musical configurations having (presumed) intentions. This relates to human intentional actions, providing a natural level at which musical meaning can be accessed. Through the description, music can be understood in relation to subjective actions. Examples are configurations that express the "inner victory of the will" or that point to cultural contexts, such as "the heroic" or "the pastoral."[3]

Interestingly, the observation that the description of subjective experience draws strongly on the notion of intentionality is not new. It has been addressed by musicologists from the continental European hermeneutic tradition (see, e.g., Faltin and Reinecke, 1973; Stefani, 1975). The main idea is that musical intentionality shows itself in musical configurations that, in a goal-directed way and through convention, are related to certain stylistic categories having a foundation in history and culture. The hermeneutic method is assumed to reveal this relationship. The method can be conceived as a projection of musical structure onto stylistic-conventional categories through the lenses of subjective interpretation. Compared with structuralist trends in musicology, this approach entails a liberation of the subjective interpretation beyond the confines of mere formal descriptions.[4]

For some musicologists, the uncovering of the music's intention is the main goal of music descriptions. Tarasti (2002, p. 24), for example, expresses this point of view clearly when he says that the reduction of a musical phenomenon to a statistical fact is anti-semiotical in nature: "For semioticians to model a phenomenon in *hard-science* terms is a kind of mystification, since we deal primarily with human, cultural, and social behaviours—not physical laws." The music's intention is considered to be a category that belongs to the mental world. Any engagement with music is a signified engagement in that it is about personal experiences, intuitive judgments, and interpretations, which are hardly accessible with scientific methods. What musicology can do is provide descriptions which are grounded in a subjective ontology of experienced musical intentions. The discourse on music thus fosters the beliefs (a) that we engage with music exclusively in the mental sphere, (b) that description has a subjective bias, and (c) that what is described is the interpreted intentionality of music.

### 1.2.4  Mediating Access to Music

The speculative pursuit of potential meanings has been the basis for a multitude of approaches that draw on music analysis, introspection, phenomenological analysis, and historical and cultural contextualization (Tarasti, 2003). The question which concerns us here is to what extent these approaches can be of practical value in a technological environment that mediates access to music. I am thinking in particular about two important contexts of mediation that form the topics of two chapters in this book: interaction with musical instruments (chapter 6) and search for and retrieval of music (chapter 7). To what extent can music description, perhaps one that is based on a speculative pursuit of potential meanings, be relevant in human–machine interactions and interactive music-making? To what extent can such a description be taken as a starting point for applications that aim at finding music in a large database? What other types of description are possible in relation to mediation technologies?

Two entirely different approaches can be considered here. One approach, attributed to subjectivism, states that the involvement with music is so subjective that it cannot be related to mediation technology. An alternative approach, which is action-based, states that aspects of subjective involvement may subsume certain regularities which can be related to mediation technologies.

## 1.3   The Subjectivist Approach

Subjectivism holds that experiences can provide a basis for speculative interpretations of how music feels and what it means. Yet such descriptions are not based on any plan or principle because the cultural bias and the personal interest of a subject do not obey such principles. For that reason, music descriptions are assumed to be highly arbitrary with respect to physical reality. Consequently, if there are no regularities that govern the relationship between experience and physical energy, then there is no ground for the development of a mediation technology. For that reason, subjectivism is rather skeptical about possible mind/matter interactions (e.g., Välimäki, 2003).

I believe that subjectivism has a point in stressing the particular subjective nature of the musical experience. Yet skepticism with respect to possible correspondences between mind and physical reality may be unjustified.

### 1.3.1   Dualism

First, consider the idea that the individual subjective experience is detached from a physical reality. This viewpoint is difficult to maintain in the light of recent insights. In particular, neuroscience has provided compelling arguments that the Cartesian division between mind and matter can no longer be maintained and that a disembodied mind as such does not exist (see, e.g., Damasio, 1999; Jeannerod, 2002; W. Singer, 2002). The brain has no center that connects the parallel worlds of mind and matter, as Descartes once suggested. In contrast to dualism, the concept of mind is seen as an emergent effect of the brain perceiving its own actions in relation to a physical environment (Erneling and Johnson, 2005). From that perspective, the subjective world of mental representations is *not* an autonomous category but a result of an embodied interaction with the physical environment.

In addition, evolutionary biologists do not find any evidence in support of a sudden qualitative difference between animals (in particular, primates) and humans. Instead, they assume a fluent evolutionary process from sensory to mimetic to more symbolic activities (Rizzolatti and Arbib, 1998; Fitch, 2005). In this evolutionary process, the body, or motor activity, is seen as the natural mediator which finally realized the development of mental representations, or mental models, of the physical environment. In other words, the mental world is not something of a different order to which humans suddenly gained access. Instead, it is the result of a gradual evolutionary process in which gradations of mental involvement, from animal to human, can be distinguished (Tomasello, 1999; Dautenhahn and Nehaniv, 2002; Meltzoff and Prinz, 2002).

By focusing almost exclusively on a disembodied mind, subjectivism puts itself into a difficult position with respect to modern insights. And apart from that, the latent fear that the subjective experience of music would be less important in an approach which considers mediation processes between physical energy and mental representation is totally unjustified, as modern science fully acknowledges the role of subjective factors in human action.

### 1.3.2  Relativism

A second point concerns the arbitrary character of musical descriptions. The idea that music descriptions relate in an arbitrary way to physical reality follows from a disembodied mental perspective and its implied neglect of a relationship with physical reality. This position may ultimately lead to a kind of relativism which holds that music descriptions cannot be argued about, that descriptions are incommensurable, and that all opinions have equal value. In other words, that there is no truth, or no truth correspondence, for music descriptions, and therefore all opinions are equally arbitrary.

I tend to avoid this kind of relativism by arguing that there are aspects of music experience that can be described and can be useful in mediation technology. Not all aspects of subjective experiences may be grasped in descriptions, yet there is sufficient room for considering particular correspondences between subjective experiences and physical reality that could be useful in a context of music mediation. The proof of this statement is contained in the subsequent chapters of this book.

## 1.4   The Action-Based Approach

A way to proceed is based on the idea that action may play a key role in mediation processes between the mental and the physical worlds. The concept of action allows sufficient room for taking into account subjective experience and cultural contextualization, as well as biological and physical processes. Actions indeed are subjective: they can be learned, they often have a cultural signification, and they are based on the biomechanics of the human body. In that sense, actions may form a link between the mental and the physical worlds.

In what follows, I argue that the action-based approach calls for a reconsideration of the notion of music description which, so far, in music signification practice, has merely been associated with linguistic-based descriptions. Three viewpoints are introduced: (a) a reconsideration of the role of linguistic music descriptions, (b) the possibility of having non-linguistic descriptions of music, and (c) the role of action in media technology, particularly in technology-mediated access to music. These three viewpoints define a general framework for an action-based account of musical involvement which will be worked out in subsequent chapters.

### 1.4.1   Linguistic Description

First consider the role of linguistic description of music. It is of interest to reconsider the basis for having linguistic descriptions of music. What is the essence of a linguistic description? What can it handle, and what does it hide? In what follows, linguistic description is approached from three different perspectives: the facts that it is proposition-based, that it is socially embedded, and that it is referentially flexible (Tomasello, 1999).

## Propositional Basis

The propositional character of a linguistic description of a musical experience implies symbolic communication. The sender encodes the experience in a symbol, a formal entity chosen by convention which the receiver decodes and understands.

The main advantage of this approach is that instead of having to undergo the experience of the sender and feel what it is like to be involved with physical energy—with all the possible positive or negative consequences that can be associated with the experience—the sender can encode the experience in linguistic format and communicate about the experience. The meaning of the experience can be clarified by describing the event and the context, and an interpretation can be given with respect to these. By the sender's doing so, the knowledge, told as a narrative, can be of great interest to the receiver. The major advance is a rapid spread of knowledge which the receiver can exploit when confronted with similar events.

As this is applied to the Beethoven sonata, I may have listened to the sonata many times, and have enjoyed the music, but I may have missed the viewpoint that the two contrasting passages, which I experienced as being rather different in expression—the one violent and the other more calm—represent inner and outer victories of spirit and will. Thanks to a story about the romantic ideal of the pastoral and the heroic, I may be able to hear the music in terms of this potential intentionality. With this knowledge, I may enhance my direct involvement with music. Whereas before, I was engaged in the episodic nature of the note sequences, or in the mimetic character of the expressiveness of calm and forceful emotions, the narrative has disposed me to hearing the music in terms of potential goals. In that sense, the narration has changed my perspective of listening because I now hear the intentions of inner and outer victory. In this way, I have access to music at the level of an interpreted (or better, attributed) musical intentionality.

The narrative can be helpful in understanding the music in terms of previously unnoticed or unknown symbols and significations. It can set the filters for having direct involvement with music. Without the narrative, it might be difficult to access this particular potential meaning of the music.

## Social Basis

The narrative discourse is furthermore a logical discourse, but being logical means that there exists a common social and cultural ground for the receiver to understand the sender's use of symbols. This common ground is characterized by projections of personal experiences onto the narration, and these projections are understood because the receiver has similar personal experiences and works with similar projections or "language acts" (Searle, 1969).

Attention has been drawn to the fact that natural language is a symbolically embodied social institution that arose from previously existing social-communicative activities (Tomasello, 1999). The grounding of the logics, and the fact that we can communicate experiences in this way, are rooted in a social basis. It means that a linguistic narrative communication rests on an understanding of other persons as agents with characteristics similar to our own. What the sender says about musical experience can be important for the receiver, because the latter is a member of the same social group. Owing to that social context, the receiver can easily understand the intentions of the sender because they can be understood as projections of the receiver's own intentions.[5]

It can be speculated that during the course of evolution, the sharing of experiences through narration must have been a tremendously powerful tool that allowed humans to react in more efficient ways to the environment, to the benefit of their survival (Donald, 1991). In the context of technology-mediated access to music, there is no reason to believe that the linguistic format of communication, through speech or text, would become less important as a method of conversation.

### Referential Accuracy

A most powerful property of linguistic descriptors is their ability to express the nuances of subjective interpretations. Much depends on the context of the signification practice, but melodies and rhythms can be brought into association with a whole world of extramusical meanings and significations. Expressing these interpretations in a clear way is one of the fundamental properties of language. Symbols are good at capturing the differences in interpretation. No other description format allows users to make distinctions between the often subtle meanings associated with music.

To sum up, the above considerations show that linguistic description has a number of attractive features that can be used in the context of modern technology-based access to music. Yet, in description of music, these features should be compared with features of the nonlinguistic description. It will turn out that linguistic description can capture only a limited aspect of the musical experience.

### 1.4.2 Nonlinguistic Description

Next, we consider the role of nonlinguistic description of music. From the above, it is clear that the linguistic description detaches, as Tomasello (1999) says, its vehicle of communication from its perceptual and sensorimotor basis. In other words, the symbols communicated from sender to receiver do not represent the involvement with music in a direct way. Symbols are not the source that gives rise to the experience. Instead, they are about the music and about the musical experience. Symbols provide a mental access to music, with the likely effect that the contact with the spatial and temporal schemes that music induces is somehow lost. Indeed, musicologists have often acknowledged that the linguistic approach to music description is in principle not capable of accurately describing or translating musical experience (Bengtsson, 1973; Eggebrecht, 1973). Do we have any alternatives, then?

**Moving Sonic Forms**
One idea, defended by Hanslick (1891; originally published in 1854), is that music consists of form relationships without defined meanings, just like architecture and dance. A building, for example, does not mean something; it just shows its formal structure. A dance does not mean something either; it just shows its moving forms. In a similar way, says Hanslick, the content of music is "tönend bewegte Formen" (moving sonic forms).

Clearly, one can interpret buildings, dances, and music as being the expression of something culturally significant. But that interpretation, according to Hanslick, is a symbolic activity and therefore cannot be anything other than a subjective potentiality. Instead, forms, and in particular moving forms, have a direct impact on human physiology because they evoke corporeal resonances giving rise to signification.

**Corporeal Engagement**
The notion of moving sonic form, with emphasis on the fact that these sonic forms move and have a physical impact on our bodies, is highly interesting. Moving sonic forms do something with our bodies, and therefore have a signification through body action rather than through thinking. Therefore, this type of signification could be called corporeal signification, in contrast with cerebral signification.

Unfortunately, corporeal signification is difficult to express by using linguistic descriptions. The reason is that motor activities are difficult to access because our awareness of them is limited. As a result, descriptions of corporeal signification can hardly be based on the hermeneutic method because the latter focuses on interpretation and symbolization of a mental awareness involving music. Therefore, if corporeal signification is indeed a genuine form of direct musical involvement, then alternative methods different from linguistic descriptions should be explored that allow us to fully capture the corporeal aspect as an aspect of meaningful signification.

A motivation for considering forms of music description that differ from linguistic descriptions is that many people do not engage with music in terms of narrative reflections or interpretations of the music's intentions. This is evident in concert halls, where people communicate mainly with their body language. It is also supported by recent research in musical social behavior (North et al., 2004) which shows that there are many different uses of music. Many people will not have the necessary background in music analysis, history, and culture that would allow them to project subjective experience onto a linguistic narrative of cultural meanings. Does this mean, then, that all these people are barred from making sense of music?

Instead, what can be noticed is that people prefer to listen to music for the sake of its direct corporeal value: for relief after a stressful day, for getting in a good mood, or simply for distracting the mind from repetitive working activities. They seek access to music for the sake of its capacity to get into behavioral resonance and for the effects it has on mood. During these activities, most people tend to engage with music in a corporeal way rather than a cerebral way. They move about, they dance, and they actively gain enjoyment from the music. They interact with musical instruments, they play, and they engage in activities that require high-level motor skills. In those situations, signification is not merely a matter of projecting one's own experience onto cultural categories, nor is it the creation of linguistic, symbolic meta-experiences through linguistic narration that counts. Signification, most often, is just a matter of focus and direct involvement, and sometimes even a deliberate avoidance of rational thinking, getting away from awareness and description. The source for these experiences is clearly not the kind of intentionality and signification practice on which subjectivism focuses; rather, it is an embodied intentionality and signification practice that closely attaches to moving sonic forms, as if such forms engage us in behavioral resonances that we cannot resist.

Corporeal engagement with music therefore broadens the perspective of what musical communication is about. It forms a basis of a whole range of interactions with music. Apart from

·    Interaction based on linguistic or verbal narrative descriptions
and
·    Interaction based on symbolic or visual signs with information stored in lists, such as scores and tables containing descriptions of musical properties based on visual icons,

we should also envision

·    Interactions based on mimetic skills, or rehearsed action scenarios, such as playing a musical instrument,
·    Interactions based on goal-directed gestures that do not require highly developed skills but nevertheless may be highly culture-dependent, such as symbolic gestures,
and
·    Interactions based on direct episodic action sequences, involving responses based on our emotive, affective,[6] and expressive capabilities.

In other words, the corporeal basis of musical involvement allows a large variety of interactions with music. The next question to be answered, then, is whether these interactions may form a basis of music description.

## Gestures and Description

If moving sonic forms engage subjects in a process of corporeal signification, then it is very likely that body movement provides the key for alternative nonlinguistic descriptions of music. If this can be combined with technology, then it may be possible to develop a proper technology-mediated access to music. Such nonlinguistic descriptions, based on body movement, can range from deliberate actions to spontaneous behavioral resonances.

A simple example of a deliberate action that could be considered as a description of music is hand movement. Hand movements were used by the ancient Egyptians to indicate melodic movement (Gerson-Kiwi, 1995).[7] They have an appeal to forms of conducting or to forms of description that allow the expression of moving sonic forms. A simple form of movement is tapping along with a finger, but most people are capable of making more elegant hand movements when listening to music.

In many cases, body movements may express structural properties of music, such as pitch going up or going down. But other properties, such as objects coming closer or moving away, or sensitive properties of objects, such as the feeling of roughness or volume, can also be expressed using body movement. Obviously, these body movements can have different degrees of sophistication. They can be spontaneous as well as planned or arranged; they can be natural as well as conventional. The latter implies imitation learning, and perhaps intensive rehearsal, in order to acquire the necessary skills. Playing a musical instrument is a typical example of a very sophisticated motor skill, and the movements of playing the instrument are likely to tell us something about the signification process of the player.

In that sense, dealing with sonic moving forms in terms of body movement provides descriptions that are based on perceptual and sensorimotor mechanisms. These descriptions can be communicated and understood by other people. They may imply cultural background as well. By means of gestures, musicians tend to put cultural knowledge in their playing. Part of this cultural knowledge is likely to be nonlinguistic, such as the knowledge of stylistic gestures (that is, sequences of elementary musical movements which are relevant for a particular style at a particular place in a particular period of time). Grace notes in the execution of musical phrases of baroque music provide a good example of this. In short, there is indeed a basis for the ideas that (a) certain aspects of music can be communicated without linguistic descriptions, using body movements as description format, and (b) that linguistic descriptions can be based on these body movements.

## Social Basis and Flexibility

It may furthermore be assumed that gestural utterances, like linguistic utterances, rely on an intersubjective basis of shared understanding. Because of that social basis, gestures may become signs that act in ways similar to linguistic symbols—sign language, for example.

Yet in comparing gestures to linguistic symbols, it is evident that gestures are more restricted in their possibilities to express different meanings. The limited referential flexibility of gestures, and the fact that they are less precise in embodying the viewpoint of an interpretation, are due to the fact that the representational format draws on corporeal realizations and their perception as spatiotemporal images rather than propositions. Gestures, unlike linguistic utterances, are not detached from their sensorimotor basis, and therefore their accuracy for describing interpretive nuances is much more limited. This connection between form and content can be seen as a limitation, but it is at the same time one of the most powerful properties of gestures.

The sensorimotor basis of gestural communication may account for the fact that music from a largely unknown culture in Africa, for example, can have a meaning for Western listeners. This meaning then draws upon gestural forms of communication which can be picked up because the physical constraints of human bodies are universal. Even if the cultural meanings of the gestures are unknown, it is still possible to experience and feel the corporeal meaning because the music has its foundation in a physical constitution that all humans share. It is not the connection with cultural context that matters at this level of musical understanding, but the fact that the physical energies of the music correspond with a physical disposition caused by being human. In addition, gestures form the basis of mutual adaptive behavioral resonances that create shared attention and are responsible for the feeling of being unified with other people. In that sense, one could say that the gestural language of music is universal, because its moving sonic forms share human corporeality.

## Multimodality of Expression

Another important characteristic of nonlinguistic communication is the fact that forms or patterns expressed in one modality can be rather easily translated into another modality. In particular, this seems to be true for moving forms which have an expressive character (Lipps, 1903). The expressive nature of sadness, for example, can be communicated through different sensorimotor modalities, such as the movements of the human body, the color palette in a painting, or sonic forms such as slow tempo and legato in music. Given the multimodal basis of expressive communication, it is therefore of interest to study possible transfers from one modality to another.

Nonlinguistic descriptions, such as body movements in response to music, rely on the transfer of sonic moving forms to motor moving forms. The motor modality is then the expression of the original auditory experience and, as such, it can be considered a description of the original music with the body. But it also may give rise to new experiences, such as the visual or tactile perception of a moving body. In that sense, nonlinguistic descriptions blur the traditional distinction between experience and description because the description of a moving form in one modality may become the source of a new experience of a moving form in another modality. It is exactly this dual capacity of sensorimotor behavior, based on the unity of form and meaning, that can be exploited in combination with technologies that allow the registration of the physical energies (light, sound, pressure, etc.) that go along with moving forms.

To sum up, moving sonic forms may be captured by corporeal articulations (gestures). This may form the basis of a kind of music description that is of interest to music mediation technology. The fact that sensorimotor-based descriptions have both form and meaning contained in a single representation is both a weakness and a strength when compared with linguistic descriptions. It is a weakness because gestures offer less referential flexibility and are vague. At the same time it is a strength because gestures in one modality can be captured and translated onto another modality. Moreover, they provide a basis for mutual adaptive behavioral resonances, which is the basis of direct social involvement with music.

### 1.4.3 Technology-Mediated Access

Finally, consider the role of technology-mediated access to music. The main argument why corporeal-based involvement with music should be studied further, in addition to linguistic descriptions, has much to do with the unique role of technology with respect to music: that access to music nowadays proceeds via digital technology. This is the case in music production, music description, and music consumption.

Media technology, the infrastructure for sound production, sound distribution, and sound consumption, has had a very profound impact on musical culture and the associated signification practices. In the course of the twentieth century, music culture became almost completely dependent on highly technical infrastructures. Every small group playing popular music nowadays has electronic music instruments and personal or portable amplifiers. Composers use computers for composition and store their scores in electronic format. Concert halls use amplifiers to improve the acoustics. Music is recorded with advanced electronic equipment and recorded sounds, and once it is captured, is burned on CDs with laser technology, or is put on large mass-storage devices from which backups are taken on magnetic tapes. Music files are put on the Internet in compact MP3 format and distributed over cables, or wirelessly, to small devices that people can carry in the palms of their hands or hang around their necks. Thus, involvement with music depends largely on technology. This situation creates dependencies as well as opportunities for musical involvement.

## Dependencies

Dependencies occur when technology becomes a necessary instrument for human action. A concrete example is Napster. At the time of its introduction in 1999, Napster was considered a revolutionary technology for music distribution because it allowed millions of users to directly share their hard disks and exchange music files over a distributed network topology. Equally revolutionary was the clear effect of this file-sharing on user behavior. Communicating music, from that moment on, became a matter of sharing files.[8] The ease and speed of the technology was the real reason for the breakthrough of file-sharing systems, with a clear effect on how people behave with music (Kusek and Leonhard, 2005). More than ever, a piece of music has become a commodity which is rapidly consumed and thrown away in order to make a place for the next consumable. Browsers have become necessary to access information on the Internet and users have become dependent on them.

## Opportunities

However, this technology has also created new opportunities. The most important, perhaps, is that a larger number of users have unlimited access to music. They can learn about music and experience a broader range of music. After all, sharing files is nonrivalrous activity. The original owner retains a copy of a downloaded file and does not affect ownership of that file by sending copies to others. Users can browse the files of other users and discuss the music in the chat rooms of online communities. The Internet thus offers a new context for the verbal description of music, and it is available at almost no cost. It allows users to read phrases about music, to learn to describe music, and thus to have direct content-based access to music. In that sense, the Internet offers a new platform for learning more about music (audio files), charts (song rankings), discussion forums, and artist biographies and information (Salavuo, 2006). This learning is based on cognitive diversity and distributed expertise. Finally, sharing files contributes to new sampling practices, such as audio mosaicing (Lindsay, 2006), and reinforces the culture of music remixes and free distribution of original sounds and musical excerpts. In short, media technology has provided a number of new opportunities for music description and for having physical access to music.[9]

### Content-Based and Experience-Based Technologies

While the Napster experiment and related experiments with recent peer-to-peer technologies indicate that user behavior is changing due to the introduction of new music distribution technology, this change in user behavior in turn has had an effect on the development of media technology. Users started to use this technology as a recommendation engine, and they may be interested in using more advanced tools in order to further facilitate access to, selection of, and retrieval of music (Lesaffre, 2005). Also, in music performance, advances in technology have gradually been extended in the direction of active resources for expressive enhancement. Examples are installations which interact with humans in an artistic/expressive way (Camurri et al., 2005).

In that sense, modern electronic infrastructures have created a new demand for a content-based and experience-based access to music, which implies a broadening of the current focus on encoding and transmission of the physical signals to content-based processing, data-mining, and interactive engagement with sophisticated systems for music generation and audio control.

Unfortunately, linguistic interaction with modern electronic infrastructures is still the dominant form of access to information. Content-based access to images and sounds is currently far underdeveloped, and most modern technology does not allow users to interact with machines in a sophisticated way involving body language. For that reason, technology is often an obstacle because it does not provide an intermediary between the human mental approach to music and the machine encoding of physical energy. What is needed is a technology which no longer is an obstacle between the human subject and the music. The technology should become a tool that enhances subjective access to music.

The call for advanced content-based and experience-based technology characterizes a recent trend in the development of music and the multimedia industry, one that will allow users to engage with virtual agents that provide access to physical information streams (audio, video, etc.), related stories (text-based contextual information, lyrics), visual data-mining tools, and controls based on the recognition of human gestures and the expressiveness of communication. This offers a challenging opportunity for music research.

### External Storage Systems

These recent developments in media technology require a reconsideration of Donald's claim (1991, p. 321) that "temporal codes and phonological codes, the two retrieval workhorses of episodic and oral memory, are largely irrelevant to managing the external storage system." Donald stressed that formal education was invented mostly to facilitate the use of external symbolic storage systems for cultural products, and that experts in a field are those who have learned to be adept in accessing and using the relevant parts of the storage systems.

However, in view of what has been said above, it is likely that the focus on linguistic and symbolic storage systems should be broadened to include storage systems that have encodings of physical energies. Such storage systems make a difference, compared with pure symbol-based systems, because they allow users to interact on the basis of biomechanical and physical energies rather than on the basis of symbolic descriptions. This interaction brings episodic and oral memory, but also motor activities and other aspects of human communication, such as moods, emotions, and affects, back into the foreground of research.

Networks of storage systems thus become sources of genuine experiences and direct access to music rather than sources of symbolic interaction. Users, for example, could sing part of a melody in order to find similar melodies, or they could describe characteristics of the physical energies of the melody with body movement, or give audio examples and recommend a list of similar melodies. Likewise, interactive music systems can interact with human users in ways that allow a fluent exchange of physical energies from human to machine and vice versa. Modern mobile devices can be extended with all sorts of visual, audio, tactile, haptic, and olfactory sensors. Thus they may provide tangible access to external storage networks and interactive machines.

If technology were able to capture aspects of subjective involvement with music, it might become a genuine device with which it would be possible to interact in ways fully compatible with human communication. From that moment on, access points to multimedia networks would no longer be passive devices based on semantic interpretation of linguistic and visual symbols. Instead, access points would have evolved to such a state that they began to become active extensions of the human mind and body, engaging in different types of intelligent interaction. Such devices would be capable of interpreting the user's intentionality and connecting it with encoded physical energy. That opens possibilities for fully exploiting different aspects of musical communication.

To sum up, the main argument for exploring corporeal descriptions of music within a framework that unifies mind and matter is that technology has created a new context in which nonverbal forms of communication can be used to access music in a physical as well as a mental way. This is a very simple argument, but a highly relevant one because it offers many new opportunities for musical mediation.

## 1.5   Conclusion

Musicology has drawn attention to the fact that direct involvement with music is a highly subjective activity which may form the basis for a speculative pursuit of possible interpretation and meaning formation. The hermeneutic methodology fosters projections of this subjective involvement to the music's assumed intentionality.

A branch of subjectivism stresses the exclusiveness of subjective involvement and interpretation, but advocates a general skepticism regarding the possibility of a technology of music mediation. An alternative position is based on an action-based account of subjective involvement with music. In this approach, direct involvement with music is assumed to be based on physical energies having an impact on the human body and mind. This action-based approach accounts for signification practices based on corporeal articulations (gestures). It further holds the promise of finding a connection with media technologies which offer ways to exchange physical energies with human corporeal articulations.

New media technologies call for a new theory for music research that goes beyond subjectivist dualism and relativism. Such a theory of music must do justice to the physical as well as the mental sources of musical involvement. The suggestion is that an action-oriented approach, based on the notion of corporeality, provides a possible epistemological foundation for bridging the gap between musical mind and matter. Music, indeed, has a large impact on behavior, and action can be seen as the corporeal component that contributes to signification. Speaking about corporeal components, however, involves speaking about physical energies. The study of corporeality requires an understanding of the relationship between mind, body, and matter, using methodologies that draw upon experimentation and computer modeling.

The task of the subsequent chapters is to develop the topics that have been introduced thus far: the relationship between a subject and its musical environment, and a model for corporeality that will allow us to make the connection between subjective apprehension and physical, physiological, and mental involvement with music.

# 2  Paradigms of Music Research

To better understand the interdisciplinary foundations of modern music research, and in particular the relationship between mind and matter and the role of the human body as mediator, this chapter provides a summary of some main research approaches. This summary is nonexhaustive and draws upon what I consider to be relevant in the context of this book.

The overview starts with Greek philosophy and proceeds with a discussion of two paradigms of cognitive research based on studies of mind and body. Since the mid-1980s, models of music cognition have been expanded with nonsymbolic approaches to musical representation, and connections have been established between sound modeling and music perception. In addition, there has been a growing awareness that gesture and motor-based processing of musical content play an important role in connecting musical mind and matter. The result is a new paradigm of embodied music cognition which goes beyond the confines of classical cognitive approaches.

## 2.1  From Music Philosophy to Music Science

The roots of the modern views on mind/matter relationships can be traced back to ancient Greek philosophers such as Pythagoras, Aristoxenes, Plato, and Aristotle. Pythagoras focused on the mathematical order underlying harmonic musical relations, and Aristoxenes concerned himself with perception and musical experience (Barker, 1984–1989). This distinction between acoustics and practice is still relevant today, reflecting the basic distinction between the focus on matter and the focus on mind. Plato comes into the picture mainly because he attributed strong powers to music, but for Plato this was a reason to abandon certain types of music because of the weakening effect they could have on the virtue of young people.

Of particular relevance to my viewpoint is Aristotle's famous mimesis theory (e.g., in *Politics*, book VIII, chapter 5), in which he states that rhythms and melodies can have similarities with the qualities of human characters. Aristotle assumes that by imitating the qualities that these characters exhibit in music, our soul[1] is moved in sympathy with it, so that we become in tune with the affects we experience when confronted with the original.

With these views on acoustics (music as ratios of numbers), perception (music as perceived structure), and expression (music as imitation of reality), there was sufficient material for centuries of philosophical discussion. This would last until the Renaissance, when science and art were inspired by a new freedom of thought.

In the early seventeenth century, rational thinking became more prominent, which implied a new start for music research. In his *Musicae compendium* (1618), the young Descartes gives a good summary of the state of the art at that time. He divided music into three basic components, each of which can be isolated for study: (1) the mathematical–physical aspect of sound, (2) the nature of sensory perception, and (3) the ultimate effect of perception on the listener's emotions. To Descartes, the impact of sound on a listener's emotion was a purely subjective, irrational element and therefore incapable of being measured scientifically.

The scientific revolution—of which Descartes was a part along with such other towering figures such as Johannes Kepler, Simon Stevin, Galileo Galilei, Marin Mersenne, Isaac Beeckman, Christiaan Huygens, and others—had a major focus on the mathematical and physical aspect of music; the link with musical experience was considered to be a practical consequence of this focus. For example, the calculation of pitch tunings for the clavichord was a mathematical exercise that impacted on musical practice (Cohen, 1984). In line with this, Leonhard Euler proposed a numerical model for estimating the degree of pleasure (*gradus suavitatis*) or sensory consonance of a given musical interval. Structural aspects of perception, such as pitch, scales, and consonance, were clearly at the borderline of mathematical and physical inquiries. Emotions or expressive gestures were not yet considered to be a genuine subject of scientific study.

Parallel with this scientific approach to sound, the traditions of Aristoxenes and Aristotle culminated in rule-based accounts of musical practices such as those of Gioseffo Zarlino, and later Jean-Philippe

Rameau (Rameau, 1722/1965) and Johann Mattheson (1739). In *Der volkommene Capellmeister*, for example, Mattheson offers a manual of how to compose in a convincing way music that expresses certain affects. These composition recipes can be seen as handbooks for creating music that makes sense. Obviously, this approach was based on musical intuition.

In the eighteenth century, the science of sound and the practice of musical sense were not connected by a common concept. Sound as energy or matter was the subject of scientific investigations, while subjective experience was still considered to be the by-product of something that is done with sound. Although there was philosophy, often grounded in different traditions related to empiricism and rationalism, there was no real scientific theory of subjective experiences, and thus the gap between matter and mind remained significant.

## 2.2   The Cognitive Paradigm

The idea that a scientific study of subjective involvement with music was possible may date from the late nineteenth century. Researchers in psychophysics and psychology launched the idea that between matter and experience there is a brain whose principles can be understood in terms of information-processing. That idea formed the basis of the cognitive paradigm.

### 2.2.1   Pioneers

The first stage of this approach is characterized by the pioneering work of scientists such as Hermann von Helmholtz, Wilhelm Wundt, and Franz Brentano, who provided the foundations of psychoacoustics, psychology, and phenomenology, respectively. With the introduction of psychoacoustics by von Helmholtz (1863/1968), the foundations were laid for an information-processing approach to musical involvement. This approach assumed that music could be seen as the product of neurophysiological mechanisms that respond to sound input. It became very influential in music research because it provided an explanation of some fundamental aspects of music perception, such as consonance and dissonance, harmony and tonality. Numerical approaches could now be grounded in physiological mechanisms whose principles were known through scientific experimentation. Mathematical functions can capture the main input/output relationships of these physiological mechanisms, thus forming a link between physics and perception. This approach provided the physiological grounding for gestalt psychology in the first half of the twentieth century, and for the cognitive sciences approach of the second half of the twentieth century.

## 2.2.2   Gestalt Psychology and Systematic Musicology

The gestalt movement was much influenced by the work of the late nineteenth-century scholars Franz Brentano and Carl Stumpf. It gained prominence by about 1920 thanks to the work of Max Wertheimer, Wolfgang Köhler, Kurt Koffka, and others. About 1930, gestalt psychology of music had achieved a solid base of knowledge, providing a foundation for research in systematic musicology. This was based on the work of Stumpf (1883–1890), Kurth (1913/1973), Seashore (1938), Révész (1944), and many other scholars. The main focus was on the perception of tone distances and intervals, melodies, timbre, rhythmic structures, and sometimes emotions (see Hevner, 1936; Watson, 1942). However, after 1945, with the rise of behaviorism and operationalism in psychology, the original gestalt approach lost much of its attractiveness. There had been too many gestalt laws and not enough solid explanations to account for these laws. Yet gestalt psychology never really disappeared, and it continued to produce works of prime importance to general psychology and, in particular, music psychology. In the 1960s, gestalt theory gradually gained a new impetus, and was found to be of particular importance in combination with then up-to-date trends in cybernetics and information science.

As mentioned, gestalt theory was one of the pillars of systematic musicology (Leman and Schneider, 1997). One may point to Stumpf's many experiments on *Verschmelzung* and consonance (Schneider, 1997), to Schumann's extensive experiments on timbre that led to the identification of formants (Reuter, 1997), to experiments on rhythm perception, tonal distances, and tonal brightness. What emerged in this approach was a thorough cognitive account of music perception based on the idea that musical meaning emerges as a global pattern from the processing of information patterns contained in sound.[2]

## 2.2.3   Technology and Information Theory

The first approach that took music technology seriously into account was conceived of in terms of information theory (e.g., Moles, 1952,

1958; Winckel, 1960). Shannon and Weaver's (1949) notions of entropy and channel capacity provided an objective account of the amount of information contained in music and the amount of information that could be captured by the devices that process music.

The interest in information theory arose in the early 1950s, at a time when composers started to use electronic music mediation technology in their music production. There was a need for tools that would connect musical thinking with sound energies. Composition implies that a mental focus on abstract concepts and structures will sooner or later be realized in sonic forms.

Information theory provided an objective description of music. This focus was not a bad choice to start with. Music, after all, has traditionally been conceived of in terms of parameters, such as pitch and duration, that allow a formal description of physical energy. Information theory provided a measurement, and thus a higher-level description, of the formal aspects of musical form (sonic as well as symbolic). For example, a melody containing many repeating notes, or instead a completely random melody, could thus be measured and communicated in terms of a measure of its entropy (the amount of uncertainty of the notes), given the notes' probability of occurrence in a number of melodies. Since parameters such as pitch and duration also reflect mental categories, it could be assumed that such measures provided objective descriptions of the formal aspects of mental content. Because media technology allowed the realization of these parameters into sonic forms, information theory could be seen as an approach to an objective and relevant content description for music mediation.[3]

## 2.2.4  Phenomenology and New Media Technology

While information theory provided a mathematical theory of music information-processing, it was musical practice that actually introduced machine technology into music research. In this context, reference should be made to the pioneering work of P. Schaeffer. While using these new tools, he noticed that an objective description of music does not always correspond to our perception (Schaeffer, 1966). In line with phenomenology and gestalt theory (Merleau-Ponty, 1945), he felt that the description of musical structure based on information theory does not always tell us how music is actually perceived by subjects. Schaeffer therefore focused on different modes of listening to music instead of the purely structural features of music, and he related the perception of sounds to the manipulation of the analog electronic sound-generating equipment of that time.

Schaeffer's approach illustrated a growing interest in capturing the role of the musical mind in relation to sonic forms. Musical imagery (representation) could serve as a basis for understanding musical meaning (signification). The main new thing was that he conceived of this in terms of the new media technology of his time.[4] Schaeffer's influential approach can thus been seen as an attempt to understand the notion of a musical object from an intentional perspective, in the framework of analog audio technology. The ambitious program was useful as a paradigm for artistic explorations, but its scientific part—how subjective musical engagement can foster access to music by means of media technology—turned out to be difficult to realize, at least within a relatively short period of time.

In fact, after an initial period of what could be called free artistic exploration, the paradigm changed in the early 1970s (see Veitl, 1997), from a phenomenology of musical sound objects to a model-based approach that fostered the development of dedicated digital technologies on the basis of scientific research. The constraints of the emerging digital-based music mediation technology would soon put much more emphasis on the development of computational tools for sound synthesis (Mathews et al., 1962; Risset, 1966; Mathews, 1969) and creative composing environments (see, e.g., Loy, 1991). As a consequence, the objective structural description of music, rather than the exploration of the subjective understanding of music, attracted the attention of most researchers, for the simple reason that it was more feasible at the time to develop practical tools for composition than to develop tools for music perception.[5]

### 2.2.5   Computational Modeling

Schaeffer's project, as I understand it, envisioned an integration of composition and perception, giving justice to subjective interaction, but the technology to fully integrate the principles of music perception with media technology was not yet available. The unfortunate consequence was that music phenomenology and gestalt theory were henceforth considered to deal with purely subjective categories of musical objects, something that was not powerful enough to fully integrate into media technology.

An alternative approach to music description was then launched by the appeal of the information-processing psychology and formal linguistics of the late 1950s (see, e.g., Lindsay and Norman, 1977). The combination of experimental psychology and computer modeling, on which these approaches were based, offered a perspective for the study of music perception that drew upon the notion of simulation of mental information-processing mechanisms. Cognitive science, as the new trend was soon called, introduced the point of view that musical processing could be conceived of in terms of a machine that manipulates representations of musical content (Fodor, 1981).

The concept of melodic entropy, for example, could now be handled as a formal descriptor that could be worked upon in terms of formal symbol manipulations. Provided that some symbol-based reasoning engine could be specified for dealing with this and similar types of descriptors, other symbols could be derived from it. Hence, derivation and reasoning were important concepts in this approach, stressing the fact that symbol manipulations were in fact simulations of mental processes. Note how in this approach the mind again comes to the foreground, now as processor of chunks of information.

### Symbol Systems for Music

The application of the symbol manipulation paradigm to music (see, e.g., Longuet-Higgins, 1987; Laske, 1975; Baroni and Callegari, 1984; Balaban et al., 1992) was very appealing because a musical score is in fact a collection of symbolic descriptors that can be put straightforwardly into a computing system. Moreover, a musical score could in fact be interpreted as the description of a mental representation of music. Once the score is put into a computer system, a heuristics of symbol manipulation can be defined on top of it, and this would simulate mental involvement with musical information.

From the viewpoint of composers, the paradigm offered the possibility of conceptualizing the compositional process as a two-phase procedure: (1) the conception of a symbol structure (e.g., a score) and (2) the transition of the symbolic structure into an audio stream. Each phase in itself can be formalized in different ways. In the first phase, for example, rule-based systems and dynamic systems of all kinds could manipulate symbols and help with, or even replace, the mental process of composing a score (Ames, 1992). Manipulation of symbols could be based on rules, probabilistic theory, or cellular automata, to mention a few possibilities. In the second phase, musicians playing traditional instruments could translate the symbols into an audio stream. Alternatively, this translation could be realized by sound synthesis rules that define mechanisms for the transition of symbols to information streams.

### Methodological Solipsism

Although modern approaches tend to integrate symbol manipulation with feature extraction tools, it is important to be aware that pure symbol manipulation depends upon what Fodor (1981) calls methodological solipsism. Solipsism is a philosophical attitude which holds that the world around us is a creation of our imagination, and thus of our mind. Methodological solipsism means that the programmer of a symbol manipulation system creates an imaginary world of symbols and meanings that is meaningful solely for the programmer or another programmer who understands the symbols and their meaning.

The programmer is forced to do this because symbols, by definition, are free of semantic connotations. Symbol manipulation works only on the formal characteristics of the symbols, irrespective of their meaning. The interpretation of a linguistic symbol is therefore due to an organism that gives meaning to the symbols. That organism—the programmer—should understand the connection between the mental world and the material world.

From that perspective, therefore, pure symbol-based computational systems do not really offer a solution to the problem of the relationship between musical mind and matter. They provide a formal framework for dealing with the musical mind, but not connections with the physical world. Symbols work in contexts where a human actor is available for interpreting them and for making the link between the symbol and the world, as depicted in figure 2.1. Pure symbol-based systems, therefore, are useful in many contexts, but they fail to provide adequate solutions in many others.

The major difficulty is that these systems work with a conceptualization of the world which is cast in symbols, while in general it is difficult to predefine the algorithms that should extract the conceptualized

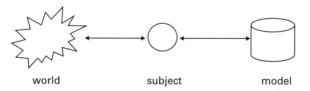

world            subject            model

**Figure 2.1**
In symbol-based modeling, human activity mediates between the world and the model. The knowledge in the model is symbolic. The relationship between the model and the world depends on the interpretation of a human mediator.

features from the environment. The predefinition of knowledge atoms and the subsequent manipulation of those atoms in order to generate further knowledge is a main characteristic of a Cartesian or rationalist conception of the world. Symbol systems, when used in the context of symbol-based modeling, should therefore be used with caution.

### 2.2.6   Empirical Modeling

The shift of paradigm from symbol-based descriptions and rationalist modeling toward subsymbol-based descriptions and subsymbol-based modeling was initiated by the interest in visual perception modeling (Marr, 1982) and the results of the so-called connectionist computation (Rumelhart and McClelland, 1986; Kohonen, 1995). Connectionism, in fact, (re)introduced statistics as the main modeling technique for feature extraction, as well as for higher-level forms of content-processing. With this approach, it was possible to study how musical knowledge gets organized in a memory. Given the limitations of symbol-based modeling, this approach was appealing for music research (Todd and Loy, 1991).

**Perception-Based Feature Extraction**
Subsymbol-based modeling provided an alternative to information theory mainly because feature extraction was no longer restricted to abstract measurements of information. Instead, feature extraction could be based on computational models that simulated the human auditory system. These models take the musical signal (physical energy) as input and extract from it the relevant features according to the constraints of physiological mechanisms of human perception. That approach, obviously, is much more justified in view of building bridges between musical mind and physical energy. Instead of abstract measurements, it focuses on those aspects of physical energy which are relevant for human behavior. The extracted stimulus-related features can then be represented as images, and dynamic interactions can be entertained that work upon those images.

The paradigm offers an empirical approach to modeling music perception. Figure 2.2 is a schematic overview of this approach. The input is a musical signal from which features are extracted, using a model that simulates the physiology of the human auditory system. These stimulus features can be called auditory images because they rely on principles of human auditory-based filtering of the audio signals. The images can be interpreted as reflecting the neuronal activations of the brain that are

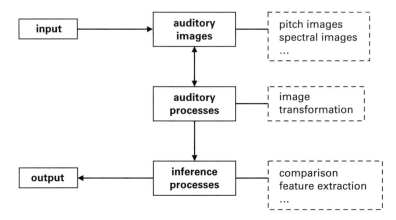

**Figure 2.2**
General schema for the processing of audio stimuli in terms of auditory images.

involved with musical information-processing. The auditory images are processed and information can be derived from them which in turn can be compared with behavioral data.

In this framework, auditory images can be further processed in different memory systems. Long-term memory would, for example, typically be conceived of as a statistical processor which extracts and keeps in memory the invariant images from the stimulus, whereas short-term memory would be conceived as a statistical processor for the immediate information content of the stimulus. The contrast between images in short-term memory and in long-term memory can be related to notions of musical meaning-formation, such as musical expectation, tension, and release of tension.

In my own work on the modeling of tonality perception, I have been using auditory models and principles of self-organization in order to simulate the growth of a long-term memory structure for tonal key relationships from audio signals (see, e.g., Leman, 1989, 1990, 1991, 1995, 2000; Leman and Carreras, 1997; Janata et al., 2002). The outcome of this research, I believe, is a challenge to cognitive musicology, in that it explains a good part of the experimental data on tonality perception from a sensory-based, bottom-up approach (Leman, 2000).

Figure 2.3 illustrates the outcome of a computer simulation that was realized in 1996 with supercomputer facilities of that time. The two maps give different views of the same "trained" long-term memory. From a computational point of view, the long-term memory is an artifi-

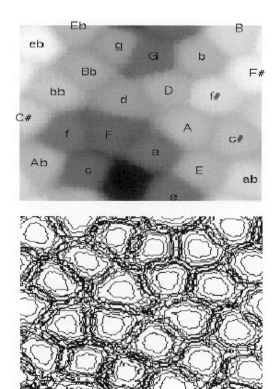

**Figure 2.3**
Long-term memory structure for tonality (adapted from Leman and Carreras, 1997). The figure on top shows the activation of a two-dimensional grid of neurons (black represents high activation). The neurons that are most responsive to a particular tonality are labeled. The figure below shows the same grid but in terms of boundaries between groups of neurons that belong to the same tonal key. (See text for further explanation.)

cial neural network, a statistical processor based on abstract principles of self-organization (the so-called self-organizing map; Kohonen, 1995). The map shows the output of the statistical processor, containing a two-dimensional grid of 10,000 output units ordered in a $100 \times 100$ array. The topology of the map is a ring. That means that units on top connect with units at the bottom, and that left units connect with right units. The map on top shows the activation of the memory, while the map below shows how the units are grouped into clusters that display similar response characteristics.

The memory was trained with seventy-two sound sequences that contained tonal cadences in all keys. The audio stimuli were first processed by an auditory model and the map was then trained, using the pitch images that came out of the auditory model. Such training consists of an adaptation of memory units to the images that represent the sound information. After training, the memory can be tested with labeled examples and the response structure of the memory can be mapped. The map on top has labels which show the response of the neurons when a cadence in the key of C is presented. The different shades of gray represent the degree of activation of the map. The cadence also activates keys that lie in the vicinity of C. Note that the map represents the keys in a structure that reflects the circle of fifths, with major and minor circles nicely related to each other. The circle of fifths is thus an invariant structure of the tonality space, and this structure can be easily extracted from the musical stimuli by a statistical method. Using musical audio as input, a trajectory of activations on the map can be followed (Leman, 1994, 1995; Gómez and Bonada, 2005).

The tonality space is low-dimensional, as shown in the experimental studies of Krumhansl (1990). From a statistical point of view, this can be demonstrated by applying the method of principal components to the pitch images. This method looks at whether high-dimensional data, such as the dimensionality of the pitch images of all seventy-two cadences used in the previous simulation, can be reduced to a lower-dimensional space. Figure 2.4 shows the solutions for two and three dimensions. In the case of two dimensions, the circle of fifths is clearly present, although the relationship between major and minor is not correctly represented. The solution for three dimensions shows how the circles of major and minor relate to each other. Once a structure has been developed, it is possible to match musical audio with it so that tonal keys can be recognized (Martens et al., 2005).

The framework allows the definition of tonal expectation, tonal tension, and relaxation of tension in terms of differences between extracted pitch images (Bigand, 2003). In Leman (2000), the calculation of tonal tension is simply a matter of a relationship between local pitch images (chords) and global pitch images (tone centers), and the amount of memory needed for this calculation is very low. Figure 2.5 shows how the index is built up by calculating the amount of similarity between local and global pitch images.

Results in perception-based computational feature extraction thus show that structural features of music, such as tonality, can be accurately

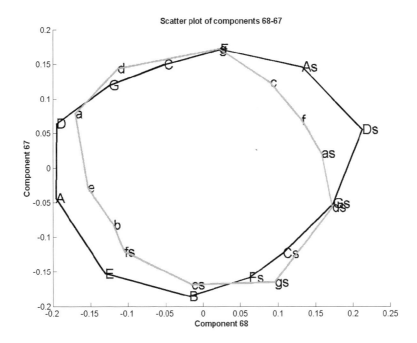

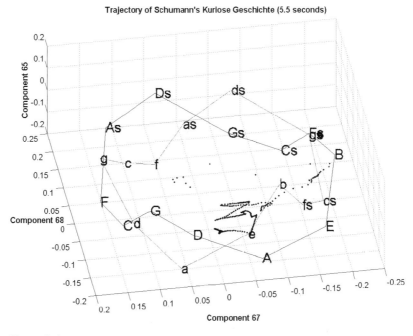

**Figure 2.4**
The tonality space is low-dimensional. The figure on top is a representation of the circles of fifths based on two components. The figure below is a representation based on three components. In this figure, the first few seconds of Schumann's piano piece "Kuriose Geschichte" have been projected onto the structure. The distance to the labeled keys allows the recognition of tonality in an audio signal.

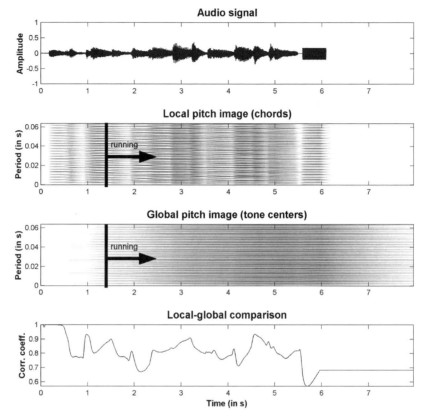

**Figure 2.5**
Tonal tension defined as a similarity between local and global pitch images. Time is represented on the X-axis. The top panel shows the waveform of the audio signal. The second and third panels show the local and global pitch images. In these panels, periodicity is represented on the Y-axis. The lowest panel shows tonal tension.

modeled and predicted using data-driven processing and empirical learning algorithms (Bigand et al., 2003). My results showed that a particular ecological approach to music cognition is possible, albeit in this case it was restricted to auditory-based processing. No multisensory processing or action-related issues were taken into account. Thus, the subsymbolic modeling paradigm conceived the simulated subject merely in terms of a passive statistical processor whose functionality is restricted to absorbing structural information from the environment. For certain applications in music engineering, this is a suitable way to handle things. However, as a basis for music cognition, this particular computational ecological approach is too restrictive because it does not allow enough room for sub-jective involvement with music or for the action-oriented bias of human perception.

## Semantic Description, Music, and Emotions

A possible adaptation is to broaden the focus on structural features of music to include emotions and semantic descriptions. Indeed, the tradi-tion on which cognitive musicology draws is not completely untouched by studies in subjective involvement. Reference can be made to research in experimental psychology in which descriptions of emotion and affect are related to descriptions of musical structure (see, e.g., Hevner, 1936; Watson, 1942; Reinecke, 1964; Imberty, 1976; Wedin, 1972; Juslin and Sloboda, 2001; see also Gabrielsson and Juslin, 2003 for an overview).

These studies take into account the subjective experience with music. Few authors, however, have been able to relate descriptions of musical affect and emotions to descriptions of the physical structure that makes up the stimulus. Most studies, indeed, interpret the description of structure as a description of perceived structure, not as a description of physical structure. In other words, description of structure proceeds in terms of perceptual categories related to pitch, duration, timbre, tempo, rhythms, and so on, categories that are also subjective.

In that respect, Berlyne's work (1971) on experimental aesthetics is important for having specified a relationship between subjective experi-ence (e.g., arousal) and objective descriptions of complexity, uncertainty, or redundancy. In Berlyne's concept, the latter provide an information-theoretic account of symbolic structures (e.g., melodies). They are not just based on perceived structures but are extracted directly from the stimulus (as symbolically represented). Modern approaches to empirical modeling tend to replace the information-theoretic account with compu-tational models of human perception (see Leman et al., 2005).

## Difference from Symbol-Based Modeling

The shift from symbol-based modeling to subsymbol-based modeling has often been understood as a matter of exchanging rule systems for statis-tics, and symbols for images. This view, however, may not be entirely justifiable, because rule systems may work on images and statistics may be applied to symbols. Instead, the main relevant distinction, in my view, concerns the status of the knowledge entities which in the symbol-based approach are defined beforehand, whereas in the subsymbol-based ap-proach, one tries to avoid the stipulation of such predefined entities.

A predefinition of the components that extract content from audio would imply that we can identify the atoms of our knowledge beforehand, that is, independently from our contact with the environment. However, such an approach would risk the programmer's deciding in advance what will come out of the system. In contrast, the subsymbol-based approach does not assume the predefinition of the knowledge atoms or an explicit description of symbol manipulation. Instead, it assumes that the perception of sonic forms can be simulated using statistical processing of stimuli-related features which are extracted from the physical environment using models of the human auditory system. Properties of a physiologically justified auditory system can be used in order to extract the relevant information from the environment by means of a statistical bottom-up methodology. This approach draws upon the idea that the statistics can find the most relevant knowledge entities contained in the stimuli.

However, the statistical processing should take into account that the information extracted from the data depends on its distribution in the environment. Indeed, the search for a tonal structure, as shown in figure 2.3, could be entirely misleading if the stimuli that are statistically processed do not already contain all possible tonal progressions. The circle of fifths would not emerge, simply because it is not contained in the data. Fortunately, tonality research can draw upon well-established knowledge from music theory which facilitates the definition of the problem domain and the distributions contained in it (e.g., Lerdahl, 2001). We know, in other words, that twelve minor and twelve major tonalities should be present in the stimuli; otherwise, the stimuli would not be relevant for the domain of our study.

Unfortunately, in many other studies it is impossible to know beforehand the statistical distributions of the categories we are interested in. This is the case, for example, in research that focuses on stimuli-related correlates of semantic descriptions of music. Single stimuli are often ambiguous with respect to the searched semantic descriptors. Typically, a very large number of musical examples would be needed in order to extract the invariant features that would account for the semantic description. Moreover, many varying examples would be needed in order to cover a broad range of semantic descriptors.

Compared with early empirical models of the 1990s (and due to the input of music engineering in this field), there is nowadays a larger and more advanced computational basis for statistical modeling of music, drawing upon statistical methods that fully deal with time dependencies and sequences (e.g., Duda et al., 2001). Modeling of musical expressiveness and performance nuances, for example, has been based on different techniques involving inductive machine learning, fuzzy logics, and different types of statistical modeling based on probabilistic methods, such as support vector machines and hidden Markov models. Computational learning of sequences can be seen as a strong computational paradigm for modern empirical modeling.

## 2.3    The Paradigm of Embodied Cognition

The cognitive tradition was criticized for its neglect of the action component in the subject's involvement with the environment. Criticism came from many different corners, but most importantly from inside cognitive science, particularly from scholars who stressed the phenomenological and embodied aspects of cognition (Maturana and Varela, 1980, 1987; Varela et al., 1991). The main argument is that knowledge does not emerge from passive perception, but from the need to act in an environment. In that sense, ecology is not merely about the relationship between a subject and its environment, but also about the knowledge which is needed to act in that environment.

The viewpoint put forward by Maturana, Varela, and others (not to forget Jean Piaget, one of the founding fathers of this idea) has generated much interest and a new perspective on how to approach the mind/matter relationship. In this approach, the link between mind and matter is based on the role of the human body as mediator between physical energy and meaning. In contrast, the earlier cognitive paradigm was less concerned with gestures and action, and more with mental processing. The Aristotelian component, which involves imitation and shared representations of action and perception, was not part of the main cognitive program, nor was multimodal information-processing.

### 2.3.1    A Tradition of Embodied Music Cognition

The idea that musical involvement is based on an embodied simulation or imitation of moving sonic forms has a long tradition that has been rediscovered only recently. In philosophy and especially in musicology, there was a school of researchers in the late nineteenth and early twentieth centuries which drew upon the idea that musical involvement is based on corporeal articulations (see, e.g., Lipps, 1903; Becking, 1928; Heinitz, 1931; Mauss, 1936; Truslit, 1938; Merleau-Ponty, 1945).

This approach differs from the gestalt theoretical ideas of that time in that it puts more emphasis on action. Like gestalt theory, this approach may be traced back to open problems in Kant's aesthetic theory (1790). Apart from the idea that beauty is in the formal structure of things, it was left open which processes would allow the translation from formal structure to beauty. Unlike gestalt theory, the emphasis of this school of researchers was less on brain processes and the construction of good forms, and more on the empathic relationship with these forms through movement and action.

For example, Lipps (1903) argues that the understanding of an expressive movement (*Ausdrucksbewegung*) in music is based on empathy (*inneren Mitmachen, Einfühlung*). While involved with moving sonic forms, we imitate the movements as expressions. By doing this, we practice using the motor muscles which are involved when genuine emotions are felt, and this gives access to the intended emotional meaning of the music. According to Lipps, the act of (free or unbounded) imitation gives pleasure because it is an expression of the self (Lipps, 1903, p. 111).[6] Thus, sad music may be a source of pleasure (*Lust*) because the moving sonic forms allow the subject to express sadness in an imitative movement. This allows the subject to participate in an expressive movement without being emotionally involved, that is, without experiencing an emotional state of sadness. To have empathic feelings with the other, the self must identify itself with it but, at the same time, must detach itself from it (Decety and Jackson, 2006). From this point of view, pleasure may result from shared representations of action and perception. Pleasure from sad music can then be understood as the result of a good match, or satisfactory correspondence, between the subject's simulated action (of sadness) and the perceived action events (of sadness) in music.

Truslit (1938) also sees corporeal articulations as manifestations of the inner motion heard in music. In *Gestaltung und Bewegung in der Musik*, he argues that in order to fully experience music, it is essential to understand its driving force, which is the expression of inner movement. The composer makes music that is full of inner movements. The musician gives shape to these inner movements by translating them into proper body gestures, and the good music listener is able to trace and imitate these movements in order to experience and understand the music properly. For example, Truslit says, "Provided the sound has the dynamo-agogic development corresponding to a natural movement, it will evoke the impression of this movement in us" (Repp, 1993, p. 52). Particularly striking is the example he gives of Beethoven, who, while

Figure 2.6
Excerpt from Truslit (1938, p. 116) that illustrates the relationship between the movements of a performer and a listener. Unfortunately, it is not clearly specified how these curves have been obtained and whether they are based on a hypothesis rather than on experiments.

composing, would hum or growl up and down in pitch without singing specific notes. This is also a phenomenon often heard when jazz musicians are playing. Truslit used the limited technology of his time to extract information from musical patterns, as well as information from body movements, with the idea of studying their correlations (see figure 2.6).

Earlier, Becking (1928) had made a connection between music and movement based on the idea of a dynamic rhythmic flow beyond the musical surface. This flow, a continuous up-down movement, connects points of metrical gravity that vary in relative weight. Becking's most original idea was that these metrical weights vary from composer to composer. Conducting movements were assumed to be based on a vocabulary of movements that allow the classification of the personal constants of different composers in different periods of history (Nettheim, 1996).

In these approaches, it is assumed that the mind/matter relationship is mediated by the human body. This largely agrees with recent thinking about the connections between perception and action.

### 2.3.2   Gesture Modeling

Since the mid-1990s, research has been strongly motivated by a demand for new tools to examine the interactive possibilities offered by digital media technology.[7] This stimulated the interest in gestural foundations of musical involvement, which form a core component of the embodied cognition approach.

With the advent of powerful computing tools, particularly real-time interactive music systems (Pressing, 1992; Rowe, 1993), more attention has been devoted to the role of gesture in music (Clynes, 1977, 1995; Wanderley and Battier, 2000; Sundberg, 2000, 2003). This gestural approach has been influential in that it puts more emphasis on sensorimotor feedback and the coupling of perception and action (Todd, 1995; Todd et al., 1999; Friberg and Sundberg, 1999). Based on modern sensor technologies, gesture-based research has become a vast domain of music research (Paradiso and O'Modhrain, 2003; Johannsen, 2004; Camurri and Volpe, 2004; Camurri and Rikakis, 2004).

Meanwhile, a number of interactive multimedia platforms have been developed (see, for example, Pure Data, Max/MSP, or EyesWeb) that have contributed to the study of the gestural and multimodal foundation of musical involvement. The platforms offer easy access to sensing devices and processing modules for rapid prototyping of experimental setups. They can be used for measuring, processing data, and integrating computational models in existing processing modules, and the results can be used in artistic applications (Leman and Camurri, 2006). Chapter 6, on interaction with musical instruments, contains a more in-depth discussion of how musical involvement relates to these interactive multimedia.

### Physics-Based Sound Modeling

Much of the recent interest in gesture modeling of music has been stimulated by advances in physics-based sound modeling, also called physical modeling. A physical model of a musical instrument generates sound on the basis of the movements of physical components that make up the instrument (for overviews, see Karjalainen et al., 2001; Smith, 2004). In contrast with spectral modeling, where the sound of a musical instrument is modeled using spectral characteristics of the signal that is produced by the instrument, physics-based sound modeling focuses on the parameters that describe the instrument physically, that is, on moving material object components (Bader, 2005). Sound generation is then a matter of controlling the articulatory parameters of the moving components.

So far, physical models are good at synthesizing individual sounds of the modeled instrument. And although it is still far from evident how these models may synthesize a score in a musically interesting way—including phrasing and performance nuances—it is obvious that a gesture-based account of physical modeling is an interesting way to proceed. Humans would typically add expressiveness to their interpretation, and this expressiveness would be based on the constraints of body movements that take particular forms and shapes—sometimes perhaps learned movement sequences and gestures depending on cultural traditions. One of the goals of gesture research related to music, therefore, aims at understanding the biomechanical and psychomotor laws that characterize human movement in the context of music production and perception. Obviously, this line of research is closely related to embodied music cognition.

## Motor Theory of Perception
Physics-based sound modeling further suggests a reconsideration of the nature of perception in view of stimulus–source relationships and gestural foundations of musical engagement.

Liberman and Mattingly (1985, 1989) assumed that the speech production–perception system is, in effect, an articulatory synthesizer. In the production mode, the synthesizer is activated by an abstract gestural pattern from which it computes a series of articulatory movements that are needed to realize the gestures into muscle movements of the vocal tract. In the perception mode, then, the synthesizer computes the series of articulatory movements that *could have* produced the signal, and from this representation, the intended gestural pattern contained in the stimulus is obtained.

Liberman and Mattingly assumed a specialized module responsible for both perception and production of phonetic structures. The perceptual side of this module converts automatically from acoustic signal to gesture. Perception of sound comes down to finding the proper parameters of the gesture that will allow the resynthesis of what is heard. Similar to the pioneering work of Truslit, features related to sound are assumed to be picked up as parameters for the control of the articulatory system. Perception of a sound, in that view, is an inhibited resynthesis of that sound, in the sense that the resynthesis is not actually carried out but simulated. The things that need to be stored in memory, then, are not auditory images but gestures, sequences of parameters that control the human articulatory (physical) system. The view also assumes that perception and action share a common representational system. Such models thus receive input from the sensors and produce appropriate actions as output. By doing this, stimuli become meaningful in relation to their sources, which are objects of action (Varela et al., 1991). Action, in other words, guarantees that the stimuli are connected to the object, the source of the physical energy that makes up the stimulus (Dourish, 2001).

The extension of statistical modeling with a motor theory of perception is currently a hot topic of research (e.g., Purves and Lotto, 2003). It has some very important consequences for the way we conceive of music research, and also, in particular, for the way we look at music perception. However, it is clear that a straightforward mapping between perceived stimuli features and sounding objects, for example, is not evident. Nor can all aspects of music perception be attributed to the recognition of the source of the stimulus. Music is often made of abstract sounds whose source may be difficult to define. Instead of the sources themselves, music often seems to focus attention on structures and relationships between sounds. It is possible, therefore, that the emphasis on source should be considered from the point of view of human corporeality and corporeal synthesis, rather than from the viewpoint of external sources (Godøy, 2001).

### Cognitive Neuroscience Research

Recent studies reveal that much of what happens in perception can be understood in terms of action (see, e.g., Jeannerod, 1994; Berthoz, 1997; Prinz and Hommel, 2002; Decety and Jackson, 2004). The hypothesis that action and perception share common neuronal codes (Hommel et al., 2001) is getting increasing empirical support from cognitive neuroscience (Jackson and Decety, 2004). The core assumption—that actions are coded in terms of the perceivable effects (distal events) rather than the stimulus properties (proximal features)—is of great relevance to music research.

It should be noted that recent empirical studies in music (e.g., Sundberg, 2000, 2003) have addressed this coupling of perception and action in musical activities, but the epistemological and methodological consequences of this approach have not been fully worked out in terms of a musicological paradigm (Reybrouck, 2001). In the chapters that follow, I intend to show that the coupling of perception and action has a number of consequences for future music research. It broadens the focus of music research quite a lot, in that it provides a new perspective for multimodal music perception, kinesthesia, affective involvement, expressiveness in music, and social music cognition.

## 2.4  Conclusion

The relationship between mind and matter is one of the main themes of the history and philosophy of music research. In this overview, attention has been drawn to the fact that three components of ancient Greek thinking provided a basis for this discussion: acoustics, perception, and expression ("movement of the soul"). Scientific experiments and technological developments were first (seventeenth–eighteenth centuries) based on an understanding of the physical principles and then, beginning in the late nineteenth century, gradually on an understanding of the subjective principles, starting with those of perception of structure, toward a better understanding of principles that underlie emotional understanding. In this context, it should be noted that the nineteenth century introduced the idea that the connection between subjective experience and matter has to do with the human brain. Cognitive science, influenced by gestalt theory, had a main focus on mental processing, whereas new approaches stress the role of the human body as mediator between matter and subjective experience.

The historical overview shows that different approaches to music research have been explored, but the major factors of progress in that field have been the introduction of the experimental methodology in the nineteenth century and of technology in the twentieth century. During the course of the twentieth century, technology had an growing impact on music culture and on the way people engage in signification practices. The latter call for more advanced mediation technologies that will close the gap between between musical mind and matter.

In recent years, the development of interactive multimedia platforms has played an important role in the shift from (disembodied) cognition to embodied cognition. Recent developments indicate that these platforms allow a straightforward use of measurement tools and modeling tools which facilitate the setup of experiments related to gestural and multimodal involvement with music. Moreover, the same interactive multimedia platform that integrates these tools can use the results from measurement and modeling in artistic applications.

A general conclusion to be drawn from this overview is that the scientific methodology has been expanding from purely physical issues (music as sound) to more subjective issues (music as experience). The connection between the two draws on fundamental relationships between mind, body, and matter.

# 3 Ecological Conceptions

While involved with music, the human body interacts with physical energy and the human mind deals with interpretations that are built on top of that corporeal interaction. But how are body and mind related? How can we bridge the gap between physical energy and mental interpretation? An understanding of this relationship forms the basis of a theory of music mediation. Such a theory is needed for building a technology that functions as an intermediary between mind and matter in accordance with the ways in which humans naturally engage themselves with music. This technology should enhance experience-based access to music rather than being an obstacle to it.

In order to develop such a theory and technology, it is necessary to understand how action and perception interfere with music. Therefore, in this and the following two chapters, action and perception will be analyzed from an ecological point of view. Ecology is the study of the relationships between the subject and its environment. The present chapter focuses on the environment, and the next two chapters will focus on the subject.

The problem to be clarified in this chapter is how action and perception interfere with regularities in the environment. It is known that some of these regularities are based on artifacts that somehow persist at a cultural level or in a cultural environment, such as a musical style. However, other regularities are purely physical or biological. Yet each type of regularity influences the other. Thus, there is a complex relationship between action and perception on the one hand, and the natural and cultural environments on the other hand. This relationship is still poorly understood because it involves physical, biological, and cultural regularities that interact with each other.

## 3.1   Direct Perception and Inference

Ecological theories of human action and perception have been developed from at least two different viewpoints, direct perception and inference. The latter is also known as the lens model.

The theory of direct perception holds that the duality between an organism and its environment can be overcome by the fact that the organism perceives the action-relevant properties of the environment (Gibson, 1979). In other words, while having access to reality, it is not the physical properties that are perceived, nor the awareness of the sensing of these properties. Rather, what is perceived is the action-relevant value of the energy that causes these sensory features. This action-relevant value is called an affordance. Direct perception thus draws strongly upon the action-oriented bias of the human organism. As a consequence, depending on the context, the same energy may lead to different affordances.

In the lens model, a distinction is made between distal stimuli, the energies in the ecological environment, and proximal stimuli, the effect of these energies on sensory input (Brunswik, 1956). The organism is not able to perceive the distal stimuli directly. Instead, it must infer the action-oriented value of the energy in the environment from the cues provided by the proximal stimuli. These cues are the lens through which the organism has access to the environment.

Differences in scope and definition of terms have been the reason, in the past, that the two psychological theories have addressed different communities. Gibson has had more influence in the psychology of (visual) perception, while Brunswik has been important in fields that address the analysis and design of human–technology interaction (Kirlik and Maruyama, 2004). The lens model has also been used as a paradigm for emotional communication in speech and music (Scherer, 1978; Juslin, 2001).

Recently, arguments have been put forward in favor of a unification of the two approaches (Vicente, 2003), but the primary difference still concerns the different modes of knowing the world. The direct perception mode is based on attunement to information, an idea which is closely related to behavioral resonance, identification, and direct access to music. In contrast, the lens model is based on judgment and inference, which involve awareness, evaluation, interpretation, and mental description of the perceived cues. Judgment is needed in order to obtain a linguistic description which, ultimately, may provide indirect linguistic-based access to mental involvement with music (see chapter 1).

In Gibson's model, the coupling of action and perception is the cornerstone of the theory. This is not the case in Brunswik's model, although it is straightforward to draw upon action/perception couplings for making inferences about reality. In what follows, the coupling of action and perception is taken to be a central concept in our understanding of the relationship between a subject and its natural environment, and both the model of direct perception and the lens model will be used for that purpose. However, a more dynamic model will also be developed which accounts for the interaction between the natural and cultural environments. This dynamic model should explain the emergence of cultural artifacts as well as the effect it has on action and perception. The result should provide a clearer understanding of the relationship between a subject and its natural and cultural musical environments.

## 3.2   The Action–Reaction Cycle

This and the following section aim to clarify subject/environment interactions by means of a case study of how musical instruments are made. Making a musical instrument involves action and perception in relation to the natural and cultural environments. It also involves the understanding of the action-relevant value of sounds, the judgment of these sounds in view of musical ideals, and shaping the physical environment that produces sound. All this proceeds within the confines of a cultural goal.[1]

The role of action and perception in an environmental interaction can be captured in a dynamic model I call the action–reaction cycle. Figure 3.1 shows this cycle applied to the making of a musical instrument. The first step of the cycle is an action (Play) that generates energy and causes physical vibrations in an object. The resulting vibrations are taken up by the air molecules that surround the object. These vibrations are received and processed by the human auditory system (Listen). A perception is then built up in the mind, and a judgment is made about the quality of the instrument (Judge). Finally, the subject can undertake an action and change (Change) the physical conditions of the instrument to optimize the judgment in terms of certain beliefs or values.

Note that this action–reaction cycle comprises aspects of direct perception as well as inference. Direct perception is involved in sound production and its perception. The sound is perceived mainly in terms of its musical value, that is, its qualities of providing direct involvement with music. In contrast, inference is involved in making a judgment about the quality of the instrument and the change in its physical conditions. In

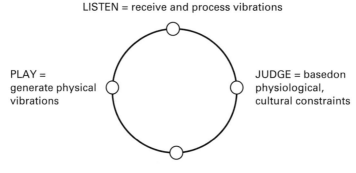

**Figure 3.1**
Action–reaction cycle.

those phases, the musical validity of the instrument is analyzed on the basis of proximal cues and inferences are made concerning the distal cues.

### 3.2.1  Ratchet Effect

Both the actual process of instrument-making (ontogenesis) and the history of how an instrument evolves (phylogenesis) can be seen as the result of a repeated cycling of Play, Listen, Judge, Change. The action–reaction cycling is a dynamic model with the capacity to subsume a cumulative process similar to a ratchet effect, which transforms physical energy into a cultural artifact (Tomasello, 1999). The ratchet image shows how skills can be accumulated, for example, through imitation learning (see chapter 5). Thus, the action–reaction cycling provides a dynamic model of how action and perception interact with the physical and cultural environments.

### 3.2.2  Intentional Actions

While a musical instrument is being built, a set of action–reaction cycles, which may occur on different time scales and perhaps in hierarchical order, transforms matter and energy into a cultural artifact for making music. This transformation often takes place as a function of the pursuit of a particular goal. In the case of making a musical instrument, the goal may be closely related to an existing instrument which serves as a model.

From that point of view, Play, Listen, Judge, and Change may be understood as an intentional activity in which the physical activities involved in playing, listening, and molding an instrument are steered by a set of cultural constraints. In that sense, the ratchet effect would be an intended effect.

However, not all effects of the action–reaction cycling can be seen as being steered by a cultural goal. Especially when dealing with the phylogenesis of musical instruments, it is clear that the instruments we know today cannot be seen as the goal-directed (or teleological) outcome of an evolutionary process. Instead, the long-term evolution of musical instruments may subsume a Darwinist model in which the long-term outcome is considered to be an effect of more local interacting forces between natural and cultural constraints. In that sense, the modern carillon, for example, is not necessarily what makers of automated chiming bells had in mind in the fifteenth century. Rather, it is the outcome of a sequence of local, goal-directed human actions that fit together and form a trajectory. Cultural evolution is involved because of the ratchet effect of multiple action–reaction cycles.

## 3.3   Nature and Culture in Interaction

The dynamic model of subject/environment interaction thus relies on the idea that a mutual relationship exists between natural and cultural constraints. To understand this relationship, the concept of a constraint needs further clarification. The question to be solved is how natural and cultural constraints can interact, and how this interaction is at work in the subject/music relationship.

### 3.3.1   Natural and Cultural Constraints

By "constraint" I understand a rule or condition that imposes limits on what is possible. In other words, a constraint can be defined as something that controls things. Natural constraints subsume the laws of physics and biology, whereas cultural constraints are rules or conditions that impose limits on what is acceptable, appreciated, and considered to be true or valid in a culture.

Natural constraints are supposed to form the study domain of the natural sciences, where the aim is to give a functional description of the cause-and-effect relationships of interacting material entities. Once these functional relationships are understood, they can be simulated using a functional modeling approach, or parts of the functional relationships can be connected with technologies. Therefore, understanding the natural constraints has direct implications for technology.

Cultural constraints, on the other hand, are of a totally different order. They are about the control of significations, attribution of meanings through habit or convention, ideals, norms, values, and worldviews. Cultural constraints control shared experiences, joint attention scenarios, goal-directed actions, intentions, and subjectivism.

In short, cultural constraints are effective in the mental domain, while natural constraints are effective in the physical domain. However, the two types of constraints are closely related. For example, assume that somebody wants to make an instrument from bronze. It is known that the natural (or eigen)resonances of bronze plates generate inharmonic tones. So how do we handle the bronze in order to make it into a musical instrument? The physical interaction with the bronze may be largely influenced by cultural constraints.

In Western culture, it is very likely that the bronze will be altered to make it sound more harmonic. The action–reaction cycle then looks as follows: Play is a matter of hitting the bronze with a hammer. Listen amounts to the perception of the sound, and Judge is about the comparison of this sound with a reference sound that one has in mind. If the sound differs too much from the harmonic ideal, the bronze plate has to undergo Change. Then a new cycle will start until the judgment produces a satisfactory comparison with the ideal model. The action–reaction cycle may be applied to the casting of a single bell. However, as mentioned, the history of bell-casting could also be seen as running through many of these action–reaction cycles until the bronze reached the form of the bells we know today. In this process, natural and local cultural constraints interact, forming a trajectory known today as the history of bells.[2]

A closer look at the steps of the action–reaction cycle reveals some further peculiarities of the interaction between natural and cultural constraints.

• *Play*  The main purpose of Play is to produce a sound. It can consist of hitting the bronze with a metal hammer. Physically speaking, the impact of the hammer causes energy to travel in the bronze plate, and the resulting vibrations are taken up by the air molecules that surround the plate. These molecular vibrations in turn can be picked up by the human ear, and are heard as the typical bell sound. However, Play can also be seen as an intentional act. It produces a sound as a function of evaluation and later musical use.

• *Listen*   This can be understood in terms of directly picking up the sound from the source that produces it. From a physiological viewpoint, this consists of picking up the vibrations of air molecules and transforming them into sensations of sound qualities. However, Listen is also a matter of direct perception, of a direct involvement with reality. What is perceived, then, is not merely the properties of sound, but also the action-relevant values of that sound. For example, what is perceived is impact and force, or sound as a function of a musical purpose. The latter focus on sound properties involves an awareness and inference. It implies that listening can focus on different aspects of being involved with sound, from its action-related values associated with survival and reward to its sound properties as a function of music-making.

• *Judge*   From the moment that physical energies give rise to the sensation of sound qualities, we enter into a new phase of the cycle, Judge. This phase is even more difficult to describe purely from the viewpoint of human physiology because judging the sound of the bronze is a matter of comparing the perceived sound quality with an imagined prototype.

To illustrate the point, figure 3.2 shows an excerpt from an assessment letter written in 1741, by the famous carillon founder Georges Duméry.[3] In this letter it is specified that ideally a good bell should have a strong bourdon, the pure octave, the minor third, the fifth, and the pure upper octave. In Duméry's mind, the judgment of a bell would have been made as a function of this ideal overtone structure. Obviously, this ideal was grounded in the theory and experience of that time.

In Judge, perceived cues are compared with the mental model. On that basis, a judgment is made about whether the distal cues are appropriate. If they are not, the bell has either to be tuned or to be remade.[4] Judge is largely culturally determined because it entails choices which depend not on physical energies but on conventions.

• *Change*   Making a bell out of bronze provides an interesting example of how physical materials should be changed in pursuit of ideal sound characteristics. However, while Change could be conceived of in terms of the manipulations that are needed to cast the bell or change its tuning, such changes involve learned skills and knowledge based on long traditions of learning by imitation.[5]

In short, natural and cultural constraints interact. The making of a bell shows how the control over natural constraints—the mastering

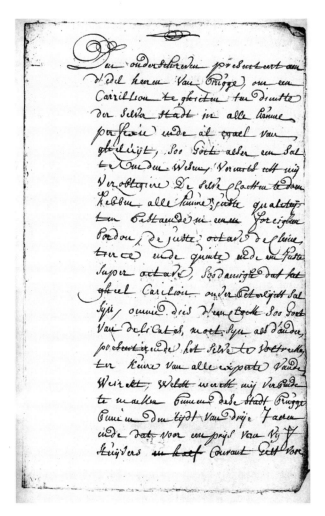

**Figure 3.2**
Assessment letter of Georges Duméry with specification of the physical qualities
of the bell he intended to cast for the city of Bruges in 1741 (manuscript at the
University of Ghent Library; reprinted with permission).

of inharmonic resonances or partial tone structures, can be seen as an action–reaction cycling. This cycling is guided by a local cultural harmonic ideal.[6] The action–reaction cycling subsumes a ratchet effect which is reflected in the accumulation of learned skills and technology. Thus, local cultural constraints and natural constraints may account for evolutionary trajectories of cultural artifacts.

The dynamic model of the subject/environment relationship holds that action and perception can turn natural constraints into cultural constraints, which in turn have an effect on action and perception. This is the motor of a cultural evolution. At the heart of this process is the human capability to translate physical energies effectively into the objects of an action- and valence-oriented mental ontology.

### 3.3.2   Explaining Cultural Constraints

Understanding the dynamics of the subject/environment relationship is complicated by the interaction of natural and cultural constraints. This interaction affects how we look at theories and how we develop explanations. In the past, explanations of particular musical phenomena were often based on cultural explanations. However, empirical and computation-based approaches in musicology have led to a better understanding of the possible relationship between cultural and natural constraints. In certain cases, such as tonality induction, physics and biology have offered a compelling hypothesis because the phenomenon may be explained as an emerging effect of biological and physical causality (Leman, 1995, 1999, 2003). In a similar way, let us look at how culturalist and naturalist explanations would work in the case of the preference for harmonic tones (Terhardt, 1984).

### The Culturalist Explanation

Why do people prefer harmonic tones rather than inharmonic tones for making music? The cultural explanation is that the instrument maker, like Duméry in the above example, will prefer pitch stability, and thus harmonic tones, because this reflects an extramusical component that points to cultural values of what is essential in the world. Reference can be made to the belief that the ultimate source of our world is absolutely pure, perfect, and immutable, and therefore stable, for change implies imperfection.[7]

However, this belief is the belief of a particular culture. Therefore, the cultural explanation puts the burden on another cultural principle, such as a worldview. But where is the worldview coming from? Ultimately, reference could be made to a dogma (e.g., stability as a property of the divine) or to the idea that cultures make arbitrary choices (cultural relativism). Unfortunately, in both cases it is hard to come up with a more fundamental or universal principle.

### The Naturalist Explanation

Instead of linking the cultural constraint to a more general cultural principle, the naturalist explanation offers a reductionist account of the phenomenon. The aim is to explain the phenomenon as an emerging effect of interactions among physical and biological entities.

Concerning the preference for harmonic tones, the first thing to understand is the nature of pitch perception. Harmonic tone complexes contain partial tones which are integer multiples of a fundamental frequency. Due to neural mechanisms in the human auditory system, the perceived pitch will correspond to the fundamental frequency of the harmonic tone complex, even if this fundamental frequency is not present in the signal (Langner, 1997).

The biological preference for stable tones may be related to the fact that few inharmonic sounds were produced before humans manufactured materials. Since perception should be conceived as an evolutionary adaptation to an environment with harmonic tones, it should not be surprising that the perception of inharmonic tones is highly ambiguous to humans. The human auditory system is simply not adapted to inharmonic tones.[8] However, even if it is true that perception is adapted to harmonic tone complexes and not to inharmonic ones, the question still remains why pitch is the main action-relevant value on which perception is mainly focused. As I see it, harmonic tones lead to the perception of a single pitch, rather than the perception of the individual overtones, because of two phenomena.

First, pitch is an easily extracted form of invariance in signals. Pitch immediately appears in the waveform as periodicity. Systems that come into resonance with this periodicity will tend to develop an emergent perception of pitch because it is the cue which is most stable over a large number of harmonic tones. During the course of evolution, stability is rewarding, and hence biological functions may develop toward the aspect of information that is most stable (less ambiguous) in the structure of physical energy. In contrast with pitch, for example, the phase structure of the harmonic tone complex is not stable. Consequently, its perception will be highly ambiguous. Therefore, biological functions will not develop toward that aspect of information because no stable relationship can be sustained between the proximal cue of phase structure and the specific structure in the energy. Concerning harmonic sounds, hearing would adapt to the hearing of pitch rather than phase structure because organisms can sustain an action-relevant relationship with the specific information contained in the stimulus. It is not possible to sustain such a relationship with the phase structure, or with inharmonic tones, because of their ambiguous information. Perceptual systems thus tend to disambiguate the information in the environment as a consequence of action-based resonances.

The action-based relationship with information contained in the stimulus is connected with the second point: that pitch facilitates communication because the reproduction of pitch is much easier than reproduction of a particular phase structure in harmonic tones. The evolutionary process by which pitch occurs as a biological adaptation is thus facilitated as a function of the resynthesis. Thus, perception will evolve as a function of this action-related value. Therefore, what is perceived is also an adaptation to the physical constraints of our own actions. In that sense, we perceive pitch as an affordance, a thing which we can handle in action. Thus, the reproduction system must also have evolved in line with perception. There must have been a mutual reinforcement of perception and action concerning pitch.

To sum up, the adaptation to pitch can be seen as the result of a resonance relationship between subject and environment. This resonance reinforces the functions that tend to disambiguate the information that is perceived in the environment. This disambiguation works as a function of action-oriented values, for example, which the organism can produce in vocalizations. From that perspective, the preference for harmonic pitch is not based on metaphysics, but instead on physics and evolution. In that sense, the preference for harmonic pitch is an emerging effect of biological and physical interaction (called mutual resonance or *entrainment*) through evolution. Thus, an explanation based on these principles reduces the cultural phenomenon to more fundamental physical and biological principles. An understanding of these principles may allow the simulation of the adaptation process. If it works, the explanatory theory may be applied to other perception cues as well. Moreover, the causal principles on which the explanation relies may be implemented in functional models that simulate the principle.

### Why Both Naturalist and Culturalist Explanations Are Needed

However, it seems that not all cultures focus on harmonic sounds. Some cultures prefer inharmonic sounds—some traditional music cultures in Indonesia, for example (Schneider, 1997; Sethares, 1998). Clearly, this focus cannot be explained in terms of a natural preference for harmonic tones. Instead, it can be assumed that other aspects of sound, different from pitch, may have played a role. For example, the amount of fluctuation may have been the focus for this culture.

What ultimately causes the difference in focus on either pitch or fluctuation is difficult to say. If it is based on principles that are external to music, such as worldviews, then we are back to the cultural explanatory level. If it is based on principles that relate to materials available in the environment, then we are back to natural constraints. More research is needed to clarify this, using a dynamic model of interactions between subjects and their natural/cultural environments.

To sum up, attempts can be made to understand cultural constraints in terms of natural constraints, using a reductionistic approach. The task is then to explain the cultural constraints as emerging effects of natural constraints. However, in matters that concern culture, we often cannot fully explain the phenomenon on the basis of a few natural constraints alone. The natural constraints that are dealt with in the explanation may be the wrong ones. For example, instead of pitch, it may be fluctuation which is important. At the end, the role of a particular natural constraint in a cultural dynamics may in turn be an effect of a dynamics of multiple subject/environment interactions. We may need to reintroduce the cultural level, or introduce at least a social level of interactions between subjects, which makes the modeling even more complex.

In short, we cannot fully understand the impact of cultural constraints on the basis of cultural explanations alone, nor can we fully understand the impact of cultural constraints on the basis of natural explanations alone. It seems that both cultural and natural constraints are needed to understand musical phenomena. Certain phenomena are grounded in natural constraints but manifest themselves as goals or values. Thus, they have the status of cultural constraints and can exert strong influence on the development of new cultural phenomena. To understand this global resonance between natural and cultural constraints, it is strategically wise to have a look at what physics and biology can offer, and then reconsider the cultural explanation from that perspective. In the case of Georges Duméry, for example, this approach offers a good understanding of why he may have chosen the harmonic tone as a reference model for the manufacturing of bells.

## 3.4   Simulating the Emergence of Cultural Constraints

The features of the ecological resonance model, which are based on subject/environment interactions, can be clarified in greater detail using computational methods. This can be illustrated with an example about the origin of musical scales.[9]

Like harmonic tone complexes, pitch scales are often conceived of as cultural constraints. Indeed, pitch scales have been assumed to be based on convention (some say logics), which is demonstrated by the fact that they have been deliberately imposed upon musical instruments such as carillons. Many carillons are tuned in the so-called mean-tone temperament, which is actually a tuning used for harpsichords. In that sense, it is justified to call the pitch scale a cultural constraint, because it controls what is considered to be the cultural "true" tuning of a carillon. Tunings based on the eigen-resonances of bells (e.g., using the methodology developed in Mathews et al., 1988) are not considered in practice.

Interestingly, two hypotheses have recently been proposed which aim at explaining pitch scales as an emerging effect of physical/biological adaptations rather than as outcomes of logical constructions or metaphysical principles. The discussion shows how computational methods can be used to understand how natural constraints interfere with cultural constraints through action and perception. The first hypothesis is based on the direct perception model: stimulus–source relationships. The second hypothesis is based on inference.

### Stimulus–Source Relationships

Schwartz et al. (2003) argue that perception is based on the disambiguation of action-relevant cues. The disambiguation is based on the accumulation of past correlations between stimulus properties and source properties, which is reflected in a probability distribution of the possible sources of the stimulus.[10]

The stimulus is what appears to the senses, and therefore it is defined by a set of proximal cues. The source is what generates the stimulus, and is defined by the distal cues. In the case of the human voice, the stimulus is the harmonic tone with its spectrum of partial tones at fixed distances corresponding to the frequency of the fundamental.

This is what the ear receives. The source is the human vocal system with its eigen-resonances, which produces the harmonic tone.

Schwartz et al. (2003) hypothesize that past experiences of the coupling of harmonic spectra with the resonance properties of the vocal tract lead to pitch representations that disambiguate pitch stimuli. In other words, the brain is assumed to build up a statistics of stimulus–source relationships and to use this statistics to disambiguate new or unknown stimuli. Thus, it is assumed that the pitch scale is based on the pitch relationships that occur most often. This point of view implies that the pitch scale is an emerging natural/biological constraint which is extracted from the direct relationships between proximal cues and distal cues.

The key component of this hypothesis comprises the idea that perception has access to the sound source. In this example, the vocal folds are the sound source. They produce a series of rapid tone pulses at rates that correspond to the frequency of the fundamental. Rapid tone pulses have many harmonic partial tones, but the vocal system (larynx and vocal tract) shapes the amplitudes of these partial tones by opening or narrowing particular resonance chambers. This gives a vowel a particular pitch and a particular color. The resonance characteristics of the vocal system—in the ideal case, the larynx and vocal tract can be seen as a tube of a certain length that is closed at one end—have peaks of maximal resonances at about 500 Hz, 1500 Hz, and 2500 Hz. Depending on the fundamental pitch at which the vocal is generated, different partials (e.g., the second, third, fourth, or fifth partial tone) may attain the maximum energy. For example, if a male produces a vowel at a fundamental frequency of 125 Hz, the fourth harmonic at 500 Hz ($4 \times 125 = 500$) is likely to have the maximum energy value, due to the resonance peak at 500 Hz. If a female vocalizes at a fundamental frequency of 250 Hz, the second harmonic at 500 Hz is likely to have the maximum energy value.

Relative to the partial tone with maximum amplitude (which emerges due to resonances of the vocal tract), the other harmonics have different but structured intervallic relationships. For example, if the maximum amplitude is at the fourth partial, the higher partial tones (5, 6, 7, 8, etc.) have the frequency ratios of 1.25 ($= 5/4$, or major third), 1.5 ($= 6/4$, or fifth), 1.75 ($= 7/4$, or harmonic seventh), and 2 ($= 8/4$, or octave) with respect to partial tone 4. The lower partial tones have the relationships of 1 ($= 4/4$, or prime), 0.75 ($= 3/4$, or lower fourth), 0.5 ($= 2/4$, or lower octave), and 0.25 ($= 1/4$, or two octaves lower). On

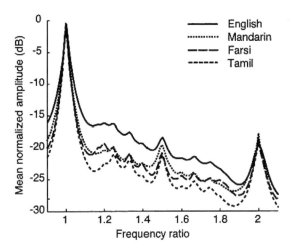

**Figure 3.3**
Statistical structure of speech sounds (Schwartz et al., 2003). (Reprinted with permission of the author.)

the other hand, if the maximum amplitude occurs at the second partial, the higher partial tones occur at 1.5 (= 3/2, or fifth), 2 (= 4/2, or octave), 2.5 (= 5/2, or octave plus major third), 3 (= 6/2, or octave plus fifth), and so on, and the lower partial tones at 0.5 (= 1/2, or lower octave), with respect to partial 2.

Schwartz et al. (2003) assume that the brain builds up a statistics of how speech sounds relate to their source. More specifically, they show that a simple summary of all these frequency ratios in vocalizations produced by males and females, old and young people, speaking different languages, in different pitches and sound colors, reflects the tone scale. Figure 3.3 shows frequency ratios in terms of their amplitude (dB). The curve shows the overall effect that certain frequency ratios occur more often than others. Of particular relevance are the peaks in the curve. For example, the prime (ratio 1) and octave (ratio 2) occur more often than the fifth (ratio 1.5), the fourth (1.33), and the sixth (1.66). The implication for music-making is that the majority of the musical intervals of the chromatic scale correspond to the mean amplitude peaks in the curve because frequency ratios at these points are less ambiguous than frequency ratios in the neighborhood.

To sum up, it is conjectured that the pitch scale arises from the statistical structure of vocalizations. Therefore, Schwartz et al. (2003) state that the pitch scale emerges from the laws of nature.

**Inference from Stimulus-Based Cues**

Although the above theory connects sound production with sound perception in an interesting way, it has not fully explained the existence of pitch scales that differ from the Western pitch scale, nor does it go into the fine details of tuning systems. For example, the pelog and slendro scales used in Indonesian gamelan music show that pitch scales are not necessarily based on harmonic relationships. A gamelan orchestra uses metallic instruments that produce inharmonic partial tone structures. Apparently, we cannot fully account for these pitch scales without taking into consideration the inharmonic tones used in this music.

Sethares (1998) has pointed out that the pelog and slendro tone scales of Indonesian gamelan orchestras can be obtained by combining the tones of metallic instruments and the human voice. In this approach, which is based on von Helmholtz (1863/1968), roughness is taken to be the proximal cue from which the pitch scale can be inferred.[11] The assumption is that the points at which the roughness is minimal (or consonance is maximal) correspond to the intervals of the scales. This approach thus begins at the proximal cue from which an inference is made concerning the actual state of the pitch scale. Figure 3.4 shows the resulting curves for slendro and pelog scales. The peaks are intervals with little dissonance or roughness. They correspond to the intervals of the scale.

### 3.4.1   Both Direct Perception and Inference?

The main difference between Sethares's approach and the approach of Schwartz et al. is that Sethares obtains the results from an analysis of a proximal cue (roughness). This cue is extracted from the stimulus, not from an analysis of a large quantity of stimulus–source relationships. In the model of Sethares, the pitch scale corresponds to the points where the roughness of two combined inharmonic tones is minimal. In contrast, Schwartz et al. (2003) do not rely on roughness perception. Instead, they assume statistics of frequency ratios in speech. They base their account on the principle of direct perception. The pitch scale corresponds to the frequency ratios that occur most often in the natural environment.

The discussion about pitch scales raises interesting questions concerning the foundation of music perception. The empirical perception approach advocated by Schwartz et al. has the interesting feature of relating stimulus to source, but thus far it cannot account for pitch scales of other cultures, nor for the fine differences between Western tuning

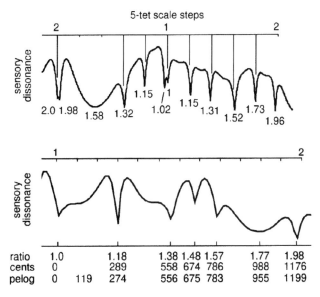

**Figure 3.4**
Slendro and pelog scales based on roughness minimalization (Sethares, 1998; reprinted with permission of the author). The downward pointing peaks of both curves indicate the intervals with minimal roughness. (Top) The combination of a generic boning and a harmonic sound generates a curve with minima close to the steps of a five tone equal-tempered scale (5-tet), typical for slendro tunings. (Bottom) The combination of a saron and a harmonic sound generates a curve with minima close to the scale steps of a pelog scale.

systems. Clearly, the theory is far from being complete since it cannot explain the pitch scales of other cultures.

In contrast, Sethares's approach (1998), based on roughness minimalization, can account for pitch scales of other cultures. In addition, it gives an account of the small differences in Western tuning systems. However, the model draws on the idea that roughness is the proximal cue from which the pitch scale has to be inferred. This may be a questionable assumption because it can be asked if roughness is indeed something that is always avoided in music. Evidence is against it, because musical practice shows that roughness is a basic part of many types of music. Just think about the use of distorted sounds from electric guitars in rock music, or the rough voices of flamenco music.

In both approaches, concepts of ecological perception have been integrated, but the one stresses the principle of sound–source perception while the other stresses inference. However, both approaches suggest that pitch scales can be seen as an emerging effect of natural constraints. Interestingly, in both cases, computational principles have been used to prove the hypothesis.

A possible compromise of the two explanatory models would consist of the idea that the stimulus–source model sets a general trend for pitch scales. But this trend may be refined or overruled using the inference techniques of a roughness-based sound analysis.

In any case, both accounts provide interesting examples of how cultural constraints may be explained as the emerging outcome of natural (physical and biological) constraints. Theories and models may be competing, but what is important is the idea that cultural constraints can, to some extent, be understood in terms of biological and physical principles. Once these principles are understood, the modeling can be used in technologies of music mediation—for example, in tools that compute pitch scales from spectral properties of sounds, as has been shown in a convincing way by Sethares (1994, 2002).

## 3.5   Culture as Resonance System

The above model suggests that the relationship between natural and cultural constraints can be further understood as something that interferes with human action and perception. This is an important observation which will be elaborated upon in the next chapter. Here it is of interest to observe that repeated action–reaction cycling may lead to a focus point, or cultural attractor, which emerges from the dynamic interplay between natural/biological and cultural constraints. Due to a ratchet effect, the interaction between natural and cultural constraints can lead to higher levels of accumulated abstraction and complexity. At the end of such a dynamic process, a cultural constraint may appear as a schema which disambiguates the complex reality of mental conceptualizations of the world. The cultural schemata thus become abstract principles which are detached from their physical origins.

While their foundation originated in physical and physiological resonances, the cultural schemata may start to generate their own dynamics. This is possible due to the accumulation of cultural artifacts and the human willingness to learn, acquire, and apply these new artifacts in human activities. Examples of such schemata are pitch scales, tonal schemes, rhythmic schemes, timbre schemes, articulatory schemes, musical styles, and musical habits. In all these examples, human perception and action seem to be the catalyst through which the ratchet effect can be realized. In other words, the ratchet which leads to the cultural attractor is moved by human action and perception.

In this dynamic ecological model, the physical, cultural, and human constraints function together, forming a dynamic which appears as a resonance system in which constraints of different types (physical, biological, cultural) interact on the basis of mutual exchange of energy. The key factor in this dynamic is that humans tend to see the world as something meaningful, and they do this because they tend to disambiguate the information stream into an ontology of action-relevant concepts. Cultural constraints related to musical ideals, structural forms in music, and even gestures emerge from this interaction as focal points or musical attractors. They are stored and cultivated, and they in turn steer learning and direct behavior toward particular goals.

The concept of a resonance system thus offers a powerful metaphor for understanding how music may have evolved. It is a big challenge to unravel the interactions between constraints because several levels of information-processing may be involved, from sensation to perception to cognition, and from simple motor reflexes to learned patterns and intended actions.

### 3.5.1   Natural and Cultural Resonances

The above model of the interactions between subject and natural/cultural constraints is summarized in figure 3.5. The subject is represented by a small circle, and the interaction with the natural and cultural environments is represented by larger circles. The lower circle (broken line) shows the action–reaction cycle in terms of natural constraints. The upper circle (solid line) shows the action–reaction cycle in terms of cultural constraints. Both circles are unified in the subject, where natural and cultural constraints interact. The horizontal line indicates that the subject is shaped through evolution.

In this model it is assumed that the social and cultural constraints engage the subject in goal-directed processes related to values, signification, and meaning (upper circle). Although it is difficult to attach time scales to this engagement, it can be conjectured that a mean time scale for goals and values to result in an effect could be on the order of several months or years, varying from a few seconds (the experienced *now*) to several decades (the experienced *me*). In contrast, the physical constraints engage the subject in action/perception processes related to action-relevant exchanges of energy with the environment. This

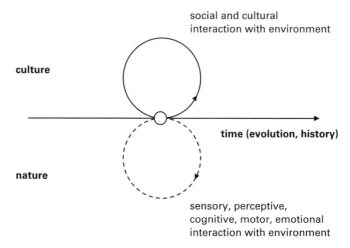

Figure 3.5
Schematic representation of an individual interacting with physical and social-cultural environments.

exchange is based on movement and motor activities, and it can be conjectured that the time scale is slightly shorter, varying from milliseconds or seconds to several hours or sometimes years (lower circle).

In this model it is also assumed that the subject is engaged in processing information streams, making sense of them in terms of goal-directed behavior. This is represented by the two circles meeting in the subject. Both circles can be conceived of as dynamic processes in which subject and environment, through action and perception, exchange energies. Reinforcements of effects that arise from this dynamic process are seen as resonances; they are the motor for the goal-directed dynamics of action and perception.

Furthermore, in the figure there is a horizontal line which represents evolution and cultural history (from left to right). The model is linked with the idea that during the course of evolution, biological organisms have become more complex and have developed interactions based on goal-directed representations and on socially and culturally determined, goal-directed, long-term behavior. It is now generally assumed that the human brain somehow accumulates this phylogenetic evolution in several layers, from sensory and brain stem locations to higher-level cognitive processing and meaning formation in the cortex.[12] The long-term effect of cultural evolution, however, is not goal-directed. Rather, it can be understood as an effect of interaction between local cultural constraints and natural constraints which may lead to the formation of trajectories toward particular cultural attractors.

To sum up, the model suggests that engagement with music involves three levels: physical energies, cultural objects, and human organisms. The action/perception processes of the subject realize the link between physical energies and cultural objects through resonances (entrainment).

### 3.5.2   Human Resonances

A main assumption of the model is that biological organisms use resonance communication to transform physical energies into action-relevant concepts that operate as a function of their reward and, ultimately, their survival. Turning physical energies into goal-directed action supports a ratchet effect at the cultural level through which natural constraints appear as cultural constraints which can be learned.

This ecological model thus puts action/perception processes at the center of how people engage with the environment. The transformation of physical energy into cultural artifacts is also reflected in the unique capability of the human mind to learn these cultural artifacts and use them as tools to signify the physical energy of the environment. In this signification process, humans use culture to turn physical energy into action-relevant representations which define an action-relevant ontology. The human brain uses this ontology for mental access to the environment at the level of cultural constraints.

Therefore, each subject can be considered to have a double identity, like two sides of the same coin.

- First, the subject's action and perception can be seen as an exchange of information and energy with the environment. Sensing and generation of energy subsume different time scales (milliseconds, seconds, years) and involve different levels of processing and memory systems (echoic, short-term, long-term, statistical, episodic).
- Second, the subject's action and perception can be seen as engagement with the cultural environment. This is the level at which we describe music as experienced and as a function of particular goals, intentions, and value systems.

The two levels suggest that involvement with music may be a highly constrained involvement in the sense that culture already provides very specific choices before our birth. The available cultural objects, such as musical instruments, musical structures, musical styles, habits in musical function, and so on, are already present. They shape the brain in the years during which the brain is fine-tuned. In many cases, such as the perception of musical styles, the brain is adapting itself to these structures by picking up invariant information that is controlled by the cultural constraints. At this level, the brain can be seen as a statistical processor trying to absorb the invariant physical structures in the environment. Culture plays a central role in that it enhances the distribution of the structures of the physical environment. Thus it becomes a determining factor of human action and perception.

To sum up, the physical/biological and cultural levels subsume constraints which define what is possible. The most important observation is that these two fields are unified in the subject through action. It is action which allows the subject to transform physical energy to the cultural level and vice versa. Associated with action is the capacity to create a mental world, which is a world of imagination, of a virtual reality composed of intentions and representations. Thus, the ecological model should be conceived of as a resonating system based on action, in which different processing systems (perception, cognition, emotion, motor systems) have effects through interaction with each other and with the environment.

### 3.5.3   Cultural Resonances

From a large number of objects in the environment, a culture will typically focus the subject's attention on particular artifacts. For example, in music, materials and objects that vibrate long enough (a few seconds) to become distinct from percussion sounds have been improved to produce even longer vibrations, until they produce pitches which can be used for music-making. However, the cultural dynamics behind all this may be hard to predict. Certain cultures, such as the Western culture, prefer objects producing harmonic structures. Other cultures, such as the Indonesian culture, prefer objects that produce particular inharmonic structures. Apart from the choice of objects, a culture will also select from the possible combinations of the vibrational structures, so the development of cultural artifacts should be seen as the result of a long dynamic process.

Given this long-term dynamics, the general idea is that culture develops in resonance with particular natural constraints. It means that natural constraints may allow cultural constraints to become more and more pronounced. During this process, natural constraints may be turned into particular cultural constraints that, due to their resonance with natural constraints, become cultural attractors. Owing to the fact that human subjects learn from cultural artifacts, these cultural constraints appear to be detached from their original natural environment. At that moment, they have become genuine cultural constraints playing a role in cultural institutions, worldviews, and significations. The pitch scale can be seen as an example of this dynamics.

To sum up, the interaction of subjects with their environment results in a complex dynamics which in turn can affect the action and perception processes of the individual subject. So far, the analysis has shown that the main mediator of this process is human action. For that reason, the notion of human action is discussed further in the next chapter. Of particular interest will be a better understanding of the way in which physical energy can be turned into objects of an action-oriented ontology. These objects define what exists in the world from the viewpoint of the mind. The general idea is that action is a mediator between matter and mind. Therefore, understanding this mediator is of crucial importance for the development of a technological mediator which will assist subjects in interactions between mind and matter.

## 3.6    Perspectives for a Technology of Music Mediation

The above ecological model offers a number of perspectives for a technology of music mediation.

A first perspective concerns the relationship between a subject and a musical environment that is embedded in electronics. Without a mediator, the subject can hardly access the musical environment in a content-based or experience-based way because music is encoded physical energy stored on a device. Therefore, a mediator has to be created which allows a more fluent interaction between subject and music. One view is that this can be realized by creating hooks which describe the encoded physical energy in terms of content and experiences. The hook is the channel through which the interaction between subject and environment can take place. It can be considered part of the musical environment, which now consists of encoded physical energy (defined by natural constraints) and descriptors of the content of music (defined by cultural constraints). The hook (like the hook of Captain Hook) is the extension of the human body into technology. Its processing capabilities should be conceived of in terms of action-relevant processes, which have meaning to the action-relevant ontology controlled by mental processes.

A second perspective concerns the relationship between the natural and cultural constraints in music. Music is pure physical energy and, at the same time, a cultural artifact. Certain features of cultural artifacts may be addressed on the basis of their physical structure. In that sense, the mediator should attempt to create hooks in such a way that regularities at the cultural level can be accounted for by regularities at the physical level. A good example is pitch scales in African music. African musicians adopt a number of different pitch scales, sometimes pentatonic, sometimes heptatonic, and so on. Assume that a large database of African music is available. By using audio-mining technology, it is possible to transform the encoded physical energy of this database into pitch representations. Thus, one can compare music in terms of pitch scales and look for similarities and geographical relationships in terms of a culturally relevant descriptor that was extracted from encoded physical energy.

A third perspective concerns the design of a music mediation technology. The designer develops a framework in which a user will interact with a musical environment. This framework will draw upon knowledge of the physical/biological and cultural constraints of the human/music interaction. Examples are modules for the extraction of pitch, harmony, and tonality; modules for onset detection, tempo, and rhythm; and modules for semantic descriptions of music. However, these regularities may subsume particular societal or cultural goals. The goal may be the design of access to African music, for example. Or it may be the design of access to an interactive music production system. In both cases the systems have functions in societal and cultural contexts. These contexts may largely define the kind of regularities that should be implemented and the kind of interactions that should be accounted for.

In many cases a description of a subjective experience may not be extracted straightforwardly from musical physical energy. It is well known that the conditions for obtaining descriptions relating to feelings, beliefs, values, goals, and personal opinions are difficult to control. In those descriptions, the focus is on subjective matters, and the description is often based on interpretations. Difference in description may reflect difference in ontology. However, it is clear that these differences should be taken into account in the development of a technology of music mediation.

A fourth perspective concerns the idea that the development of a technology of music mediation is similar to the development of a musical instrument. A musical instrument can indeed be seen as an extension of

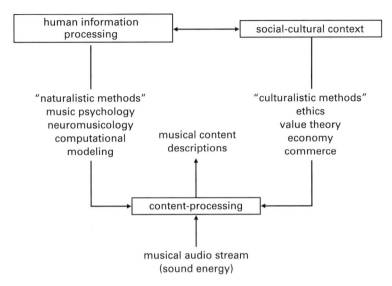

**Figure 3.6**
Content processing involves naturalistic and culturalistic approaches.

the human body, and it contributes to the creation of cultural artifacts, using the principle of a ratchet. That is, it builds upon earlier results. Hence, the dynamics of the action–reaction cycles, as well as the idea of the ratchet effect, may be used as an analysis model for a system-engineering approach to music mediation. Mediation technology can be seen as an artifact evolving on the basis of accumulated knowledge.

In more abstract terms, it seems that the ecological model may provide a general concept for the development of content-based mediation technologies. The natural and cultural constraints are reflected in general methodologies, called naturalistic and culturalistic methodologies.

Figure 3.6 represents this relationship between naturalistic and culturalistic methods in general terms. The naturalistic methods are used to study human information-processing. The resulting knowledge may provide basic principles of how sound energy can be transformed into musical descriptions. The culturalistic methods are used to study social, ethical, and economic behaviors—in other words, to study how the subject behaves in a social and cultural context. This behavior is considered to be goal-directed. Finally, research in human information-processing is carried out as a function of the values and significant actions of the social-cultural context. The schema assumes that music content description is a function of these naturalistic and culturalistic methods. In the development of a particular music information retrieval system, for example, human factors are brought into focus. They may largely determine the kind of information-processing tools that need to be developed, and the kind of mediation technology that can be used in a particular context. The schema shows that the design of a technology for music mediation may depend largely on the goals of a project. Obviously, these goals are constrained by the context in which that particular technology is going to be used.

## 3.7   Conclusion

In this chapter, involvement with musical reality has been discussed from the viewpoint of an ecological framework for subject/environment interactions. The focus has been on the roles and interaction of natural and cultural environmental constraints. The model developed in this chapter has been based on the notions of direct perception, inference, the action–reaction cycle, and resonances. The result is a powerful dynamic model that relates action and perception to natural and cultural environmental constraints.

This dynamic has shown how action/perception processes may disambiguate stimuli–source relationships encountered in the environment. Furthermore, through action, humans are able to turn physical energy into action-relevant concepts and cultural artifacts. Resynthesis and imitation of action-relevant values of physical energy play a key role in the construction of a culture. Action thus forms a basic component of culture. It allows the creation of cultural artifacts, of technology, of the sharing of attention on goals, intentions, and significations.

The ecological model put forward in this chapter implies that involvement with music is embedded within a dynamic of multiple constraints impacting each other. This makes the model complex. The dynamic assumes resonant interaction between different components of that model. In developing tools that allow human beings to enhance their interaction with stream-based musical information through modern technology, these resonances have to be studied and exploited in more detail.

# 4 Corporeal Articulations and Intentionality

In the previous chapter, involvement with music was dealt with in terms of subject/environment relationships. The emphasis was on the interaction of a subject with natural and cultural environmental constraints. It was found that human action can realize the transformation from physical energy to cultural abstractions, and vice versa. This chapter emphasizes that transformation, and goes deeper into the mechanisms of action and perception of the involved subject.

This chapter starts with an analysis of three different types of music description—first-person, second-person, and third-person—which express different approaches to intentionality. Of particular relevance is the distinction between first-person and second-person descriptions. They reflect the distinction between the (cerebral) interpretation of an intended act and the (corporeal) articulation of an intended act. In the second section, it is argued that corporeal articulations may be seen as an expression of a corporeal understanding of music as intentional being. This understanding is grounded in the human bias to attribute intentionality to things that move and with which we move or which we imitate. In the third section, attention is given to the engine that allows corporeal understanding. This engine is based on the coupling of action and perception, the underlying system of which is a coupling of motor and sensory mechanisms. In the final section, attention is again focused on the intricate link between corporeal articulations and linguistic descriptions of music. Examples of music description are given and the parameters are set out for a theory of music perception and a technology of music mediation.

## 4.1 Descriptions

Intentionality refers to a nonexistent content, as Brentano (1874/1955) noted. Mental attitudes, such as thinking, believing, wanting, and desiring, are about something that is physically nonexistent. They are about a virtual world, about intended things. For example, I can think about the face of a musician, his or her posture, and even particular movements, but the face, the posture, and the movements exist only in my imagination. My thinking does not create these objects in the real world. And no observer will ever be able to see these objects in my mind. In a similar way, I can imagine music and mentally simulate its temporal deployment as if I hear it. But again, this mental operation does not create existing music, except in my mind. The reality of my mind is, from a physical point of view, a purely imaginary reality.

In a similar way, I can attribute a mental attitude to other subjects. By looking at how a person moves and behaves, I can understand that person as an intentional being. My understanding of his or her intentions allows me to predict his or her actions and understand them as part of an understanding of my own actions.

This attribution of intentionality can also be extended to material things that move, such as cars. In traffic, another car is not just a moving object. It is an object with particular intentions which I can understand by using the experience of my being a driver. Responsible drivers aim at understanding the intended movements of other cars, and on that basis predict their future behavior. It is likely that for a dog, a car is just another moving object. It is not an intentional object because the dog is not involved with driving a car. The moving car is not something that the dog can relate to its own actions. Hence, it may not have an understanding of it in terms of a mental simulation.

Like cars, music can be understood as an intentional object. Indeed, the literature on music aesthetics and the phenomenology of music (e.g., Wellek, 1963; Schaeffer, 1966; Broeckx, 1981; Scruton, 1997; Cumming, 2000; Tarasti, 2003) provides a wealth of introspective descriptions concerning intentionality related to music. The descriptions are based on the perception of a differentiated set of qualia, which range from structural attributes such as pitch, melody, harmony, tonality, and rhythm up to semantic attributes which relate to our affective, expressive, or even emotional life. In this literature, involvement with music is basically described in terms of purposes, values, beliefs, and feelings.

Clearly, these attributions of intentionality to music somehow reflect the typical way of being involved with music. This involvement tends toward the perception of what is intended, rather than what is. In addition, musicologists tend to give interpretations of what is intended.

They tend to understand the source of what is supposedly intended in music.

### 4.1.1  First-Person and Third-Person Descriptions

The musicological literature draws on a distinction between two types of description: first-person and third-person.

The first-person descriptions in musicology draw upon interpretations of intentions attributed to music, such as an attribution of "inner victory of the spirit" to a passage in Beethoven's Piano Sonata in A (see chapter 1). This attribution is possible because the information picked up from physical energy is used to define properties of objects that are relevant in view of the subject's action-oriented bias. Thus, moving sonic forms receive the status of actions to which intentionality can be attributed.

Interpretation aims at finding the source of the attributed intention. In doing this, it often puts intentions in a historical and cultural framework. Through the lens of subjective interpretation, personally experienced intentions enter into the domain of a linguistic-based description of the world. Thus, music description acquires the status of a meaningful but personal narrative which other people can understand because they share similar interpretations of the environment. The description results from a subjective interpretation. It is both intention-based and symbolic/linguistic.

In contrast, third-person descriptions are about repeatable measurements of phenomena. These measurements, in principle, can be obtained by any observer, or can be made by a machine or with the help of a machine. By putting knowledge of human information-processing mechanisms, as well as knowledge of user conventions, into a machine it is possible to measure high-level structural and semantic properties directly from physical energy such as pitch, loudness, tempo, and particular affects such as "sad" or "happy". In addition, subjective involvement with music can be observed from the third-person viewpoint. For example, a subject's movement of arms and legs in response to music, or brain activity, can be recorded and further analyzed from a third-person perspective.

Figure 4.1 gives a schematic overview of the differences between third-person and first-person descriptions. To the left, physical energy is measured and the resulting descriptors are third-person. To the right, the first-person description is based on the subject's attribution of

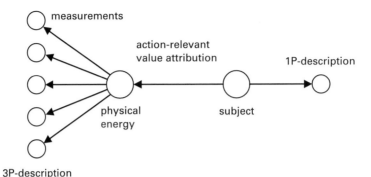

**Figure 4.1**
Model of first-person and third-person descriptions.

action-relevant cues to physical energy. In this case, the action-relevant cue is related to moving sonic forms that are seen as being intended. This attribution is an effect of direct perception, the bias to perceive our world in terms of affordances. The next step is an interpretation of the intended action-relevant cue in terms of a possible source or cultural context.

Clearly, the first-person and third-person descriptors have entirely different purposes. The first-person description may provide a narrative of musical involvement, whereas the third-person description provides the results of a measurement of the physical energy.

## Correlating Interpretations with Measurements

A main reason that correlations between first-person and third-person descriptions might be of interest is that such correlations would facilitate the interaction between subjects and their technological environment. For example, access to music as encoded physical energy in a database (a third-person description) would be easier if access could be based on first-person descriptions that specify content and experience. Indeed, our action-oriented understanding of the world is in terms of content and experience rather than in terms of measurement of physical energy. Correlations would link this action-oriented understanding with aspects of physical energy and facilitate the interaction. Along with that practical objective, there is the pure scientific argument saying that we have no complete theory of music if we cannot account for this connection between mind and matter (Chalmers, 2004).

However, it may be difficult to discern regularities in speculative interpretations. In fact, this is exactly what subjectivism claims (see the

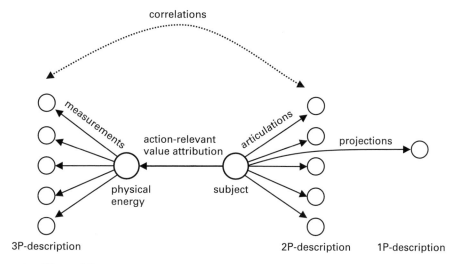

**Figure 4.2**
Model for first-person, second-person, and third-person descriptions (see text for explanation).

discussion in sec. 1.3). The speculative character of interpretations introduces a level of arbitrariness which may be difficult to grasp in terms of underlying rules or regularities. As a matter of fact, if there are no rules or regularities, it becomes difficult to develop a statistics that makes associations. In that case, no data-mining technique will be able to extract something useful. As a result, if no regularities are available, speculative interpretation will remain a private method of meaning-formation. This may still be something of interest for the subject who makes these interpretations, as well as for a group of interested subjects, but it is probably less appropriate to use as a hook (an action-based connection point) in a technology of music mediation. In that case, the link with interpretation may be problematic.

### 4.1.2   Second-Person Descriptions

The question is whether it is possible to have a form of description which involves intentionality but is less linked in that way to interpretation. In what follows, I draw upon the idea that an important form of description may be based on corporeal articulations.

The model for this type of description is presented in figure 4.2. The figure integrates the first-person descriptions (right) and the third-person descriptions (left). However, the new aspect is that perceived action-relevant values can be articulated, and the resulting articulations are called second-person descriptions.

The main difference between first-person and second-person descriptions concerns the distinction between experience as interpreted and experience as articulated.

Second-person descriptions are used to show, express, and articulate the private experience from one subject to another. They imply a "me-to-you" relationship. Both subjects have a disposition to show, express, and articulate music, and therefore can understand the experience on the basis of such a shared expression. It is like a doctor who asks a patient to describe what he or she feels. The nonverbal and verbal articulations of the patient express what is perceived and experienced. Based on that information, the doctor should be able to make a correct diagnosis. The patient's articulations should avoid interpretations and associations. At the lowest level, the articulations can be related to bodily behavior which the doctor observes. At the highest level, they may involve verbal descriptions of corporeal feelings. Second-person descriptions reflect involvement with physical energy in a context of intersubjective communication. Yet, in being subjective, these descriptions can be elusive and bound to a number of subjective factors.

Note that second-person descriptions comprise nonverbal articulations as well as verbal descriptions. Verbal descriptions of observed states of the human body involve self-observation and sometimes interpretation, and in that sense they may come close to first-person descriptions. Indeed, it may be possible to consider a continuum of steps from low-level corporeal articulations, to vocal utterances, to high-level conceptualized self-observations, and, finally, to interpretations which relate bodily behavior to cultural topics. In my definition, only the latter would be considered genuine first-person descriptions. Clearly, not all verbal descriptions rely on hermeneutic interpretations. There is sufficient room for considering a self-contained category of nonverbal as well as verbal descriptions that have their origin in corporeal articulations rather than in cultural associations. The intimate nature of these descriptions is in agreement with a social context where two subjects interact; hence the name "second-person description."

### Correlating Articulations with Measurements
The model of figure 4.2 assumes that correlations can be made between second-person and third-person descriptions (top). If correlations are

found, then prediction models may be built that allow the prediction of subjective (second-person) descriptions, starting from an analysis of the physical properties of the music. In principle, this could be done for each individual subject. These models could then be used in databases and interactive machines. The link from relatively high-level subjective articulations to descriptions of physical energies would then allow each subject to have an individualized technology-mediated access to music.

Ultimately, the main goal of music research might be to work out causal models of the relationship between physical energy and subjective experience. Such models would imply the physical modeling (models that are functionally equivalent to causal processes) of the biomechanics of the human body. Whether this is possible remains to be seen; it is an important research question.

## Reducing Ontologies

Now assume, for a moment, that associations between corporeal articulations (for example, arm movements) and objective descriptions of musical structure (for example, percussion events) have been found. Have we then reduced the subjective involvement with music to a measurement of some aspect of the physical energy? In other words, is intentionality then made equal to an aspect of physical energy? Obviously not, for the simple reason that corporeal articulations and descriptions of physical reality rely on fundamentally different ontologies. Articulations express something that is created in the mind of a subject whose action is directed toward some aspect of the physical energy. The description of the physical reality, however, does not take into account the intentional orientation of a subject. Nevertheless, correlations between corporeal articulations and physical energy can be useful in music mediation technology. They may help facilitate the extension of the human body into the virtual world of electronic media, thereby closing the gap between the human mind and the machine-encoded physical energy contained in that virtual world.

To sum up, in this section a distinction has been made between subjective and objective descriptions of music. Objective descriptions are related to measurement and repeatable observations, while subjective descriptions are related to the reporting of unique experiences of action-relevant cues in music. These experiences can be either articulated or interpreted. Articulations are more spontaneous, more socially functional, and more body-based than first-person descriptions. The latter stress interpretation and the link with cultural topics. In connection with music, these descriptions are based on awareness. They focus on private life, provide insight into culture, and imply a cerebral-based approach. The hope is that part of the human subjective involvement with music can be captured in terms of articulations. Given their subcognitive and social character, I believe there is a chance that meaningful correlations with objective descriptions can be discovered.

## 4.2   Corporeal Intentionality

Until recently, the philosophy of intentionality seems to have emphasized the cerebral aspect of intentionality, which closely adheres to thinking and interpretation. The relationship of this type of disembodied mental activity with the real world has always been slightly mysterious and, for that reason, a mostly unsolved problem in philosophy (Erneling and Johnson, 2005). However, recent developments in neurophysiology provide evidence for the role of human movement and human action in explaining the phenomenon (Berthoz, 1997; Metzinger and Gallese, 2003; Jeannerod, 2003; W. Singer, 2002; Berthoz and Jorland, 2004; Gallese, 2006). In this approach, intentionality refers to an action-based understanding of the world, while cerebral intentionality can be seen as a layer on top of it. My notion of corporeal intentionality is much in line with these approaches.

In what follows, I argue that corporeal intentionality can be conceived as an emerging effect of action/perception couplings, the underlying engine of which can be defined in terms of a sensorimotor system. The engine turns the physical energies of music into an imaginary world of objects having qualities, valences, goals, and intentions, and vice versa. Corporeal articulations can be seen as expressions of this process of turning physical energy into an action-relevant and, as a consequence, action-intended ontology.[1]

Corporeal intentionality can be distinguished from cerebral intentionality—which, in music, explores the speculative pursuit of potential interpretations. The essence of cerebral intentionality is interpreting the source of intentions attributed to music. The essence of corporeal intentionality is the articulation of moving sonic forms, with the emphasis on movement in relation to behavioral resonances of the human body. Corporeal intentionality can be seen as an emerging effect of the coupling of action and perception. If action and perception are indeed tightly coupled (probably due to overlapping neuronal codes), then it should be possible to derive action sequences from perception in order to see how intentionality is reflected in the action sequences. If corporeal intentionality can be captured in articulations, it may provide a key to communicating with technologies that mediate access to stored, encoded physical energies. I will show that this approach is feasible in music research and is likely to become a major research area.

## 4.2.1   The Intentionality Engine

A useful model for understanding the engine behind corporeal intentionality is based on the notions of outer space and inner space. These spaces should be conceived as representational spaces of a subject's outer and inner environments, respectively.[2] The knowledge of the outer, environing world is determined by receptors and effectors that define what becomes a stimulus or sign for a biological organism. The inner environing world is created by the directing apparatus of the biological organism, that is, the movements and actions in the environment. Corporeal intentionality can be understood in terms of a coupling of these two spaces.

### Inner Space
First, let us look at the inner space. The sensing of our body movements leaves traces of motor activity in memory, and the sum of these motor traces defines an internal model (or internal representation) of possible movement trajectories.

The sensing of our own body movement is called kinesthesia. It is done by receptors which capture body movement. Basically, this capturing proceeds in two ways: a relative way, through the sensing of body movements that change with respect to ongoing body movements, and an absolute way, through the sensing of body movements that change in relation to the environment (Berthoz, 1997). (See figure 4.3.) The proprioceptive receptors located in muscles and joints produce the relative sensing of movement, while the receptors in the vestibular system, the organs for equilibrium and gravity—more particularly the semicircular canals and otolith organs—produce the absolute sensing of movement.

At the same time, however, the inner space is also a reservoir for the execution of body movements (Jeannerod, 1994). The reservoir of biomechanical possibilities contains schemata or learned sequences of elementary movements that can be executed.[3]

The inner space is a center for afferent and efferent processing of information. In afferent processing, the sensing of movement proceeds

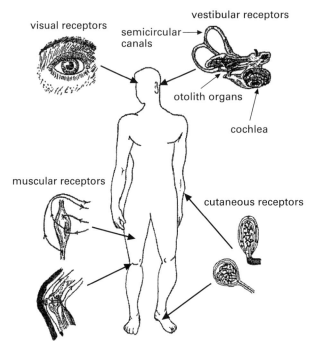

visual receptors

vestibular receptors

semicircular canals

otolith organs

cochlea

muscular receptors

cutaneous receptors

musculo-articulatory receptors

**Figure 4.3**
Human receptors. (Reprinted with permission from A. Berthoz, *Le Sens du mouvement* (The brain's sense of movement), translated by G. Weiss. © O. Jacob, 1997, p. 26.)

from the periphery to the center. In efferent processing, the execution of movement proceeds from the center to the periphery. Efferent processing can be blocked at a late stage: all processing can be carried out until the last moment when the body would start to move. In terms of the functional apparatus of the human body, it is as if the movement had taken place, except that the very last stage is blocked. Several studies show that the execution of movement can be blocked at different levels of the efferent processing pathway. Jeannerod (1994) distinguishes between central and peripheral mechanisms for motor images. Berthoz (1997) refers to gamma motor neurons that modulate the sensibility of kinesthesia or movement sensing. The activity or non-activity of these neurons induces an activity or a non-activity in the neuromuscular nerves. Kinsbourne (2002) observes that the younger the child, the less the inhibition, and the greater the overt movement overflow.

## Outer Space

Apart from kinesthesia, the sensing of the external world is based on visual, auditory, and tactile receptors. This sensing also leaves traces. The sum of these traces defines the outer space, that is, an internal model (or internal representation) of the external world.

The inner and outer spaces both rely on sensing, but the main difference is that the inner space has the power to set the body into covert or overt action (using capabilities of efferent processing and inhibition at different levels of the efferent processing pathway), while the outer space is basically an afferent device.[4]

## Coupling Inner and Outer Spaces

The coupling of afferent and efferent processes creates a very powerful enacting device from which intentionality may emerge (Metzinger and Gallese, 2003). A core idea of the coupling is that perception and action share common neuronal event codes, that is, a common representational medium for perceived events (perception) and intended or to-be-generated events (action) (Hommel et al., 2001).

Let us first look at what happens when sensory trajectories activate motor trajectories. The physical energy of a stimulus provides information to the sensory system, which, on the basis of previous experiences, can form a percept. The coupling with inner space and the activation of a motor trajectory allow the system to react on the physical energy of the environment, through either execution of an action or the simulation of an action. In simulation, efferent processes are activated but blocked at a certain level. As a result, the percept becomes an object of an action-directed bias, and via that bias it becomes an object of an action-oriented ontology. This ontology defines an a priori framework for any subjective goal-directed bias, and thus for perception and action.

The notion of action-intended ontology goes beyond the statement that perception focuses on the action-relevant cues of physical energy. Instead, it states that perception induces the simulation of intentions that may be attributed to the environment. In fact, perception can be seen as the creation of a motor image of the world that is based on sensory information. The world is seen from the viewpoint of intentional actions.

The sharing of neuronal event codes for perception and action is consistent with the viewpoint that perception is simulated, or emulated, action (see, e.g., Berthoz, 1997; Meltzoff and Prinz, 2002; Wilson and Knoblich, 2005). This view entails that through the coupling of action and perception, percepts are directly related to predictions and to actions. It is also consistent with the viewpiont that perception in terms of motor images may have the additional advantage of reducing the large number of sensory parameters to a few control parameters needed for motor-based resynthesis, or imitation (Liberman and Mattingly, 1985). This implies that important aspects of the outer world, particularly music, would in fact be captured in terms of actions and, thus, in terms of embodied resynthesis.

All this implies that motor trajectories may turn a (proximal) stimulus into an action-intended percept rather than an action-relevant percept. This view embraces the idea that the perception of the world fundamentally induces intentionality and anticipation (Hawkins and Blakeslee, 2004). In other words, the world is conceived from the viewpoint of action and prediction rather than merely based on the construction of gestalts (good forms).

Obviously, the sensorimotor system also works the other way around. When a trajectory in the inner space is simulated—for example, a walk from the front door of the university building to my office—I can associate this motor image with a trajectory in the outer space. I can explore the visual-audio-tactile features of the objects I encounter along my imaginary walk. In that sense, the sensorimotor couplings allow the transition from imagined movement to predicted sensory qualities. If the moving sonic forms can engage humans in body movements, then it is straightforward to assume that this movement will engender sensory qualities which can be attributed to music as well. If corporeal imitation of movement in sound is possible, then the association with sensory qualities is straightforward (Godøy, 2003).

Figure 4.4 summarizes the model presented so far. The boxes on top represent inner and outer space, and contain trajectories of movement and of sensory information. These trajectories should be conceived of in terms of neural representations. The inner space holds trajectories of movement, while the outer space holds trajectories of sensory information. The spaces are connected with each other and perhaps partly overlap at defined levels of representation. Both spaces are also connected with the environment. Physical energy provides input to the systems that perceive movement and sensory information. In addition, motor responses provide access to the environmental energy. These motor responses, however, can be inhibited at different levels.

As a result of this motor feedback, physical energy will be captured as objects and events (distal cues) rather than as physical cues or sensory

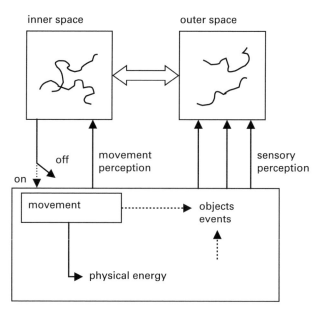

**Figure 4.4**
Coupled action and perception model.

cues (proximal cues). In other words, the stimulus properties are turned into recognition of the stimulus–source relationships through active involvement of body movement on the physical energy. Through learning, the subject can rely more on a statistics of previous observations.

Furthermore, the object may become a goal when movements are simulated to grasp the object. The movements become actions and are directed toward a goal. The object may further acquire a valence because it exerts reward or punishment. Acting upon the object, in other words, forms the basis for turning physical energy into an object of the subject's action-oriented ontology (Gallese and Metzinger, 2003).

### 4.2.2   Evidence for Action/Perception Couplings

The sensorimotor model assumes a tight coupling between low-level motor movements and sensory perception. It can be conceived of as the neuronal equivalent of the action/perception model at a higher mental level. Evidence in favor of the model comes from different fields: (1) from behavioral studies, particularly from observations of imitation in newborn infants, and (2) from the discovery of so-called mirror neurons in monkeys and humans.

### Native Imitation

Meltzoff and Moore (1977) showed that newborn infants imitate facial gestures such as lip and tongue protrusion. Numerous studies also have confirmed that newborn infants can, in addition, imitate mouth-opening, hand gestures, hand movements, cheek and brow motions, eye-blinking, and components of emotional expressions (see Meltzoff, 2002a for an overview). The studies provide evidence that the coupling of observation and executed movements is innate. Newborn infants spontaneously imitate actions they have never seen before by overt behavior. Later in life, this ability is inhibited.

### Mirror Neurons

The discovery of so-called mirror neurons provides direct evidence for the existence of a common neural structure for action and perception. They were discovered during studies that focused on the activity of motor neurons in a particular brain area of conscious monkeys (e.g., Gallese et al., 1996; Rizzolatti et al., 1996). During these studies, the monkeys were allowed to reach for and grasp objects in a seminaturalistic context. Rizzolatti et al. (2002) summarize how the neurons of this area were related to specific actions, such as grasping-with-the-hand, grasping-with-the-hand-and-the-mouth, holding, poking, and manipulating. A certain percentage of these neurons also respond to visual stimuli, in particular when the monkey observes graspable objects. The visuomotor neurons thus encode a motor representation of an action suitable for interaction with a particular object. Mirror neurons form part of this second category of visuomotor neurons because "They activate when the monkey observes another individual (the experimenter or another monkey) making a goal-directed action either with the hand or, in some cases, with the mouth" (p. 249).

Mirror neurons do not code a simple parameter of movement, such as force or movement direction; rather, they encode the intended action of an agent toward an object. For example, the beginning of the grasp action executed by the experimenter may be observed by the monkey, but the end of the action, the actual grasping, may be hidden behind a screen. The observed grasp action should not be completed, but should give the impression of being completed in order to induce an intention, and thus an activation of mirror neurons. Furthermore, it should be done by a monkey hand or the hand of a human experimenter, not a mechanical object. The neurons discharge during the execution of the goal-directed action and during the observation (auditory, visual) of the same goal-directed action. The mirror neurons thus represent both the monkey's own executed action and the observed action, providing a common neural structure for action and perception. Hence the name "mirror neurons": they encode the connections between intended trajectories of the inner space and associated intended trajectories of the outer space (Gallese and Goldman, 1998; Iacoboni et al., 2005).

After this discovery in monkeys, it was shown that similar regions subserving perception and action couplings are present in the human brain. In figure 4.4, mirror neurons would be situated in the area between inner and outer space.

Kohler et al. (2002) localized audiovisual mirror neurons in area F5 of the macaque brain that encode actions independently of whether these actions are actually performed, but rather through association with the sound of the action. Calvo-Merino et al. (2005) showed that the mirror system integrates observed dancing actions with a personal motor repertoire. Thus mirror neurons draw upon learned action sequences, as the work on dancing actions suggests. Blakemore et al. (2005) showed somatosensory activations during the observation of touch. There is evidence, in other words, that mirror neurons are amodal, in the sense that they can encode the mirroring of multiple sensory channels.

A few authors have made a connection with language development. For example, Rizzolatti and Arbib (1998) have suggested that the mirror system is the precursor of the crucial language property of parity: that an utterance usually carries similar meaning for speaker and hearer. Mirror neurons have been assumed to be part of a vocabulary of action that contains the image (the simulated motor trajectory) of how to perform an action in terms of their goals. Mirror neurons perform sensorimotor integration and transformation as the basis of imitation. Recent findings seem to support the idea that such neuronal functions would be able to execute and observe not only the action itself but also the expressiveness of the action (Calvo-Merino et al., 2005) and emotions (Wicker et al., 2003).

### 4.2.3   Action-Oriented Ontology

The move from sensorimotor couplings to intentionality, and ultimately to subjective descriptions, is best understood by considering the notion of action-oriented ontology once more.

## Social Origin

An action-oriented ontology is about entities that exist on the basis of an intended action toward the physical energy in the environment. This intentionality can be attributed to subjects as well as to objects (or, rather, events). Attribution of intentionality is likely to occur on the basis of mirroring, that is, on the basis of a simulation of the perceived action in the subject's own action. Actions of others are understood as intended actions because the subject can simulate them and understand them as its own intended actions. Yet the identification is not complete, because if it were, the sense of self, or ownership of the body, would be lost. Therefore, several levels are probably involved. They imply partial overlap but should leave room to distinguish one's own actions from the actions of the other (Decety and Grèzes, 2006).

Obviously, music is not another human subject, but it provides "moving sonic forms" which, through corporeal articulations, are associated with our actions. In that sense, music can be considered a virtual social agent whose actions can be emulated. Based on these actions, the proximal sonic stimuli can be turned into distal action events, which provide cues for attributing intentionality. The possibility of human social communication, using subjective expressions and descriptions, is based on the fact that humans come to their action-oriented ontology in more or less similar ways. In other words, ontologies partly overlap among subjects and thus may create a repository for semantic communication. The latter assumes that the emulated actions are somehow self-observed, conceptualized, and, finally, verbally described.

## Values and Drives

The coupling of action and perception shows that the construction of an imaginary world is not purely a matter of structures and forms, but of actions and action simulations as well. In addition, we may assume that there are also drives involved. Thus, the drive to handle real-world objects as action-oriented objects (or goals) is mainly due to the fact that the physical things in the environment give a return, and therefore become associated with a valence (good or bad). The objects encountered in the environment (and represented in outer space) thus acquire the status of goals with associated valence and energy. Objects are then perceived in terms of actions directed at objects-with-valence-and-energy. The internal models that we build of such objects have the status of experienced values to which we refer in intentional attitudes (Gallese and Metzinger, 2003).

To sum up, the engine for turning physical energy into subjective experience, and thus for intentionality, is a mirroring system based on the coupling of action and perception. Thus, a virtual or intended world is created as a function of an action-oriented ontology. Corporeal intentionality can be defined as action-based involvement with music. This involvement is based on the creation of a virtual world of moving sonic forms. Corporeal articulations and (second-person) verbal descriptions are expressions of this involvement.

## 4.3   Expressive Meaning Formation in Music

The above theory suggests that subjective involvement with music may be partly captured by corporeal articulations that reflect actions. These actions are induced by a mirror system that translates moving sonic forms into motor activity. But how are corporeal articulations related to linguistic descriptors? I introduce this intriguing question in this section, and I return to it in more detail in the next chapter, where I deal with the notion of empathy, and in chapter 7, where I deal with verbal descriptions in view of music information retrieval.

Broeckx's (1981) theory of expressive meaning formation in music provides a useful contribution and a starting point. It makes a distinction between different levels of second-person descriptions.[5] According to Broeckx, listeners become engaged in the process of signification because the music appears to them as an intentional organism, that is, as a kind of material organism with sensitive attributes such as an acting subject that is involved in events. Subjective description of music, in his view, is the verbal description of experienced musical expressiveness. It is based on three processes: synesthetic, kinesthetic, and cenesthetic. A fourth process is involved with interpretation.

•     Synesthetic processing involves multisensory integration. Physical properties of musical audio—such as frequency, duration, spectral density, and loudness—are first perceived as auditory categories of pitch, duration, timbre, and volume, which then lead, via synesthetic (or multisensory) integration, to impressions of visual and tactile space, such as extension, density, weight, smoothness, roughness, hardness, softness, liquidity, and ephemerality.

•     Kinesthetic processing concerns the sensing of musical dynamics. Music is dynamic in the sense that physical properties (frequency, amplitude, and so on) evolve through time and generate in our perception segregated streams and objects that lead, via ideomotor processing, to impressions of movement, gesture, tension, and release of tension.

•        The cenesthetic process allows the experience to be turned into a linguistic description. It allows the description of the general feeling or awareness of the properties of multimodality and the properties of kinesthesia.[6]

•        A fourth process, analogical thinking, is based on cognitive interpretation and association.

Although the above theory appears to focus on structural cues and cognitive processing, there is a direct link with affective processing as well. This link is due to the fact that the perception of qualia and movement is related to reward. In this theory, the sensing of movement is strongly associated with reward functions.

While Broeckx's account of expressive meaning-formation was inspired by phenomenological and gestalt-theoretic approaches to music, its intuition sounds surprisingly actual. The essence of this theory is that a description of musical expressiveness and signification can be a report of how it feels when your brain is engaged in the valenced multimodal and kinesthetic processing of the musical audio stream. It provides a general schema of how synesthetic and kinesthetic corporeal articulations can be turned into linguistic-based second-person descriptions and, finally, into first-person descriptions (analogical thinking). A broadening of this theory toward the measurement and analysis of corporeal articulations is straightforward. Also, the link between music-driven expressive movements and self-observed verbal descriptions of these movements needs further attention in terms of the distinction between self and the other (here understood as a virtual other which is induced by music).

To sum up, the sensorimotor-based account of intentionality has a number of consequences for how we look at the communication and description of music. If perception is indeed covert action, then there may be certain techniques or tricks that may turn this covert action into overt action. What could be revealed are descriptions of corporeal intentionality, that is, articulations of how the world is perceived in terms of synesthetic- and kinesthetic-relevant cues. Such corporeal articulations are certainly very subjective, but it is in a sense objective for the subject, because the subject measures the physical energy as such. On top of these articulations, a linguistic description may be based, as proposed by Broeckx. And on top of those linguistic descriptions, interpretive projections into cultural signification are possible. In that sense, the progression from second-person to first-person descriptions is layered. It involves corporeal articulations which can be captured as descriptions and turned into linguistic descriptions, and, finally, into meanings that situate the perceived moving sonic forms in a cultural and historical context.

## 4.4   Music, Movement, and Intentions

The above theory provides a powerful model for understanding direct involvement with music. In what follows, the theory is linked with further scientific findings and some personal experiences I had with playing music, dance, and listening.

### 4.4.1   Playing Music

Playing a musical instrument is a highly skilled activity that is based on long-term and intensive rehearsal of motor patterns. This rehearsal aims at forming an inner space of motor trajectories that can be recalled and generated automatically—that is, without paying too much conscious attention to them. Rehearsal of motor actions (e.g., playing arpeggios on the violin) is needed in order to automate the motor patterns so that the musician can concentrate on the musical goals—the expressive intentions—rather than on the gestures or movements.

Music educators often distinguish between technique and musicality. A good technique should allow the musician to concentrate on musicality. In this process, the prediction of motor trajectory as an internal simulation of a motor trajectory, and the simulation of the expression before the actual execution of the expression, are essential aspects of making music. The driving force (perhaps one among many) is a particular aesthetic reward.

Recently, several studies have focused on the intrinsic relationship between playing music and brain activity. Some studies show that extensive procedural and long-term motor learning, and continued practice, based on imitation and rehearsal, seemingly have an observable effect on the human brain which is reflected in the brain's plastic reorganization (Schlaug, 2001; Pantev et al., 2001). Other recent studies (Lotze et al., 2003; Kristeva et al., 2003; Langheim et al., 2002; Hickok et al., 2003; Haslinger et al., 2005) indicate that primary motor and auditory areas become tightly coupled with executed activities during musical training. When one primary area is activated, the other also activates.

The studies also show that motor training leaves traces in inner space that can be used in imagery tasks.

Prediction of movement trajectories and goal-directed action toward expressiveness form an important part of the musician's ability to deal with music as expressive information. More than ever, playing music has been related to the tight coupling of action and perception. Recent brain research seems to confirm that playing music is embedded in a goal-directed ontology of involvement with music.

### 4.4.2   Dance and Response

Playing music, listening to music, and moving along with the music draw on sensory information (trajectories in outer space) and synchronized motor resonances (trajectories in inner space). The coupling of motor trajectories to any of these sensory traces provides a rich basis for behavioral resonances with music, either through synchronization and motor movement that goes along with the local physical energy in music, or through higher-level forms of attuning and goal-directed movements. During these musical activities, perception seems to induce a transition from musical audio streams to trajectories of auditory sensing in the brain, to motor trajectories in the inner space. The movements may be simulated (inhibited) or actually executed through movements of the head, the hands, the feet, or the whole body.

Interestingly, moving along with the music is what most people naturally do when they hear music. In contrast to the movement trajectories of playing an instrument, these movements are often not learned, but result from a spontaneous and natural "moving along." It is only when learned or rehearsed movements are involved that we speak about dance. Spontaneous movements, including "motormimetic sketching" (Godøy et al., 2006), may be closely related to predictions of local bursts of energy in the musical audio stream, in particular to the beat and the rhythm patterns.

Thus, when the music is violent and aggressive, we tend to perform movements (either simulated or executed) that go along with the violent and aggressive sounds. We move as if we produce the violent and aggressive sounds ourselves. These movements can be performed slightly ahead of the music, especially if we happen to know the music well. Through these movements, we become aware of violence and aggression because these movements invoke the sensing of acceleration, change of gravity, velocity, and force—parameters of movements that we would sense in actual violent and aggressive acts. The hypothesis is that we construct motor models of musical expressiveness on top of the sonic structures in music.

Here, too, the link with intentionality is straightforward. When sensory information evokes motor traces (either simulated or executed), it is likely that the perceived objects or processes are experienced as objects of an action-oriented ontology—as if the music is the product of our own action, as if we generate the music ourselves. Based on our natural inclination to predict and anticipate, these objects acquire the character of goals with valence (positive or negative character) and activity (high or low energy).

### 4.4.3   Pure Listening?

Do we really perceive music as if it is generated by our own actions? From my personal experience with music, I would be inclined to say that the better we know the music, the more we enjoy its simulated control, as if we were the musician or the conductor. Music thereby offers the proximal sonic cues and engages us to move along with the distal action that could have produced these cues.

This feeling of resonance, control, and anticipation may be important in explaining aesthetic pleasure. According to the sensorimotor theory, the senses provide the information to create action-related models of our environment, and these models allow us to anticipate the consequences of our actions. Thus, the better we know the music (or the musical style), the more (and the better) we are inclined to predict on the basis of movement. Work by Repp and Knoblich (2004) provides evidence that pianists recognize their own performance out of a number of other performances. The sense of control, and thus of overlapping of performed actions and perceived actions, may well be the origin of aesthetic pleasure, as was observed by Lipps (1903).

The listening experience is, moreover, a typical example of multisensory association because our auditory perception forms part of our fundamental multisensory perception of the world. We may assume strong associations not only between sensory information and motor information, but also between multiple modalities of sensory information. The nature of music, when performed in its natural environment, is basically multimodal.

Music will typically generate energies that are detectable by different sensory receptors. Different modalities of the stimulus, such as light and vibration, are transduced by the receptors into neural signals that follow separate processing paths. Multisensory integration implies that at a certain moment, responses to one mode of energy modify, enhance, or inhibit the responses to another mode of energy (Meredith, 2002).

Sensory integration, which is another aspect of the sensorimotor theory, makes it possible to experience music not only as pure sound but also as sound in association with other properties, perhaps basically visual, tactile, and motor experiences. In an excellent concert hall, equipped with an orchestra of loudspeakers around the audience and an appropriate spatial distribution of electronic music, I once experienced vivid sensations of myself moving in spaces with different forms, objects, and colors changing and moving. This experience, close to a (controlled) hallucination (Metzinger, 2003), was more vivid when I closed my eyes while listening, so that I was not disturbed by the scene around me. Introspection teaches me that sounds are indeed strongly related to different forms of sensation. In my case the sensation was perhaps more visual than tactile and not at all olfactory, but movement was the basic component. A colleague told me that his experience was more tactile than visual, although he agreed that movement was the main issue.

Shapes, colors, textures, and spaces are all in motion, and at least on that single occasion I experienced my own body as moving in these spaces. Electronic music may work particularly well to elicit this kind of experience because the sound is often detached from known instruments and other direct causes of the sounds. The abstract nature of electronic music often invites one to imagine the distal action event that could have produced the sound. Being surrounded by sound may give the feeling of immersion and being driven by another source, which is close to a feeling of ownership ("I am moving") without the sense of agency ("I am not causing the movement") (Gallagher, 2000).

Scientific evidence for multisensory integration comes from studies in synesthesia (Cytowic, 1989) and, more recently, in brain science. Multimodal neurons encoding space or related characteristics of stimuli have been found in several cortical and subcortical areas. But the best-understood mammalian neurons for multisensory integration are probably those of the superior colliculus (Patton et al., 2002). This nucleus receives inputs from the visual and somatosensory systems that are derived from cortical and subcortical brain regions. The neurons are known to be organized topographically according to the location in sensory space of their receptive fields. Visuotopic maps of the visual space, and maps of the body surface and of auditory space, have been found.

Due to the convergence of the sensory inputs, it also appears that many neurons in this nucleus can be activated by natural stimuli coming from more than one sensory modality—for example, by a visual stimulus or an auditory stimulus. The superior colliculus integrates converging inputs and triggers orienting movements of the eyes, head, body, or pinnae of the ears toward the source of stimulation.

The spatiotemporal relationship between the stimuli is critical for their sensory integration and enhancement. It is generally assumed that integration uses time windows updated at regular intervals (see also Berthoz, 1997). Spatial proximity also plays a role.

## 4.5    Consequences for a Theory of Music Perception

The principles discussed so far contribute to an ecological theory of the relationship between the subject and its musical environment. This theory, explained in the previous chapter, assumes that the subject's action and perception are entirely embedded and constrained by the natural and cultural environments. The ecological embedding has an effect on how music perception can be conceived of. In particular, the following aspects should be taken into account:

•     Perception serves to disambiguate the stimuli in our environment. This is necessary for survival actions.
•     Perception involves prediction in that it is based on past experiences rather than on logical analysis of the present stimulus.
•     Perception reduces the information to control parameters that can be used for resynthesis or action.
•     Perception is an emerging effect of resonance communication by means of which natural constraints and cultural constraints interact with each other.
•     Perception of our own actions generates internal representations of intentionality (goal-directed actions) which are associated with valence attributions.
•     The perception of the actions of others proceeds in terms of our own ontology of intentions, and hence in terms of prediction and anticipation. By extension, moving sonic forms are perceived in terms of our own ontology of intentions.
•     There is a bias to perceive physical movement as being intentional, especially if physical movement comprises biologically relevant movement patterns.

- Corporeal articulations are expressions of the intentional (anticipatory) nature of perception. They form the basis for a synesthetic and kinesthetic appreciation of music. Through self-observation (different from interpretation!), certain aspects of this appreciation can be turned into verbal descriptions.
- The sharing of attention paid to goal-directed activities (such as music) forms the basis of social bonding and cognition. It has a grounding in gestures and actions, and linguistic communication.

## 4.6   Consequences for a Technology of Music Mediation

The theory of intentionality put forward in this chapter may have far-reaching consequences for a technology of music mediation. Of particular relevance is the idea that perception and action are strongly coupled. Corporeal articulations are conceived as reflecting the action-oriented ontology that is induced by moving sonic forms in music. They exhibit prediction and anticipation of stimulus properties. The view entails that physical energies can be experienced in terms of structural, multimodal, kinesthetic, and affective properties, thereby forming the phenomenal basis for the subjective involvement with music. These properties form the target of the subject's ability to describe music in a corporeal and verbal way.

What this approach seems to promise for music research is a description layer which holds the middle course between objective and subjective. The question is whether there exists a method which allows the capturing of this medium description layer. So far, a single method has not been proposed, but our analysis suggests that corporeal articulations could be the key to a solution. In particular, if perception is indeed simulated (or covert) action, then methods should be developed which turn covert action into overt action (in other words, which turn perception into action or, better, into articulations). The intentional character of perception would then be revealed in the properties of the articulations—for example, in their anticipatory or mirroring character.

Turning perception into action holds the promise that correlations between corporeal articulations, verbal descriptions, and measurements of physical energy can be studied. Indeed, if corporeal articulations (corporeal second-person descriptions) can be captured and perhaps linked to verbal (second-person) descriptions and measurements of physical energy (third-person descriptions), then interesting applications become feasible for technologies of music mediation. It would mean that technologies can be accessed by means of descriptions that closely adhere to the natural expression of human subjects. However, research in this domain has just begun, and the implications of a theory based on musical corporeality are not yet fully incorporated into music research.

The resulting descriptions would include corporeal as well as verbal descriptions which draw upon subjective experience, but are sufficiently intersubjective and related to the properties of physical energies that they may become functional in a social context based on semantic communication. This is very different from first-person descriptions, which express speculative potential interpretations of a private experience. The following possibilities may be considered.

•    Verbal description based on motor behavior. It implies the sensing of movement—in other words, kinesthesia—and the subsequent description of this sensing with respect to space. Such descriptions have to be based on relationships between structural properties of the physical energy and an intersubjective set of motion terms.
•    Verbal description based on multisensory properties that in turn are based on sensed qualia related to mainly visual and tactile descriptors.
•    Verbal description based on affective qualities associated with the objects of the subjective action-oriented ontology. This is based on the idea that motor and multisensing properties are related to reward. It can be assumed that a particular set of affective descriptions, when properly used in attribution descriptions, is sufficiently intersubjective.
•    Corporeal articulations that mirror synesthetic and kinesthetic processing. It is of interest to explore the idea of having a description of music based on synesthesia and kinesthesia, without having to rely on linguistic descriptions. There are several contexts in which these notions might be important.
—In music information retrieval contexts, motor movements can be a source of description—for example, for defining a pattern of expressiveness or for indicating the tempo. Singing and vocal imitation imply motor movements of the throat.
—In interactive multimedia, motor movements are a central issue, mainly in terms of generating music (the music-playing paradigm).
—In brain research, motor responses form the key to the study of musical execution and imagery.

## 4.7   Conclusion

Through motor resonances, the complexities of the physical world are related to our personal experiences. Intentionality, therefore, can be conceived of as an emerging effect of this communicative resonance. It is grounded in the coupling of action and perception. Through this coupling, the human brain creates an action-oriented ontology of the world that forms the basis of musical communication.

The theory of action/perception couplings has a high potential to explain typical musical activities, including playing music, musical social engagement, the connection between music and dance, and the multisensory basis of listening to music. In addition, the sensorimotor theory provides a tool to turn musical phenomenology into a genuine musical content-processing science.

At the same time, the theory is limited because not all subjective descriptions can be straightforwardly related to an action-oriented subjective ontology. Associations between moving sonic forms and context descriptions, such as linguistic descriptions of historical conventions or stylistic categories, may be difficult. In contrast, there is a particular subset of semantic descriptors which, I believe, can be related to experiences of content. In that sense, the focus is on semantic content descriptors rather than semantic context descriptors.

The step from physical energies to description forms a primary challenge because the subjective ontology on which semantic descriptions are based associates values, goals, and signification practices with experiences. In this context, a distinction was made between first-, second-, and third-person descriptions. First-person descriptions focus on the subjective interpretation of these experiences. Third-person descriptions focus on structural properties of the physical signals. Second-person descriptions involve the description of a subject's multimodal and kinesthetic engagement as socially expressive engagement. These descriptions can be corporeal as well as linguistic. The latter assume a translation of experience into language, which involves an awareness and cognitive filtering of the corporeal articulations.

# 5 Corporeal Articulations and Imitation

In the previous chapter, it was suggested that people engage with music in a way similar to the way they engage with other people. Specifically, the behavior of another person can be understood when it can be mirrored in the subject's own action-oriented ontology. The valence-related goal directedness contained in this mirrored action can be attributed to the behavior of the other person. Thus, the other person is seen as having intentions, beliefs, values, and meanings. Likewise, changes in sound energy can be mirrored in the subject's action-oriented ontology. On the basis of this mirroring process, sound patterns can be understood as having intentionality. The process forms the basis of an appreciation of music which is strongly based on body movement, and to which cerebral appreciation and interpretation can be added.

This chapter goes deeper into the mirroring processes that underlie corporeal articulations. First, the nature of mirror processes is considered in terms of recent research on imitation. It turns out that different aspects of imitation can be discerned in relation to music. Second, an attempt is made to distinguish different types of corporeal articulation according to different degrees of musical involvement. The proposal is to distinguish among synchronization, attuning, and empathy. Third, corporeal articulation is related to musical expressiveness. After all, if articulations are a kind of expression, how do they relate to expressiveness in music? Finally, consequences are drawn for music research. It is argued that the understanding of corporeal articulations in response to music is related to a number of challenging questions requiring an interdisciplinary approach.

## 5.1 Corporeal Articulations as Imitation

Corporeal articulations have been defined as expressions of the attribution of intentionality to music. They are indications of synesthetic and kinesthetic action-relevant processes, having a predictive and anticipatory character. Such articulations manifest themselves as activations in the human body—for example, as brain activations, as physiological responses (such as cardiovascular responses manifested by changes in blood pressure, pulse rate, galvanic skin resistance, and breathing patterns), or as overt behavioral responses (observable movements of body parts).

In what follows, the focus is on the underlying theoretical model of corporeal articulations, no matter at which level they are observed (neural, physiological, behavioral). The theoretical model assumes that involvement with music is based on a mirroring process (realized in the coupling of action/perception), which allows the attribution of intentionality to music. Corporeal articulations, as indicators of intentionality, can be studied in terms of this mirroring process. Thus the central notion to start with is mirroring and imitation.[1]

### 5.1.1   True Imitation

There is a famous paragraph in Aristotle's *Poetics* (chap. 4) in which he says

Imitation is natural to man from childhood, one of his advantages over the lower animals being this, that he is the most imitative creature in the world, and learns at first by imitation. And it is also natural for all to delight in works of imitation. (2001, p. 1457)[2]

The passage sounds surprisingly similar to modern ideas. Recent empirical findings in child psychology and brain research support the view that true imitation (to be distinguished from mimicry and motor contagion) (1) is innate, (2) is well-developed in humans, (3) fosters learning, and (4) yields pleasure. An overview of the modern conception of imitation is given below.

### Imitation Is Innate

Since 1980, the experiments by Meltzoff on imitation behavior in newborn human babies, repeated by laboratories worldwide (for an overview, see Meltzoff, 2002a), have initiated a silent revolution in thinking about early childhood. Developmental psychologists now believe that Piaget's time scale (set up by Piaget in the 1950s) was too conservative in the sense that at an early age children are much more cognitively competent than was previously thought. Infants seem to be attuned to other persons from birth, and they seem to be capable of entertaining interactions by means of imitations via body movements, vocalization, and facial expressions. Based on experiments, imitation is believed to be a basic form of corporeal articulation which is goal-directed and based on purposeful action (Meltzoff and Moore, 1997). Many authors believe that imitation is an innate mechanism because, in certain experiments, actions such as tongue protrusion have never been seen by children, and yet, when they observe it, they imitate it. In other words, they can turn new visual information directly into a motor action.

## Imitation Is Most Advanced in Humans

According to Tomasello (1999), who studied the behavior of chimpanzees, the capacity to understand conspecifics as intentional/mental agents like the self is species-unique. A developed form of this ability in humans is perhaps the only characteristic that distinguishes modern humans from premodern human beings and animals. Animals indeed do imitate, but their imitation is less often directed toward the attainment of goals.[3]

Trevarthen (2004) assumes that human newborns' neural systems enable them to establish communication with their caregiver, to the benefit of their own survival. He argues that imitation is a function of the newborns' bias toward active experience and communication—in other words, to get a response from the person they are dependent on. The advanced form of gestural imitation in humans is assumed to presage the emergence of symbolic language (Rizzolatti and Arbib, 1998). This capacity underlies the development of social cognition.

## Learning Through Imitation

Imitation which allows learning is sometimes called true imitation because it differs from behavior, which draws upon contagious action sequences, such as yawning, and from imitation, which draws upon mindless repetition, or mimicry, such as the sounds of a parrot.[4]

(True) imitation is known to be extremely important for newborns, first to provide a sense of connectedness with social partners and then to allow the acquisition of information about other people's actions and intentions (Rogers et al., 2003; Trevarthen et al., 1999). In understanding the process of imitation, a distinction can be made between imitation that copies the task structure and hierarchical organization, and imitation that copies movements (Byrne and Russon, 1998). True imitation focuses on the goal, rather than on the means through which the goal is attained (Mitchell, 2002). Imitation thus involves a complex process of observation that is coupled to action prediction, followed by the execution of the action as a function of the goal. In that sense, imitation can be part of a learning process. This process contains several components (Bekkering et al., 2000):

- First, imitation involves a decomposition of the observed sensory action into constituent components that are encoded in motor components. This is followed by a reconstruction of the action pattern from the motor components.
- Second, decomposition is guided by an interpretation of the motor pattern as a goal-directed behavior. Thus, the constituent elements involve the goals of the action rather than the means through which the action achieves its goal.
- Third, goals are represented in hierarchical patterns.
- Fourth, the reconstruction of the pattern is subject to resource constraints. Dominant goals remain when resources are limited.

## Imitation Is Pleasure

Finally, Aristotle referred to delight, or pleasure, as a form of satisfaction or reward.[5] There is ample direct scientific evidence that corporeal imitation in music is a source of pleasure for humans. Yet, several hypotheses can be formulated.

The first hypothesis assumes that imitation facilitates communication and learning. The human newborn's bias to actively seek interaction, and the reward it gets from that, is one example of seeking communication. The communication between parent and newborn is very similar to musical communication. It involves specific patterns, and repetition and imitation of patterns in a two-way communication between parent and child. Trevarthen (2004) describes these communications as musical communication. When in a face-to-face interaction with an adult social partner, the adult suddenly holds a neutral, still face for one to two minutes, infants as young as two months respond with increased negative affect and gaze aversion. This is often interpreted as a disruption of a positive feeling or pleasure that the infant has while engaged with the adult (Striano and Tomasello, 2001).

A second hypothesis is that imitation may provide access to domains of reality that otherwise remain closed. An example is young children making a "telephone call" using a shoe instead of a real cell telephone. What is imitated is clearly the telephone-calling behavior, and the shoe is only a means to achieve that behavior. The essential thing is that through corporeal imitation of adult behavior the child mirrors the adult world with its own world. Thus the child gains access to the adult world. The child can now look at the world with the eyes of the adult, which supposedly can be very beneficial for its development. By analogy one could say that music may give access to aspects of reality which are otherwise difficult to access. Particular expressions, feelings, and affects can be experienced which are otherwise difficult or dangerous to experience (for example, a state of hubris). A further extension of this idea concerns ritual performances. Ritual performances create a context of mirroring and allow subjects to see the world from another viewpoint. In rituals, mirroring may provide access to knowledge that can be described and experienced through corporeal imitation. Symbols, in that context, facilitate mirroring just as a shoe facilitates the imitation of a telephone call.

A third hypothesis states that corporeal imitation forms the basis of seduction (that is, display of genetic fitness) and a whole palette of automatic communication patterns that is also operative in sexual display and attraction (Grammer et al., 1998, 2000). It is likely to assume that such behaviors work with music, not only in a social context, where partners use movements and gestures to evoke interest, but also in the individual context, where subjects can engage in similar movements and gestures with moving sonic forms in music. Music provides an excellent context in which to train these corporeal imitation behaviors and later to display them in a context with potential partners. By imitating expressiveness in music, the subjects are increasing their own viability.

The fourth hypothesis is based on the notion of self-motivation. In learning to play a musical instrument, often there is a balance between skills and challenges. Playing a musical instrument starts with the imitation of low-level skills and low-level challenges. However, as skills improve, the challenges can rise to a higher level. When skills and challenges are in equilibrium, this gives rise to an optimal experience or pleasure. Csikszentmihalyi (1990) calls this a negentropic state of consciousness which is intrinsically rewarding. Thus musical learning is done for pleasure; it changes mood or provides consolation.

To sum up, a major feature to keep in mind is that true imitation has a focus on goals rather than on the means by which the goal is attained. Furthermore, imitation gives rise to pleasure. An understanding of the relationship between pleasure and imitation is crucial, but further research is needed in this domain.

### 5.1.2   Music and Imitation

Given the modern view on imitation, it is of interest to take a closer look at how imitation manifests itself in music. Apparently, imitation in music can be approached from different viewpoints, and straightforward distinctions can be made between imitation of skills, imitation of musical figures, imitation of symbols, imitation of moving sonic forms (corporeal imitation), and imitation of group behavior (allelo-imitation).

**Imitation of Musical Skills**
Learning to play a musical instrument is a typical example of true imitation. It draws on the ability of the student to focus on what is essential in the teacher's example. Even if the instrument is not the same—for example, the teacher plays trombone and the student plays trumpet—it is still possible to imitate particular behaviors and playing styles because the student has more of a focus on the goals and less of a focus on the precise movements. However, the student's ability to see the movements and gestures of the teacher may be an important component in learning to play a musical instrument. The visual observation of expressive movements may facilitate the mirroring of the teacher's intentions to the student's intentions.[6]

The role of mirroring in music education has been confirmed by a brain imaging study (Buccino et al., 2004). Playing of a musical instrument was used to show that the decomposition into elementary motor components was encoded by the mirror neurons. When the action to be imitated corresponded to an elementary action already present in the mirror neuron system, this act was forwarded to other structures and replicated. In that case, no learning was needed. However, when imitation required the learning of a new pattern, further mechanisms were required. Unfortunately, the precise neural circuits of imitation learning are not yet fully understood. This study shows that true imitation does not always involve learning.

**Imitation of Musical Figures**
Imitation of musical figures is often studied in connection with music analysis. The aim is to find and characterize the musical (melodic, rhythmic, harmonic) figures which are repeated and varied in different layers of the musical structure. Musical figures are said to be imitated by other voices or instruments.[7]

Figural imitation largely draws upon formal structural similarities. In recent years, measurements for structural similarity in music have been formally defined. More and more, the study of figural imitation forms part of a mathematical viewpoint of similarity measurement (e.g., Berenzweig et al., 2004).

Obviously, figural imitation differs from corporeal imitation in that it is purely about musical structure rather than human behavior. Nevertheless, figural imitation, as practiced in fugues and counterpoint, is (intuitively) known to have a large impact on corporeal imitation. As far as I know, however, this has not yet been demonstrated by experiments.

## Imitation of Topics

The idea that art is mimesis has been very influential. Nature, people in action, emotions, and even styles have been used as reference models for imitation in music. Classical examples are the imitation of thunder in Vivaldi's *Four Seasons* and of a train in Honegger's *Pacific 231*. Emotions also have been imitated, such as the exclamation of desperateness in Berlioz's *Nuit d'été*. Even musical features have been imitated, such as the style of a composer (e.g., Stravinsky imitates the style of the baroque composer Pergolese in the *Pulcinella Suite*), or the musical style of a particular aesthetics (e.g., in postmodern music). However, it can be debated whether this is a form of imitation or, rather, citation or paraphrase.

Clearly, topical imitation is often based on habits that may have become a cultural constraint creating their own dynamics and referential system. Once the habit is lost, due to changing social conditions, the habit may still live in the cultural repertoire as a symbol. Hunting, for example, was a common practice in earlier centuries, but it is no longer part of the daily life of most people in industrialized cultures. Therefore, references to hunting in music have become part of a symbolic cultural repertoire (Monelle, 2000). The horn call reflects a conventional meaning, a topic, that is referred to in music through the imitation of the original model. The musical imitation of hunting behavior uses a sonic form similar to the sonic forms used in real hunting traditions. In that sense, the imitation could be called an icon. However, it is also a symbol in that it brings to mind a cultural context which is associated with aristocracy, nature, horses, and courtly virtues.

The above examples show that particular gestures may become imperative for the style. Interestingly, these gestures may be typical musical gestures that become cultural constraints, and therefore, according to cultural habits, ought to be imitated in many pieces. In such a context, particular articulations may become referential articulations. Although these stylistic articulations by themselves do not imitate an extramusical model or refer to a particular affect or emotion, they may still function in a stylistic framework, and therefore they can become carriers of the stylistic reference (Hatten, 2003).

Examples can be found in the singing styles of many pop stars. Ornaments used in these styles are often imitated by young amateur singers who tend to adopt, with different degrees of success, the ornamental singing styles of their models.[8] The ornaments are examples of stylistic gestures that achieve the status of cultural constraints. If you perform that music, you must perform it using the singing style of a particular pop star. Imitation of typical musical gestures, therefore, is not excluded from a referential context.

### Imitation of Moving Sonic Forms (Corporeal Imitation)

The main characteristic of corporeal imitation is body movement, which manifests itself in brain activity, physiological responses, and behavioral responses. It is based on a process of mirroring which in turn is based on both multisensory information-processing and the sensing of movement (kinesthesia).

As mentioned, imitation can refer to a historical remainder of something that originally had a great appeal to habitual behavior. While the link with the habit may have been lost, listeners unaware of the original historical content may still engage in corporeal imitation and therefore have access to the original.

Take the way Mozart characterizes men and women in action in *Le Nozze di Figaro* (Allanbrook, 1983). Swaying rhythms evoke in the listener an engagement which is the corporeal basis of understanding the essential nature of the action. In addition to that experience, the audience can associate the particular rhythms with their specific cultural context.

Natural associations connect with certain universal habits of human behavior, and their historical associations are largely in the possession of the educated operagoing audience today. A minuet, for example, is characterized by covert, gracious behavior, easy to imitate in a corporeal way, but for those who know the context, it may be a symbol of the aristocracy. In contrast, a rhythmic folk dance tune is characterized by fluent, overt behavior, also easy to imitate corporeally, which may be a symbol for the peasant class. Could the assumed universality of music be related to its capability of inducing motor responses in listeners which are strong enough to easily connect with cultural conventions that are still part of our society? Topical imitations may thus become more easily accessible when they are fully embedded in corporeal imitations. In Mozart's *Le Nozze di Figaro*, one could say that the corporeal and symbolic characters of the music go together. The empathy experience of corporeal imitation facilitates the *aha* experience of a contextual interpretation.

### Imitation in Groups (Allelo-imitation)

Corporeal imitation may be a key concept for the understanding of musical behavior in groups. Group articulations such as synchronized dancing of thousands of people during pop concerts can be explained as the sum of each subject's individual corporeal imitation of the moving sonic forms in music and each subject's corporeal imitation of his or her neighbor. This is a type of global group attuning, or allelo-imitation, known to generate global effects of group behavior. Though it has been little studied in music, emerging group behavior has been studied in animals. Theraulaz and Spitz (1997) provide mathematical simulations of animal imitation and mimicry behavior.

Allelo-imitation can be assumed to play an important role in ensemble playing. Good ensemble playing requires attentive listening to the other performers, as well making adequate gestures that bind the actions of the performers. The latter aspect can be related to corporeal imitation and mirroring in the sense explained above. What is imitated is likely to be related to the nature of the playing gestures with which one performer expresses gestural communication.

To sum up, imitation in music is multifaceted, and its study calls for much more detailed investigations in a larger framework of imitation research. In what follows, I concentrate on direct corporeal imitations of moving sonic forms. The reason for doing so is that corporeal imitation is a basic form which can be assumed to underlie all other forms of imitation in music.

## 5.2   Degrees of Empathic Musical Involvement and Imitation

The idea that musical involvement is based on the corporeal imitation of moving sonic forms has a long tradition (see chapter 2). A school of researchers in the late nineteenth and early twentieth centuries had a conception of musical involvement based on corporeal articulations (see, e.g., Lipps, 1903; Truslit, 1938).

In more recent accounts, movement in response to music is often seen as a gestural expression of a particular emotion (sadness, happiness, love, anger) that is assumed to be imitated by the music (e.g., Clynes, 1977; Friberg and Sundberg, 1999; Friberg et al., 2000; Camurri et al., 2003). Yet, the expression of emotion is only one aspect of corporeal involvement with music. In the next section, I show that corporeal articulations can also be used to annotate structural features, such as melody, tonality, and percussion events.

In what follows, I propose to make a distinction among three levels of corporeal imitation: synchronization, attuning, and empathy. They all involve imitation, but in different degrees of participation and identification. Where possible, brief examples are given of research that aims at capturing and understanding these types of corporeal articulation.[9]

### 5.2.1  Synchronization

The low-level resonances of the motor system refer to the ideomotor principle, according to which the perception of movement will always induce a tendency to perform the same or similar movements (Knuf et al., 2001). This principle is responsible for people's tendency to move in synchrony with auditory rhythms. Repp and Penel (2004) found evidence that synchronization of movement with purely visual rhythms is rare, whereas synchrony with auditory rhythms is more common. This suggests that there is a particular effect of sound energy on the human motor system. The effect is clearly observable in the tendency to tap along with the beat of the music. The beat is the most natural feature for synchronized movement because it appeals to fundamental biomechanical resonances (Thaut, 2005).

### Tapping the Beat

Tapping the beat while listening to music is a corporeal articulation called synchronization.[10] Many subjects, without being aware of it,[11] tend to move body parts in synchrony with patterns in the physical stimulus (Fraisse, 1963; Michon, 1967). A common practice is to ask listeners to tap the beat of synthesized patterns of music and then to measure the beat in terms of grouping and interonset intervals (Essens and Povel, 1985; Parncutt, 1994).

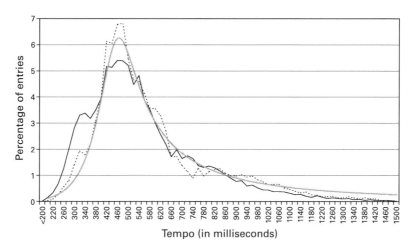

**Figure 5.1**
Resonance curve for beat. The graph shows distributions of tempi from different musical sources. The fluent solid curve is a model approximation (adapted from Van Noorden and Moelants, 1999).

While earlier research on tapping focused on frequency ranges (Fraisse, 1982), and on deviations of tapped values from regular values in the physical stimulus (see Desain and Windsor, 2000), more recent studies have stressed that tapping the beat is an elaboration of a more general sensorimotor faculty of the human brain (Todd et al., 1999, 2002). In line with this idea, the origin of the preferred tapping tempo has been related to biomechanical resonance properties of the human body.

van Noorden and Moelants (1999) found that tapping along with the beat in music fits well with the hypothesis of a resonator. The resonator forces beat perception to be structured by a period of about 2 Hz, which equates to about 120 beats per minute (bpm) (figure 5.1). Most of the tempi used in popular music have been found to be in agreement with the eigenfrequency of the assumed biomechanical resonator. Measurements of tempi in different musical genres show a distribution that comes very close to the resonance curve.

The resonator model predicts that subjects tend to tap the beat in agreement with the optimal range of the eigenfrequency of the resonator. Experiments show that in order to better fit the eigenfrequency of the resonator, the beat in slow music may be tapped twice as fast as the beat induction pattern in the physical stimulus. For much the same reason, the beat in fast music may be tapped twice as slowly as the actual beat induction pattern in the physical stimulus.

The effect of beat tapping can be measured further in respiration. Music with a faster tempo will speed up the respiration pattern, which in turn affects the affective judgment of music as being more pleasant and exciting (Gómez and Danuser, 2004). This interesting finding shows that body resonance has an real effect on the induction of pleasantness and intensity of emotion.

From the viewpoint of annotation, the tapped beat is an annotation of a particular structural feature of music. Though the beat has received little attention in traditional musicology,[12] it is now considered to be a relevant feature. Indeed, in the framework of a technology of music mediation, the beat may serve as a reference frame for musical timing relationships. Starting from the beat, structures can be subdivided into smaller units or compose part of larger structures. In both cases, binary and ternary divisions in compositions are very common.

To sum up, the beat pattern may function as a first entry point to get into the music, to synchronize biomechanical resonances with the music. Tapping the beat allows the subject to feel and understand (in a corporeal way) a basic element of structure in music (Thaut, 2005). This can be seen as a first step in alerting the human resonance structure to be ready to follow along with the music.

## Inductive Resonance

While many studies on tapping have focused on synchronization, it is likely that human movement in response to music may involve much more than passive adaptation to the pulses of physical energy. Indeed, what is often observed in movement responses to music is a fairly good understanding of the underlying structure and expressive timing patterns (Clarke, 1989; Palmer, 1997). Listeners seem to expect to hear music as expressively timed, and they will compensate for the absence of such timing (Repp, 1998).

In other words, resonances of the motor system may imply an understanding of the intended action. This is called the induction principle (Knuf et al., 2001; Prinz, 2002). It means that a subject listening to music tends to perform actions suited to realizing what the subject wants to happen. For example, when we turn our tapping along with the beat into conducting movements, the focus is no longer on the passive following of some feature in music, but on active control and short-term prediction of musical sequences that immediately follow what we hear. Obviously, the active control is an illusion. It is a manifestation of the inclination to attribute intentions to music.

In the above definition, synchronization can be conceived of as a type of corporeal articulation which closely adheres to low-level sensorimotor mechanisms. Synchronization, in principle, is possible without paying too much attention to the physical stimulus. It is a natural (sensorimotor-based) inclination to move along with a given pattern in the physical environment.

### 5.2.2  Embodied Attuning

In contrast with synchronization, embodied attuning implies corporeal movement in accord with music, such as drawing along with the moving sonic forms of music or, perhaps more typical, singing along with the music. Attuning brings the human body into accordance with a particular feature of music. It can be seen as navigation with or inside music. Attuning may be considered a form of synchronization in the sense that it aims at being as much as possible in harmony with features of the moving sonic forms of music, a kind of playing together with the music. Whereas synchronization is based on low-level sensorimotor activity, attuning aims at addressing higher-level features such as melody, harmony, rhythm, and timbre, or patterns related to expressiveness, affects, and feelings. Attuning, more than synchronization, draws upon the idea that the world is perceived in terms of cues relevant to the subject's action-oriented ontology. It assumes that the perceived cue is relevant insofar as it can be reproduced. This involves a more active role for the subject and an engagement in higher-level intentional processes.

Two examples may help to clarify this. Next I present a brief report of two pilot studies in which attuning was first used to uncover the perception of structural features in music. The first study is about tonality, and the second is about melody and rhythm.

### Probing Technique

To date, much research on tonality perception has been based on the probe-tone technique (Krumhansl and Kessler, 1982).[13] In the probe-tone experimental setup, a tonal context is given and is then followed by a probe tone that is one of the twelve chromatic tones of an octave. The listener is then asked to rate the similarity between the probe tone and the tonal context on a scale from 1 to 7. If this is done twelve

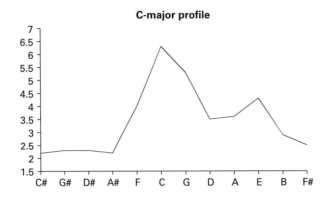

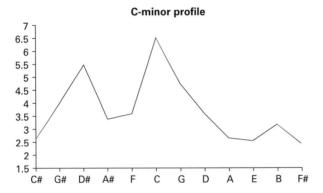

**Figure 5.2**
Profiles of the tonality in C-major and C-minor chord progressions, obtained by the probe-tone technique (Krumhansl and Kessler, 1982). The horizontal axis shows the pitches; the vertical axis, the subjective ratings.

times—once for each chromatic probe tone, a profile is obtained that measures how similar the twelve chromatic probe tones were with respect to the musical audio sequence.

Figure 5.2 shows the profiles of a musical context that consisted of chord progressions in the key of C major and C minor (based on data provided in Krumhansl, 1990). The horizontal axis represents all chromatic notes; the vertical axis, the means of subjective ratings. In the key of C major, for example, the notes C, G, F, and E are more prominent than D and A, and the latter are more prominent than C♯, E♭, F♯, A♭, and B♭. The profile, as it was originally conceived, was assumed to reflect the cognitive structure of tonality in long-term memory.

The probe-tone methodology has been expanded to include continuous measurements (Toiviainen and Krumhansl, 2003).[14] During a period of continuous measurement the subjects listen to music, and from time to time a probe tone appears along with the music. At that moment, the subjects are expected to rate how well the probe tone fits with the music. However, most subjects find the continuous method rather difficult. At least in my lab, it was hard to replicate the results of the continuous probe-tone measurement of tonality. A major difficulty was that the timbre of the probe tone interfered with the timbre of the music. As a result, it was not always very clear whether the probe tone was part of the music or not. Moreover, the method is rather time-consuming because in order to get the profile of a single piece, subjects have to listen to the same musical example twelve times. In principle, they have to do this for several pieces.

## Vocal Attuning

The attuning technique (Heylen, 2004; Heylen et al., 2006) offers an alternative approach which is more spontaneous because it is based on low-voice singing or humming along with the music. The method is easy and fast. Subjects are asked to sing a low tone which they feel is in tune with what they hear. In a recent experiment, twenty-nine subjects were asked to sing a note while listening to thirteen musical pieces in a major key and thirteen musical pieces in a minor key. For evaluation, the sung melodies were translated into a score, using software for melody transcription (De Mulder et al., 2004). All pitches were then reduced to the octave and the total duration of each chromatic note was measured for each piece. These data were then transposed to the key of C (because the musical pieces were in different keys). The final result is shown in figure 5.3. The horizontal axis shows the pitches, and the vertical axis shows the pitch duration as a percentage of the total duration of vocal attuning. The figure on the left (solid line) shows the profile obtained from the vocal attuning task of the musical excerpts in the major key. The figure on the right (solid line) shows the profile obtained from the vocal attuning task of the musical excerpts in the minor key. The dotted lines are the outputs from acoustical models based on spectrum analysis (dotted lines) and auditory analysis (dots and dashes). Comparison with the spectral and auditory models[15] shows very high correlations for both major and minor (0.95 and 0.96 for the major and minor of the spectrum model, and 0.96 for both major and minor of the

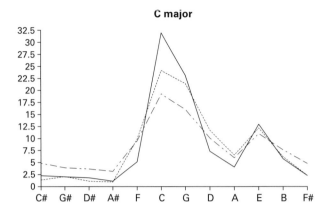

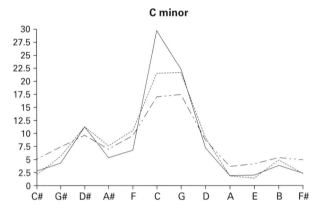

**Figure 5.3**
Profiles of the vocal attuning to musical excerpts in major and minor tonality.
Left: the tonality profile for C major. Right: the tonality profile for C minor.
The horizontal axis shows the pitches, and the vertical axis shows the pitch dura-
tion (in percentage).

auditory model).[16] The results suggest that listeners are able to accurately attune to tonality cues, and that these cues are contained in the
audio signal. This finding supports the idea that the induction of tonal
sensitivity is largely determined by sensory input.

The pilot study shows that a structural feature of music as complex
as tonality can be captured by means of vocal attuning. Vocal attuning is
easy, fast, and suitable for any kind of music. It involves the subject in a
pleasurable state of behavioral resonance, invoking significations based
on corporeal articulations. The study suggests that tonality in music is

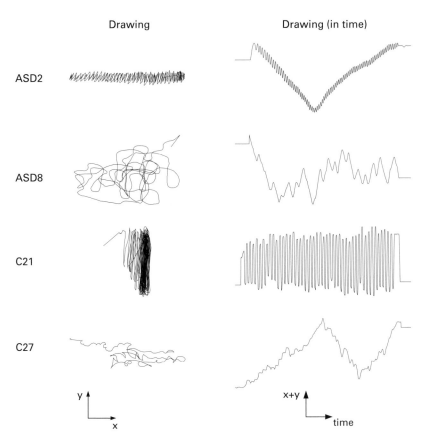

**Figure 5.4**
Graphical attuning to the rhythm of a single musical excerpt. The rows show the results for four subjects. The left column shows the design on the tablet. The right column shows the design as it develops in time.

an important perceptual cue because it can be easily replicated in a imitation task.

## Graphical Attuning
A second pilot study was based on graphical attuning, using an electronic pen and tablet. This study aimed at investigating possible differences between subjects with autism spectrum disorder (ASD) and a control group (C) of normal subjects (De Bruyn, 2005).

Figure 5.4 illustrates a graphical attuning task in which subjects were asked to move the pen in accord with the rhythm heard in music.

Two ASD subjects (ASD2 and ASD8, first and second rows) are compared with two control subjects (C21 and C27, third and fourth rows). The left figures show the actual design on the tablet. The right figures show the development of the design over time. The horizontal and vertical axes are summed and plotted over time. The figure shows that subjects ASD2 (first row) and C21 (third row) develop a more or less similar attuning pattern consisting of fast up-and-down movements in response to the beat. In contrast, subjects ASD8 (second row) and C27 (fourth row) develop more circular movements. The attuning is less clearly focusing on the beat.

Figure 5.5 illustrates a graphical attuning task in which subjects were asked to move the pen in accord with the heard melody. Subjects

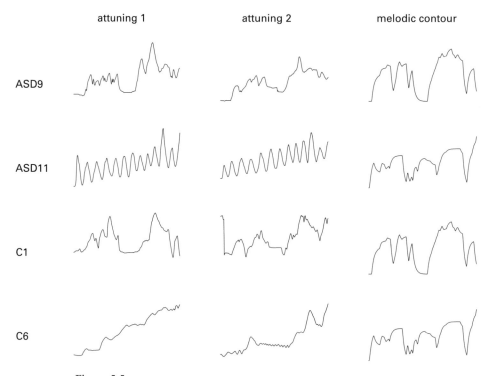

**Figure 5.5**
Graphical attuning to melody. The rows show the results for four subjects and two melodies. Subjects ASD9 and C1 attune to melody 1. Subjects ASD11 and C6 attune to melody 2. The first and second columns show the design of a first and second attuning session. The third column shows the melody contour of the musical stimulus.

ASD9 and C1 attune to melody 1. Subjects ASD11 and C6 attune to melody 2. The first and second columns show the results of two different attuning sessions. The third column shows the melodic contour as extracted from the audio signal.[17] Subjects ASD9 and C1 perform this melody attuning task rather well. The contours of the drawings resemble the pitch contour. In contrast, ASD11 synchronizes with the rhythm, and C6 has difficulties attuning to either melody or rhythm. ASD9 is very accurate in the design of the melodic contour.

The results suggest that in graphical attuning to music, subjects with autism spectrum disorder (but normal motor abilities) display little or no difference from a control group of normal subjects. In both groups there are subjects who can attune to aspects of rhythm and melody in a reasonable way, while other subjects (a minority) fail to do so. It was found that the attuning of the ASD subjects to the melody was often more accurate than that of the control group. These results seem to confirm earlier research (e.g., Heaton et al., 1998, 2001; Bonnel et al., 2003) which showed that subjects with autism spectrum disorder have an enhanced sensitivity to pitch, which enables them to perform better on pitch categorization and pitch discrimination than a control group. It is likely that ASD subjects display more attention to the notes of the melody rather than to the melodic contour.

However, in another task where subjects had to verbally describe music using affect-related adjectives, ASD subjects who performed well in attuning typically needed four times more time to complete the task than the control subjects. Furthermore, the control group performed this task more spontaneously and faster, with fewer errors.[18] The main difference between ASD subjects and a control group thus concerned a task which involved the processing of particular observed and experienced affective or emotional characteristics in music. The finding suggests a clear distinction between corporeal attuning to structural and affective cues in music and experiencing affect in music. The latter can be considered a component of empathy with which ASD-subjects have particular difficulties (De Bruyn and Leman, submitted).

## 5.2.3   Empathy

Empathy (*inleven* in Dutch, *Einfühlung* in German) is the ability to share another person's feelings or emotions as if they were one's own (see, e.g., Berthoz and Jorland, 2004). Empathy assumes participation, identification, and understanding, as if the other's state of experience is one's own.[19]

Empathy is often related to emotions and feelings. Thus empathy with music would mean that humans have the ability to identify with the emotional expressiveness contained in the music, as if it could be shared with the music. It is very likely that subjects can have the impression of being involved in an empathic relationship with music. This question is not unfamiliar in musicology, for emotional expressiveness is one of the central concerns of musical aesthetics.

### Phenomenology of Empathy

Aristotle's observation that imitation gives rise to pleasure deserves some attention in this context. Apparently he had in mind two types of experiences: the *aha* experience, which implies that pleasure is due to the sudden recognition of the original (evoking the common exclamation *aha!*), and the empathy experience, which implies that pleasure is due to a process of identification in terms of an attuning of the soul (or self) to the original. In this context, it is the latter kind of experience which interests us.[20]

I will interpret Aristotle's concept of soul as an emerging effect of embodiment, a process that turns physical energies into objects of an action-oriented ontology by means of a body. From that perspective, the empathy experience, in which the soul, or the action-oriented bias, is attuned to the original, can be seen as a kind of imitation of emotional intentionality based on action. Empathy with music would thus refer to an imitation of the music's emotional intentionality.

### Empathic Involvement

In recent studies it has been suggested that empathy is related to emotional identification and feelings of intimacy or social connectedness (Berthoz and Jorland, 2004). This can be studied through third-person observation, using brain scans. Recent results (e.g., Carr et al., 2003; Leslie et al., 2004) suggest that the motor system may access the emotional system with different degrees of engagement, depending on whether the affect is observed, imitated, or properly felt. This offers a layered view of how behavioral resonance to affect and emotion in music could be accessed.

**Observation of affect**   Perception of music, as argued before, can be conceived of as a covert simulation of the perceived moving forms (chapter 4). According to this approach, identification of affect in gestures would be a matter of comparing the affective content of the simulated moving forms with a set of affective forms in memory. The one that is more similar is the affect recognized. This view is closely related to cognitive similarity theories of expressiveness. It is based on recognition of forms associated with affects rather than on the actual experience of the affect.

**Imitation of affect**    If the motor component is not inhibited, then simulation of affect in music may turn into overt corporeal movement, or corporeal articulation. In this case, the corporeal articulation expresses the affect. This is similar to the articulation of structural features such as tonality, melody, or rhythm-attuning examples. Music which expresses joy would then be replicated, perhaps through the movement of arms, head, or legs. What is sensed by the subject are the physical movements of the body in terms of force and acceleration. This may have some similarities to earlier experiences of force and acceleration when real joy was experienced. Hence, it may provide knowledge of the affect that is articulated. Note that the actual movement provides a stronger embodied understanding of affect than the observation does. Observation would involve the memory of the force and acceleration, while corporeal articulation would make that aspect physical, and thus stronger.

**Feeling of affect**    A next step would be that the corporeal articulation, and the sensing of force and acceleration, impact the emotional system. The experience of the acting body (kinesthesia) is then combined with the emotions that are actually felt. There is neurophysiological evidence that centers for action representation and execution (mirror neuron areas) are anatomically connected with centers for emotional processing (limbic system) (Carr et al., 2003). Empathy is thereby assumed to be mediated by affective qualities rather than by sensory qualities (T. Singer et al., 2004).

Furthermore, empathy is likely to be based on degrees of intimacy and social interaction. National hymns, for example, contain strong gestural forms for many people. The fact that they are easy to imitate is only one aspect of their power to elicit empathy. The other aspect is their association with social connectedness. The contexts in which hymns are played are often ritualized manifestations in which allelo-imitation plays an important role. This context may open the door for feelings of social connectedness and intimacy. Empathy may largely depend on these so-cially related forms of imitation.

In the above study on autism and music, it was found that subjects with autism spectrum disorder had problems with assigning affective adjectives to music. They were able to assign an affective adjective to music (see also Heaton et al., 1999), but they needed much more time to complete this task. These findings agree with those of Capps et al. (1992), which showed that children with autism spectrum disorder need much more time to understand emotions than children in a control group. Normal subjects do a very fast evaluation of the affective character of music, whereas subjects with autism spectrum disorder seem to reason, evaluate, and compare. It is as if they rely less on motor and emotion imitation, and more on observation and associated (disembodied) cognitive processing.

### Embodied Listening, Having Empathy with Music

Recent studies suggest that empathy is not a simple match between the self and the other, but involves an explicit representation of the subjectivity of the other, as well as principles that regulate the distinction between self and other. Translated into neural code, it means that empathy draws on shared as well as distinct representations of perception and action, as well as on a regulation mechanism that allows for different degrees of empathic involvement (see Decety and Jackson, 2004, 2006 for reviews). Music is a domain where aspects of empathic involvement can be demonstrated.

In a pilot study (Leman et al., submitted), listeners were asked to express perceived music through corporeal articulations. The hypothesis was that listeners would be able to improve their performance as a result of implicit learning, and that subjects would be able to access the quality of their performance. To test this hypothesis, we asked listeners to move an arm along with three short pieces ($P_1$, $P_2$, and $P_3$) of Chinese *guqin* music. Each piece was presented as two performances (e.g., $P_1P_1$, $P_2P_2$, $P_3P_3$).[21] Movements were recorded with a joystick and the movement velocities of the first and second performances were compared, using correlation as measure. It is important to mention that listeners were unfamiliar with the music, and that the music did not have a real beat.

It was assumed that listeners who moved in harmony with music in the first performance would not change their motor strategy in the second, which immediately followed the first, and that listeners, who found

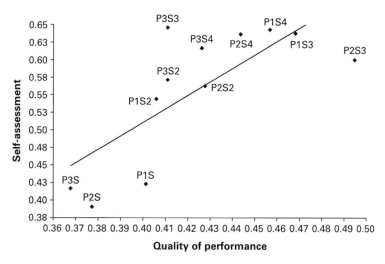

**Figure 5.6**
Scatter plot illustrating the relationship between (1) the quality of performances measured as the average of the significant correlations ($p < 0.01$) between subsequent trials (X-axis), and (2) the self-assessment as the average of all subjective ratings that correspond to the selected significant correlations (Y-axis). The labels refer to the piece and the session of each task. For example, P3S4 stands for piece 3 in session 4. (See text for further explanation.)

that their corporeal articulations were not in harmony with music would move differently in the second performance. Thus, statistically significant correlations ($p < 0.01$) between the movement velocity patterns of two successive trials would mean "good" performance, and nonsignificant correlations ($p >= 0.01$) would mean "poor" performance. The quality of performance could be investigated and compared with the listener's self-assessment.

Thirty subjects had to perform the task in four sessions ($S_1, S_2, S_3, S_4$) that followed one after the other. Figure 5.6 shows a scatter plot and regression line of the relationship between "good" performances and self-assessment. The correlation is very significant, which means that a subject's awareness of the quality of performance corresponds to the objective measurement of that quality. This correlation is not revealed with "poor" performances. Note that the quality of the movement and the subjective ratings are low in the first session and higher in the last session. This is an indication that implicit learning took place.

The results imply, first, that embodied listening is prone to implicit learning and, second, that subjects tend to be aware of the "quality" of their movements. Third-person descriptions of movement thereby strongly correlate with their second-person verbal description, provided the movement is of good quality. In the present context, the latter means that the movement draws on a repeatable motor strategy. The study suggests that subjects can compare a representation of their own movements with a representation of the (distal) moving forms that they perceive in music, and that this comparison is accessible mentally. Since emotions are not directly involved in this task, it is reasonable to assume that embodied listening is a preempathic activity.

The above findings agree with the notion of self as a mental model having access to a proprioceptive and kinesthetic representation of one's own body in combination with a representation of intended relationships with the other (Gallagher, 2000; Metzinger, 2003). Both aspects of the self, its inward and outward directedness, can be considered aspects of the action-oriented ontology. In the present context, the other is of course the music. The above findings are consistent with the idea that empathy involves regulatory mechanisms by which the subject keeps track of the self in relation to music. These regulatory mechanisms are assumed to play an important role in social contexts where the subject, in view of social facilitation, will tend to adapt his or her expressive behavior to the expressive behavior of other social agents (Bargh and Chartrand, 1999). In short, there are strong indications that music can be conceived as a virtual social agent, and that listening to music can be seen as a socializing activity in the sense that it may train the listener's self in social attuning and empathic relationships. Presumably, this training is an important component in social music cognition—more specifically, in forming the personal self of young people—as well as in the forming of social bonds among groups of people.

Concerning the latter aspect, it is likely that embodied listening by a group of people may directly foster social interaction. Indeed, if movements of individual subjects are harmonized with music, one may expect that the movements among subjects would tend to be harmonized as well. Mimicking the behaviors of others is known to increase liking between interaction partners (Lakin et al., 2003). If music indeed drives a group of subjects to harmonize their expressive behaviors, then music-driven embodied attuning can be said to train the social capabilities of attuning and self-regulation. In that sense, embodied listening may provide an understanding of music's role in the forming of group identities and social bonding (Gregory, 1997; Hargeaves and North, 1997; Freeman, 2000).

To sum up, different degrees of empathy with music can be distinguished, depending on whether the motor system and the emotional system are involved. This allows the distinction between empathy as observation, as imitation, and as actual feeling of the emotional component of music. Subjects seem to be aware of the relationship between themselves and the music when they engage in an empathic relationship with music. Ultimately, the emotions involved in empathy with music are likely to be based on the feeling of intimacy and social connectedness, but self-regulation may guide the degree of empathic engagement. Embodied attuning and empathy with music are likely to open up new directions in the new field of social music cognition.

### 5.2.4   Distinctions Between Synchronization, Attuning, and Empathy

The above distinctions among synchronization, attuning, and empathy are tentative. Further research is needed in order to determine how they relate to each other. In fact, it could be argued that there is a continuum of corporeal articulations which is associated with low levels of sensorimotor processing and subsequent higher levels of sensorimotor processing, up to action/perception couplings that account for higher levels of intentionality. Alternatively, it could be argued that synchronization, attuning, and empathy are three aspects of imitation and intentional involvement with music which can coexist. After all, the assumption is that these manifestations of corporeal articulation rely on different levels of the sensorimotor system and action/perception couplings, as well as on different levels of emotional processing. Further research is needed to fine-tune these concepts.

So far we have assumed that synchronization does not need to involve the emotional system. The attribution of intentionality is low-level, based on local energy patterns in the stimulus, and not very demanding in terms of attention. Synchronization is a genuine aspect of the ideomotor principle, which states that body movement is the result of resonances. Thus, it can be seen as something that the subject largely undergoes, such as a sensation. In contrast, empathy seems to involve the emotional system. It implies commitment, identification, and participation in the attributed intentionality.

Attuning occupies the middle position between synchronization and empathy. Similar to perception, attuning implies an active role for the subject. The activity of the subject is in harmony with a particular aspect of the music, such as singing along or moving in time to the music.

Although it is a kind of participation, attuning may be less involved with identification. For example, when subjects are asked to sing along with tonality, this implies the processing of structural information at a high cognitive level. However, when subjects are asked to draw along with music, or move a baton or laser pen, it is likely that they can engage in an emotional empathic relationship with music as well.

The degree of musical involvement amounts to a degree of identification with the attributed intentionality. Research at different levels of corporeal articulation (neural, physiological, behavioral) is needed in order to obtain more insight into different degrees of mirroring processes and imitation.

## 5.3    Mimesis Theory and Expression

The above account of corporeal articulation focused on the subject's involvement with music through movement and movement sensing. Parallel to this, mimesis theory holds that music is capable of imitating and expressing aspects of reality, in particular affects and emotions that, in turn, can be picked up by subjects listening to music. This has been discussed above, but it needs further consideration because it can be a source of confusion in music research.

Mimesis theory assumes a transitivity relationship: (1) music imitates something, (2) the subject imitates the music, and hence (3) the subject imitates that same something (see figure 5.7). A related version of this transitivity relationship is based on the notion of expressiveness: (1) music expresses something, (2) the subject captures that expression, and (3) the subject captures the source of that expression.

This idea of art as mimesis reflects some of Aristotle's most central views on imitation. In the *Politics* (book VIII, chapter 5), for example, Aristotle suggests that rhythms and melodies contain similarities to the true nature of qualities in human character, such as anger, gentleness, courage, temperance, and the contrary qualities. When we hear

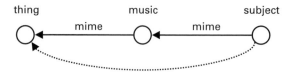

**Figure 5.7**
Mimesis theory.

imitations—and, according to Aristotle, the objects of imitation in art are men in action, emotions, and characters—our feelings move in sympathy with the original. When listening to music, the soul thus undergoes changes in tune with the affective character being imitated. This is possible because real human characters move our souls. Aristotle assumes that by imitating the qualities these characters exhibit in music, our souls are moved in a similar way, so that we become in tune with the affects we experience when confronted with the original.[22]

This view incorporates the idea that subjects are involved in an empathic relationship with music because music itself is an imitation of something. Mimesis theory assumes that music is pointing to some external referent, typically an expressive character, an emotion, or an affect. This assumption of external reference is one of the cornerstones of many theories of musical expression. It deserves further critical analysis in the light of an alternative viewpoint which holds that an external reference may not be necessary for experiencing expression.

The mimesis theory contains two claims which deserve attention: that (1) music imitates or expresses something (e.g., an emotion) and that (2) musical expressiveness can be captured (observed and experienced).

## Music Imitates, Music Expresses

The claim "music imitates" or "music expresses" often accompanies another claim about music: that music performs an action and that this action is about something. However, one should be careful when saying that music performs an action. Indeed, the musical audio stream is not an organism equipped with intentional capabilities. Music as pure physical energy cannot intend something, and therefore it cannot imitate or express, because the act of carrying out an imitation or an expression involves goals, prediction of motor trajectories, and intentionality. It is only when the physical energies are related to the action-oriented ontology of the subject (and this by itself is carried out by a far more complex physical/biological system) that music can appear to be an imitation or an expression of something. In order to say that music imitates or expresses, music must be considered as a relational modality, more particularly a relation of physical energies to a subjective action-related ontology. In other words, it is only with respect to the subjective action-related ontology that music imitates or expresses. Therefore, it is better to say that music is an imitation of something, or that music is an expression of something, than to say that it imitates or expresses (Kivy, 1980).

But when we say that music is an expression of something, we silently assume that some external reference is the source of the music's expression. As a result, the assumed reference to something calls for a subsequent construction of an interpretive context and a search for a possible reference model that is imitated or expressed (e.g., a character, an emotion). This assumption of transitivity (thing ← music, music ← subject, therefore thing ← subject) is problematic because it assumes that music relies on a reference model.[23]

However, the need for a reference model may be challenged. Indeed, as I have argued, the perception of expressiveness may have its origin in motor resonances to physical energy. These resonances underlie a mirroring effect by which perceptions are coupled to the action-relevant ontology of the subject, and hence to intentions of the subject itself, and not necessarily to the intentions of an external source. This viewpoint entails that the experience of expression is rooted in the subject's action-oriented perception of the world—in other words, that the assumption of a reference model is induced by the subject's inclination to attribute intentionality to music.

Corporeal imitation may be seen as a sufficient source for the induction of expression. In corporeal imitation, moving sonic forms (the changing physical energy) are fully taken into the body, and via the body they are turned into action-oriented percepts that associate with expressions. The next step, the search for a possible source of this expression, is of a different order. It implies an interpretation which may not be needed and which is perhaps not always justified. Indeed, searching for the possible intended meaning of music forms part of a signification practice which can be useful but is not necessary in order to make sense out of music. As argued, the search for the possible intended meanings is a speculative enterprise which is likely to be based on corporeal experiences of music. This viewpoint implies that the quest for the reference model behind musical expression is an option, not a necessity, for experiencing music and making sense out of it.

In short, the idea that music is an imitation of something cannot be held as a rule, and therefore the unconditional acceptance of the transitivity relationship is unjustified. Music is sometimes an imitation, but in many cases it is not. Frequently, it is the subject's action-oriented ontology which turns physical energy into expression.

Just think about a suite by J. S. Bach. This is abstract music, albeit related to dance. It is not imitating something specific, nor is it the expression of something specific (e.g., an emotion). Nevertheless, many listeners are able to capture a very concrete expressiveness from the way they articulate that music. Moreover, the music appears to have an intentional character, but this character attributed to music is an emerging effect of the fact that perception is coupled with an anticipating memory, that is, the action-relevant ontology. In that sense, the attribution of expressiveness is an effect of how our body and mind work together with sound energy.

To sum up, listeners can engage in different degrees of involvement with music without having to draw upon a reference or to know what this music expresses. Nevertheless, the music is recognized as expressive. This is possible because expression can be captured by the mirroring system (motor resonances) and corporeal imitations. It provides a basis for corporeal understanding without any need for a reference. In contrast, cerebral understanding (cognition) often results from a search for something that is imitated.

## Capturing What Is Expressed in Music

The second claim, that musical expression can be captured by a subject, focuses on the mechanism. I have proposed corporeal imitation as a mechanism, but it is of interest to relate this to other accounts of musical expressiveness.

Obviously, the landscape of theories of musical expressiveness is varied (Budd, 1992; Kivy, 1980). Some theories adhere to the mimesis theory and assume that the capturing of expressiveness is possible because music is an imitation of something (e.g., a feeling or emotion). These theories often refer to mechanisms of resemblance which are grounded in cognitive appraisal and arousal. Other theories do not assume imitation and tend to explain expressiveness on more formal dynamic grounds. Also, a distinction is often made between cognition (e.g., disruption of thinking) and arousal.

For example, in different grades of subtle argumentation, Kivy (1980, 2001) has argued that music resembles expressive behavior because the properties of the imitated joy in music are similar to sensory properties of real joy. Kivy seems to hold that we know this because we animate our perceptions. If this is the central message, then Kivy indeed comes close to my own account. Yet it is unclear to me whether Kivy would subscribe to corporeality, or whether his account would be closer to Meyer's (1956, p. 82) viewpoint that "there appears to be nothing autonomous and independent about the motor response to music. Everything which occurs as a motor response can be accounted for in terms of mental activity and, since the converse of this is not true, music is best examined in terms of mental behaviour."

In defense of an arousal theory of musical expression, Panksepp and Bernatzky (2002, p. 135) say that "music derives its affective charge directly from dynamic aspects of brain systems that normally control real emotions and which are distinct from, albeit highly interactive with, cognitive processes." In their view, music is uniquely efficacious in resonating with our basic emotional systems, and they see music as largely dependent on direct and indirect (i.e., cognitively mediated) effects of subcortical emotional circuits in the human brain. These statements raise the question of whether music really needs to invoke the emotional system in order for us to recognize in music the expression of joy. Indeed, the arousal theory says that the imitated joy in the music arouses the listener in a way that resembles the arousal of real joy.

In my opinion, both the cognitive appraisal and the arousal theory of musical expression may profit from considering the role of corporeal imitation behavior. The latter considers different levels of intentional involvement (synchronization, attuning, empathy) as well as different levels on which emotional involvement is built up (from observation, to imitation, to feeling or arousal). Motor-processing forms an integral part of this theory, even when real emotional states are considered. While music is being experienced, associations with real emotions, affects, feelings, gestures, and images can be made. In those cases, music can be said to be expressive of something. But in most cases, perception sets action-oriented processes in motion while the final goal or underlying intention remains undefined. Expression is then understood in a corporeal way through motor resonances.

## 5.4    Consequences for Music Research

In terms of technology, measurement is no longer an obstacle to the study of corporeal articulations. Over recent decades, advanced sensing techniques for the measurement of brain activity and physiological responses, as well as capturing movement, have become accessible to an increasing number of researchers. Technology nowadays allows the measurement of almost any kind of physical manifestation of corporeal articulation. This is no longer a problem. Instead, the main problem is the theoretical approach, the experimental paradigm, and the interpretation of measurements within a context of mind/body/matter relationships.

The theory put forward here assumes a tight coupling between action and perception. It differs from the disembodied cognitive approach in that it takes into account the human body as an active component of experimentation.

In the disembodied approach, the subject was often conceived of as a passive observer whose mental representation could be mapped in terms of perceived similarities in the stimuli. The human body was thereby seen as a disturbing factor, but necessary to provide responses, either corporeal or verbal. For example, subjects had to press a button, move a slider in response to the stimulus, or give a verbal response. There was little confidence in the subject's possible creative or active contribution to perception.

In contrast with the concept that the subject is a passive observer, it is possible to conceive of the subject as an active observer having an action-oriented bias to music. This active bias is reflected in corporeal articulations. The principal task of the researcher is to steer this action-oriented bias in directions that allow quantification. This can be done by asking subjects to focus on a particular structural cue. For example, in the tonality attuning experiment described above, the subjects are asked to sing along with music in a low voice and rather slowly. Their singing is constrained within certain limits, which allows a quantified processing of the attuning data. Interestingly, such experiments, because they involve the human body, are felt to be very natural because many subjects tend to sing along with music that way. Similarly, in a motor-attuning experiment, subjects can be asked to move along with a particular musical feature. By doing so, their perception becomes overt in corporeal articulations which can be observed.

The measurement of corporeal articulation also requires new forms of analysis. In this respect, the development of techniques that extract action-relevant features from physical energy are important because they allow an action-relevant comparison with neural, physiological, and behavioral recordings of corporeal articulations. The same extraction techniques can also be used as analysis tools. For example, in the tonality attuning experiment, tonality profiles are obtained with software that transforms the recordings of sung melodies into Hertz or cent values[24] from which the profiles can be derived. Thus, the melody extraction software allows very precise measurements of the singing in response to the musical stimulus. Corporeal articulations can thus be compared with action-relevant cues which are automatically extracted from the musical stimulus.

Similarly, it is possible to compare recordings of movement with a large number of perceptually relevant features extracted from polyphonic audio, so that the biomechanics of movement can be studied in close relationship to the moving sonic forms. This offers a number of highly interesting possibilities for music research, both for the refinement of a theory of musical involvement and for the application of findings to a technology of music mediation.

The above theory can be refined by a better understanding of the mirroring processes and imitation in response to music. Here lies the key to a number of important contributions in fields such as music education and music therapy. Also of particular interest are practical applications in the field of gestural control of audio and multimedia devices.

Related to the above problem is the relationship between corporeal articulations and language. It is generally assumed that corporeal articulations can be conceptualized by the subject that undergoes them, but the mechanism of self-observation is still poorly understood. Linguistic descriptions of music are useful for search and retrieval in databases. Therefore, the linguistic characterization of corporeal articulation needs much more attention.

To sum up, the above approach shows that the study of the relationships among mind/body/matter is a huge challenge in terms of measurement, analysis, theory formation, and practical application.

## 5.5   Conclusion

The theory put forward in this chapter states that the sensorimotor system and the action/perception system (one connected with ideomotor resonances, the other with intended behavior) form the basic processing engine for interaction between a subject and its musical environment. During the development of a child, this interaction results in an action-oriented ontology which is, moreover, intention-oriented. This ontology forms the basis of the child's, and later the adult's, self.

One of the main features of this motor system is that changes in physical energy can be mirrored as motor resonances, which allow the understanding of the physical energy as a function of its biological value. As a side effect of this mirroring process, intentionality is attributed to the physical source. It is assumed that this machinery of intentionality attribution is reflected in corporeal articulations.

In this chapter, the emphasis has been on mirror processes and imitation. Several notions of imitation can be distinguished: such as skill imitation, figural imitation, topical imitation, corporeal imitation, and allelo-imitation. Corporeal imitation has been assumed to underlie many of the other forms of imitation.

Corporeal imitation was then analyzed in terms of synchronization, attuning, and empathy. Attuning has a high potential in annotation and experimental research. Empathy with music is a most fascinating topic. Subjects may attribute aspects of their own expressive intentionality (such as affects and feelings) to physical energy. This attribution is an effect of the mirroring processes which allow subjects to translate moving sonic forms into components of their action-oriented ontology. These processes may call on the emotional system so that human subjects become emotionally involved with music. Intimacy and social connectedness may enhance the empathic engagement with music.

The above theory allows us to understand why the empathic engagement with sad music may provide consolation, and thus a source of pleasure or relief. A subject in a sad mood may use this music to express the inner feelings of sadness in a corporeal way, which consoles and gives relief. Thus, music becomes a therapy. The theory offers a perspective for understanding this healing power of music.

# 6 Interaction with Musical Instruments

Corporeal articulation and intentionality, two concepts introduced in the previous chapters, provide a framework for understanding musical involvement. They allow us to understand the direct impact of physical energy on the human body and the subsequent translation of this sensing into action-oriented values, meanings, goals, and mental representations. A central part of the embodied music cognition theory concerns the role of the human body as a mediator between the human mind and forms of the physical environment. It provides an understanding of how the physical energy of music can be related to an ontology of action-oriented behavior and how a subsequent conceptualization of this relationship may lead to verbal descriptions of musical experience and further use in symbolic communication.

Now the question is how the above theory of musical involvement can contribute to practical applications in mediation technology, that is, to tools that can provide access to (technologically encoded) music. Two chapters aim to give a provisional answer to this question. The present chapter is about how human subjects can enhance artistic expressiveness with the help of interactive music systems. Chapter 7 is about how human subjects can search for and retrieve music from a database.

In both chapters, it is assumed that machines may be furnished with tools that become extensions of the human body. In addition, these tools may be conceived of as more or less independent agents with which humans can interact at a level in agreement with the assessment of intentional actions and nonverbal corporeal communication. Flexible human–machine communication is still far beyond the capabilities of any existing system, yet the concept of intentional verbal and nonverbal interaction is an important and useful metaphor in human–machine communication research. It draws upon the idea that a machine could be developed as a *you* (a second person, or social agent) with whom the subject interacts and communicates. In both cases corporeal articulations and verbal descriptions play an important role. This chapter and the next show how the human body, as a natural mediator between the mental world and the world of physical entities, can be extended with technology, thus allowing a more flexible access to music encoded and stored in machines.

An important aspect of technology-based mediation is concerned with interactivity. Playing a musical instrument is an interactive activity, and the musical instrument can be seen as the technology which mediates between human mind (musical ideas) and physical energy (music as sound). In recent decades, acoustic instruments have evolved to electronic instruments to music environments and multimedia platforms. In this development, interactivity has been a central concern, as well as one of the driving forces for innovation in music research and far beyond.

In this chapter, interactivity is investigated in relation to music systems. It is assumed that the foundations of interaction can be found in acoustic instruments and that the detailed study of the way in which performers handle acoustic instruments may reveal basic components of an embodied interaction and communication pattern that can be exploited for the development of electronic interactive systems.

This chapter has four sections. In the first section, involvement with music is considered in terms of multimodal experiences and multimedia technology. It defines a global background for the second section, in which a model of musical communication is worked out. This model starts from a case study in which the relationship between playing an acoustic musical instrument and corporeal attuning to the resulting sound is studied in detail. The third section is concerned with an analysis of the constraints that define musical communication. These constraints are related to problems encountered in electronic instruments, environments, and multimedia systems. Finally, in the fourth section, the model and its implied constraints of musical communication are applied to a concrete example of an interactive multimedia system.

## 6.1  Multimodal Experience and Multimedia Technology

The idea that musical communication involves all senses, and therefore is a multimodal experience, is not new. It is a central concept of ethnomusicology, in which music and sound are seen as part of a multitude of energies and events having social and cultural signification (Merriam,

1964). In most cultures, music is integrated with dance and social/ cultural functions. Music forms part of visual and tactile events, such as actions, movements, and interactions between performers and listeners. Moreover, even if the music is limited to a single energetic channel such as audio (as in radio, CD, or iPod), then the musical experience can still be said to be a multimodal experience. Music moves the body, evokes emotional responses, and generates associations with spaces and textures. Music as sound involves all senses, but often music is also embedded in other physical energies that have an impact on how music is experienced.

In Western culture, there has been an interesting development toward an integrated use of different media technologies in the production of music. In the early seventeenth century, Florentine humanists introduced the concept of *opere* (works) as a new and strategic attempt to integrate media of expression—such as singing, reciting, movement, and musical accompaniment—in close synergy with each other. This set the stage for an important development which in the nineteenth century culminated in Wagner's concept of *Gesamtkunstwerk*, the unification of all the arts into a single medium of artistic expression (Packer and Jordan, 2001). In the 1950s, with the development of electronic equipment, composers of avant-garde music explored the integration of electronic media technologies in musical spectacles and music theater. This was based on the use of tape players, film projectors, light organs, and other devices that allowed the electronic manipulation of reality. Popular musical culture also became increasingly involved with electronic media. Meanwhile, most pop music concerts became spectacles of sound, drama, dance, light, smells, and tactile modalities, using electrically powered multimedia engines. Recent developments indicate that avant-garde music moves in the direction of multimedia performances and virtual reality. The link between multimodal experiences and multimedia technologies can be seen as an extension of a long tradition that puts the human body (again) at the center of musical activity, as it is in many non-Western music cultures.

The connective thread in these developments seems to be the desire to enhance the expressive power of music, using technology as a means. For that purpose, the integration of sound with other types of energy can be seen as enhancing the effect of peak experiences, of being immersed within the music (see section 1.1).

Of particular interest in this context is the increase in stimuli levels, which runs parallel with the development of multimedia. During the course of the nineteenth century and the first half of the twentieth century, orchestras grew in size, and musical instruments increasingly produced more energy as manufacturers broadened their sonic and dynamic ranges (Sabbe, 1998). In the second half of the twentieth century in particular, with the advent of modern dance music, the sound intensity at concerts came to have an ever-increasing range.[1]

In fact, both the increase of sound intensity and the integration of multiple media are likely to facilitate peak experiences. They are examples of the human predilection for using music to become totally immersed in energy. Other approaches include phenomena such as trances and drugs. In what follows, however, I restrict my account to technology, and in particular to interactive technologies, whose development can be seen as an extension of the human body to reach peak experiences.

### 6.1.1   Multimedia Micro-integration

Before going deeper into the interactive aspect, it is of interest to mention that the contribution of modern digital technology to music and multimedia is particular. Compared with previous stages in the history of multimedia and music, the main novelty of modern digital technology is concerned with the encoding, exchange, and integration of energy, using different levels of description. In the modern concept, multimedia are no longer conceived of as a juxtaposition, the placing together, both synchronically and diachronically, of different media related to sound, acting, decor, and lighting, but rather as a micro-integration, or close linkage, of different media. This micro-integration is possible because of computational platforms that allow the processing of different media at different levels of description which are mutually exchangeable, from low-level descriptions of physical energy to high-level content-based descriptions of artistic expressiveness.

Micro-integration is an important concept because it offers new opportunities for artistic exploration. For example, it allows the parameters of musical expressiveness to be extracted from one modality, say sound, and then to be reused in another modality, for example, in computer animation, where it is used to modify the expressive movement of an avatar on a screen (Mancini et al., 2006). All this can be realized in real time, and the computational platform can be configured so that it acts as an independent agent or a virtual environment with which the artist can interact.

Micro-integration allows humans to communicate with machines that extrapolate, enhance, or transfer aspects of our multimodal experience in real and virtual environments. Mixed and virtual realities use machine technology to cope with the multimodal nature of corporeal articulations, intentions, expressions, and expressiveness. Thanks to the availability of digital electronic technology (sensors, computers) and software applications, a whole new area for artistic exploration has become available. In this, the interaction between multimodal experiences and multimedia technology plays a key role. How should we conceive that interaction, and how does it relate to the human body? What are the invariant components in that interaction, and what are the constraints that confine it?

### 6.1.2    Approach

In this chapter, multimodal experience and multimedia technology are related to the theory of corporeal articulation, thus providing a foundation for practical applications in musical interaction in terms of embodied cognition. This is conceived from two different viewpoints: (1) in terms of a human subject, which stresses the multimodal component in interaction, and (2) in terms of an interactive technology, which stresses the multimedia component in mediation.

•    The multimodal aspect of musical interaction draws on the idea that the sensory systems—auditory, visual, haptic, and tactile, as well as movement perception—form a fully integrated part of the way the human subject is involved with music during interactive musical communication. It is hypothesized that through corporeal articulation, multimodal experience of music (through movement, vision, audio) is translated into components of our subjective action-oriented ontology, and vice versa. Corporeal articulation should thus be seen as a unified principle that links mental processing with multiple forms of physical energy.

•    It is straightforward to assume that any technology which mediates between mental processing and multiple physical energies should be based on multimedia, that is, on tools that take into account the different ways energy manifests itself as a function of human interaction. These tools can function as an extension of the human body, the natural mediator between musical energy and mental representations. In what follows, musical instruments are conceived of as multimedia mediators. They evolved from acoustic musical instruments to electronic music instruments to multimedia environments and multimedia platforms.[2] They rely on common principles of human interaction and mind/body/matter transitions. The main problem to be solved is why, and to what extent, multiple media (e.g., audio, visual, haptic, tactile) are necessary for music mediation, and how these media can be designed such that they cope with principles of human interaction.

In what follows, I show that principles of multimodal and multimedia human/technology interaction can be studied in acoustical music instruments and that the implied principles are relevant to the development of electronic musical instruments and environments, and multimedia platforms.

## 6.2   The Communication of Intended Action

In this section, music interaction is considered in terms of the communication between a musician and a listener, using a musical instrument as mediator. The relevant questions are to what extent this communication can be measured and to what extent we can infer from it a model of musical communication and interaction that can be extended in the electronic domain.

In what follows, I start the discussion with a case study which suggests that musicians may encode gestures in sound, while listeners may decode particular intended aspects of these gestures through corporeal resonance behavior. The study suggests that these encoding/decoding processes may enable the communication of intended actions.

Since the mid-1990s, the study of musical intentions has focused on the study of musical expressiveness and, related to that, the study of gestural control and performer nuances (e.g., Dannenberg and De Poli, 1998; Widmer, 2001; Widmer and Tobudic, 2003; De Poli, 2004; Widmer and Goebl, 2004). In several experiments, it was shown that the musician's intentions are reflected in the sound structure and the cues that can be extracted from it, such as timing, articulation, loudness, and sound color (e.g., Canazza et al., 1997a, 1997b). Research on musical expressiveness has been stimulated by studies that envision the automatic performance of a musical score. A piece of music played without expression sounds dull and boring, but with expressiveness added, the music may acquire a more lively character. The idea is to capture expressiveness in performance rules, and to use these rules to drive the synthesis of musical scores (Friberg, Colombo, et al., 2000; Sundberg et al., 2003;

Zanon and De Poli, 2003). Studies also show that listeners are capable of capturing important aspects of the intended expressive meaning in music. They may recognize what kind of expressive intention the musician wanted to communicate (Gabrielsson and Juslin, 2003). This finding suggests that the musician can encode particular intentions which the listener can decode. More particularly, these message may relate to something as elusive as expressiveness.

What is not clear, however, is how decoding could work as a mechanism, and how the listener may have knowledge of the particular intention that is encoded in the music. In most studies on musical expressiveness, the underlying assumption is that the listener has in mind a representation of the symbolic structure of the music—as a score, say—which is used as a reference frame to compare performance nuances. From that disembodied comparison, the listener would be able to infer the expressive character of music.[3] This approach assumes that listeners hold a cognitive map of deviation patterns which they use for the recognition of expressiveness in the music. A second hypothesis has been proposed by Juslin and Laukka (2003), who claim that the expressive code used in music can be derived from that used in speech.

I propose a third account, based on the idea that the listener is able to decode aspects of the performer's expressive intentions on the basis of corporeal resonances with the implied moving sonic forms. This account assumes that perception and understanding of musical expressiveness is based on corporeal resonance behavior which relates sound energy to the subjective action-oriented ontology. The decoding process can be effective if the encoding process is effective as well, that is, if the composer and performer succeed in translating aspects of the subjective action-oriented ontology into sound energy. Evidence for this theory would consist in showing possible links between the intentions of the performer's gestural control and the intentions of the listener's embodied perception. This idea is studied in more detail in the following case study.

### 6.2.1  *Guqin* Music

The case study is based on an analysis of *guqin*-playing. The *guqin* is a Chinese plucked string instrument of the zither family, considered to be the oldest such Chinese instrument, with a history of about three thousand years. The *guqin* can be roughly described as an instrument which is played by plucking the string with the right hand and by manipulating the string with the left hand in order to produce different pitches.[4] The *guqin* is very suited for this type of study because the sound reflects the player's subtle gestural control in a direct way. In contrast with the violin or guitar, the *guqin* involves no other mediating device, such as a bow or frets.

In *guqin*-playing, as with many other instruments, the short-term goal of a performance is to produce a sequence of tones. All movements that contribute to the formation of a tone can be considered as constituent of a tone gesture. The whole piece can be conceived as being produced by a sequence of such tone gestures. However, when looking at individual tones, in particular tones with pitch-sliding, it becomes clear that the tone gesture itself consists of several more elementary movements (Li and Leman, submitted). For example, a single *guqin* tone may first go up in pitch, then go down in pitch, and end with a vibrato (fast up-and-down of pitch). Gestural control is then accomplished by moving the left thumb on the string from left to right, and from right to left, followed by a rapid repetitive movement from left to right and back. Each movement, from left to right or from right to left, can be considered an elementary movement.

Figure 6.1 shows a short fragment of a piece of *guqin* music in Western notation. In this score, arrows are used to indicate pitch-sliding effects. Sonic entities that define a *guqin* tone are described using one or more notes, and bars should be read as rough indications of the meter. The tones are numbered from 1 to 20. Table 6.1 provides a summary of how these tones were produced: which finger was used, which string was played, whether the string was pressed/stopped by left-hand fingers or

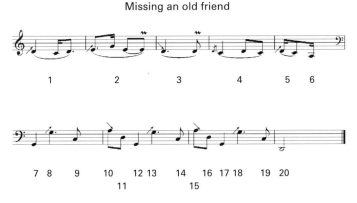

**Figure 6.1**
Western notation of a short *guqin* piece titled "Missing an Old Friend."

**Table 6.1**
Description of twenty sound entities (called tones) in terms of control characteristics

| Tone | Finger | String | Open/ Stopped | Pitch movement | Finger movement (left hand) | Type of gesture (left hand) |
|---|---|---|---|---|---|---|
| 1 | 1 | 7 | S | UVDUV | RVLRV | E |
| 2 | 1 | 7 | S | UVUDV | RVRLV | E |
| 3 | 1 | 7 | S | DVV | LVV | E |
| 4 | 1 | 7 | S | DVUVDV | LVRVLV | E |
| 5 | 1 | 7 | S | UDV | RLV | E |
| 6 | 4 | 7 | S | / | /(press only) | / |
| 7 | | 4 | O | | | AP |
| 8 | 4 | 6 | S | UV | RV | E |
| 9 | 4 | 6 | O | | | EP |
| 10 | 4 | 7 | S | D | L | E |
| 11 | 4 | 7 | O | | | E(A) |
| 12 | | 4 | O | | | AP |
| 13 | 4 | 6 | S | UV | RV | E |
| 14 | 4 | 6 | O | | | EP |
| 15 | 4 | 7 | S | D | L | E |
| 16 | 4 | 7 | O | | | E(A) |
| 17 | | 4 | O | | | AP |
| 18 | 4 | 6 | S | UV | RV | E |
| 19 | | 6 | O | | | |
| 20 | | 2 | O | | | |

Note: The number of each tone corresponds to the number in the score of figure 6.1.
4, left hand ring finger (*Ming*); 1, left thumb; S, stopped string; O, open string; U, pitch up; D, pitch down; V, vibrato (pitch, hand); R, movement to the right; L, movement to the left; E, effective movement; P, preparatory movement; A, ancillary movement.

not (open), if pitch goes up or down, if the finger goes left or right, and if gestural control is executed by the left hand.

The gesture that produces a sliding tone will typically consist of a sequence of coordinated movements of left hand and right hand. For example, to play tone 1, the finger of the right hand will provide energy by plucking the string at onset time. The thumb of the left hand (finger 1) will press the string and move to the right, so that the string becomes shorter and pitch goes up to note d. This will be followed by a rapid alternation from left to right, that is, of shortening and lengthening, which results in a short vibrato. Then the thumb will move to the left, so that the string becomes longer and pitch goes down to note c, and then again to the right (note d), which again involves a vibrato.

### 6.2.2   Corporeal Articulations and Elementary Movements

In what follows, gestural control of the *guqin* is analyzed in terms of its constituent elementary movements, so that it can be related to the corporeal attuning of listeners.

### Elementary Movements

An elementary movement can be defined as the movement of a body part between two points in space (Gibet et al., 2003). This movement is characterized by a bell-shaped velocity pattern (figure 6.2). In a typical pointing task, where a finger moves from point A to point B, the velocity of the finger will increase, reach a maximum, and then decrease in order to arrive at point B. Moving a finger on the string of a *guqin* can be considered a pointing task. In this example, the asymmetric form of the bell-shaped curve of figure 6.2 may reflect the fact that the initial (more or less linear) part of the movement is largely preprogrammed, while the second (nonlinear) part is influenced by sensory feedback after touching the string shortly after the maximum speed is reached. In general, while playing, the movements of the left finger on the string of a *guqin* can be considered as a multipoint movement constrained by sensory feedback. In essence, playing is then reduced to a sequence of elementary movements.

### Gesture and Action

Whether an elementary movement can be considered a gesture (that is, a movement with a defined meaning that stands on its own) or a gesture component (that is, a movement which forms part of an action) depends on the level at which one looks at the gesture. Clearly, a displacement of

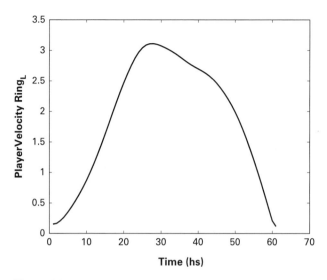

**Figure 6.2**
Elementary movement. The horizontal axis represents time in hundredths of a second, the vertical axis represents velocity (in relative units). The curve represents the movement of a finger in a more or less straight line from point A to point B.

the finger from point A to point B is often just an element in a sequence of movements which together characterize the gestural control of a *guqin* tone. When a gestural control has a particular goal—to play a *guqin* tone—it is called an action.

### Monitoring Gestural Control in *Guqin* Music

The displacement of a marker attached to a particular body part (e.g., finger, wrist, elbow, head) can be monitored with an infrared camera system (figure 6.3).[5] From this displacement in three dimensions, it is possible to derive the velocity (first derivative), and thus to obtain a displacement and velocity curve of each marked body part. The top panel of figure 6.4 shows the displacement curve and the velocity curve of the (left) thumb during the first part of the piece. The top panel of figure 6.5 shows the displacement curve and the velocity curve of the (left) ring finger[6] during the second part of the piece.

### Segmentation of Gestural Control

Given that playing music is a continuous activity, the camera will record a continuous displacement from which a continuous velocity pattern will be derived. In view of the concept of elementary movements, this

**Figure 6.3**
Infrared recording equipment and *guqin* player.

continuous velocity pattern can be interpreted as a sequence of bell-shaped forms. The zero crossings, the points at which the curve goes through the horizontal line, suggest a segmentation of the continuous movement in terms of elementary pointing movements.

Zero crossings can be used as a criterion to segment the measured velocity of a marker into elementary velocity patterns.[7] In figures 6.4 and 6.5, only large movements have been segmented. Smaller movements, which are typical for vibrato, are neglected. In fact, it is straightforward to consider vibrato as a self-contained movement after all.

### Sonogram of *Guqin* Music

The bottom panels of figures 6.4 and 6.5 show sonogram representations of the *guqin* music. The vertical axes show frequency in hertz, and the horizontal axes show time (amplitude is in black). The onset of each tone generates a short burst of energy over all frequencies. This can be used as a segmentation marker for tones. The tone numbers are written below each sonogram.[8] The dashed vertical lines indicate segmentation marks of the gestural control (displayed in the top panel). On the sono-

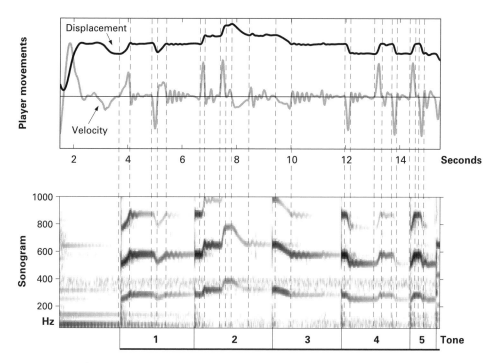

**Figure 6.4**
Player movements and sonogram of the first part of "Missing an Old Friend" (figure 6.1). The top panel shows the displacement and the velocity of the thumb. The bottom panel shows the sonogram. Vertical lines indicate segments at zero crossings of the velocity curve. To facilitate reading, only large movements have been segmented. Vibrato is not segmented.

gram representation they clearly mark the difference between gestural control and sonic output.

### 6.2.3   Gestural Control and Its Effect on Sound

A tone can be conceived as the sonic encoding of an action. It starts with the pluck, and all pitch shifts within the tone are considered part of the tone.

In order to have a better view of the relationship between the player's action and the resulting tones, tones have been analyzed according to the descriptions summarized in the legend of table 6.1. The following considerations should be taken into account:

•     A string is played open (O) or stopped (S). An open string is often plucked by the right hand (R). In that case, the left hand (L) does not

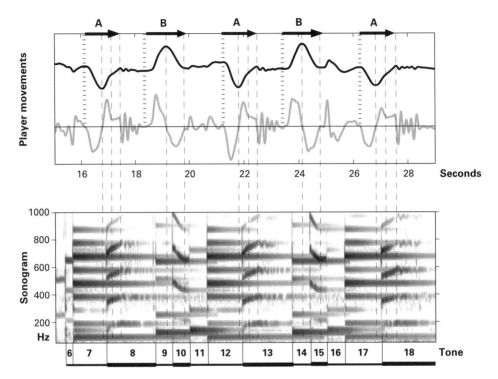

**Figure 6.5**
Player movements and sonogram of the second part of "Missing an Old Friend" (figure 6.1). The top panel shows the displacement and the velocity of the ring finger. The bottom panel shows the sonogram. Vertical lines indicate segments at zero crossings of the velocity curve. To facilitate reading, only large movements have been segmented. Vibrato is not segmented. The arrows in the top panel indicate control gestures that contain countermovements. (See text for further explanation.)

touch the string. The resulting pitch is then only the pitch of the string. However, there are cases where an open string is plucked by the left hand as well.

• In this piece, the stopped string is played by two fingers of the left hand, the thumb (finger 1) and the ring finger (finger 4). The first five tones are controlled by the thumb and the other tones are mainly controlled by the ring finger. In all stopped tones of the example, the left hand controls the pitch.

• The *guqin* has seven strings, numbered from 1 to 7, which correspond to the notes c, d, f, g, a, c, and d.

• The vibrato (V) is defined as a sequence of fast up-and-down pitch (or hand) movements. It is considered as a self-contained movement (or hand movement).

• The pitch of stopped tones can go up (U) or down (D). This corresponds to the movement of the finger to the right (R) or to the left (L).

• The gesture made by a finger of the left hand is called effective (E) when it actually produces a tone. It is called preparatory (P) when it is preparing the production of a tone. A movement is called ancillary (A) when it is neither effective nor preparatory.

Using these labels, the musical fragment can be described as follows:

• Tone 1 is played by the thumb (finger 1) on string 7. As shown in the sonogram of figure 6.4, the tone first goes up in pitch, followed by a vibrato. Then the pitch goes down and up and ends in a vibrato. The corresponding movement can be seen in the displacement curve (top panel). The thumb moves to the right, makes a vibrato, moves to the left and then to the right, and finally makes a vibrato. The velocity curve shows the change of movement. Displacement to the right (upward on the displacement curve) corresponds to positive bell-like curves, while displacement to the left (downward on the displacement curve) corresponds to negative bell-like curves. The horizontal line corresponds to zero velocity (no displacement). Note the interesting negative curve just before the start of the first tone, right where the arrow indicates that this is the velocity curve. This shape indicates a typical preparatory movement which anticipates the effective gesture. As can be seen on the displacement curve, the anticipation movement is in the opposite direction from the effective movement. Note also that the onset of tone 1 starts a fraction of a second later than the actual start of the upward movement. In *guqin*-playing, this technique is known as hidden head sliding. It is used to avoid the emphasis on the beginning of the tone, and thus produces a light, smooth, and gentle tone quality. The same technique, often more pronounced, is used in tones 5, 8, 10, 13, 15, and 18 (figure 6.5, top panel).

• Tones 2 to 5 can be described as similar to tone 1. These tones have no preparatory movements, which can be explained by the fact that their pitch starts at the pitch level on which the previous tone ended. The player already knows the starting position.

• Tone 6 (figure 6.5) has a stable pitch. This tone is plucked by the left thumb while the left ring finger is pressed 10 cm to the left of the left thumb on the same string. There is very little movement because the ring finger is about to press on the string, and it is very close to the pressing point.

•     Tone 7 has a stable pitch which results from plucking open string 4, using a finger of the right hand. The left ring finger first makes ancillary movements but during the second half of the tone, it anticipates the generation of the next tone.

•     Tone 8 goes up in pitch and is followed by a vibrato. This tone is produced by the left ring finger on string 6, by a movement which goes to the right and is followed by a rapid left/right movement. This movement is effective for sound control. Note that the first part of the movement has been anticipated by a fraction of a second. Indeed, the tone starts when the velocity of a movement to the right (upward) is at top speed. The pitch shift consists of two parts, a rapid rise followed by a slower rise. This is reflected in the displacement curve as well as in the velocity curve. In order to be able to perform this subtle gestural control, the movement had been prepared at the end of the previous tone. The anticipatory movement seems to start from the position where the tone will end, and the time to perform this countermovement is about equal to the time to perform the movement that allows the finger to touch the string and thus to generate the sound.

•     Tone 9 has a stable pitch which results from plucking string number 6 with a finger of the right hand. Meanwhile, the movement of the left ring finger is anticipating the production of tone 10.

•     Tone 10 goes down in pitch. It is controlled by the left ring finger on string 7, through a movement to the left. The gesture is effective for the sound production. Also, the tone starts when the speed of the movement to the left (downward on the displacement curve) reaches its maximum. This gesture is also anticipated during the sounding of the previous note, and the anticipation has the character of a countermovement in space and in time.

•     Tone 11 is a stable pitch which results from plucking string number 7 with the left ring finger. This plucking movement is reflected in a sharp peak in velocity.

The sequence of tones 12 to 16 is a repetition of the sequence of tones 7 to 11. For example, in tone 12, the left ring finger makes an ancillary movement and then a preparatory movement. Apart from a salient ancillary movement in tone 16, the two sequences are almost exactly the same. At tone 17, the sequence is again repeated.

These detailed descriptions show the following:

- A tone in *guqin* music can be analyzed in terms of its gestural control. The action which produces a sliding tone consists of a sequence of elementary (point-to-point) movements.
- Some *guqin* tones start with low velocity, as shown in tones 1 to 5. In this type of tone, the maximum velocity tends to be obtained somewhere in the middle of the upward or downward pitch shift. The pitch shifts of tone 5 are faster than those of the other tones.
- Other *guqin* tones are characterized by starting when the velocity is maximum. This is the case for tones 8, 10, 13, 15, and 18. In order to produce this tone, the effective movement has to start in advance. Furthermore, all these tones are preceded by a countermovement, whose displacement is in the opposite direction from that of the effective movement. For example, if the effective movement goes to the left (pitch goes down), the preparatory movement goes to the right (tones 10 and 15). The duration of this countermovement is almost equal to the duration of the effective movement.[9]
- Upward and downward pitch shifts may differ with respect to their speed. Their nature is defined by the effective movements that underlie the pitch shifts. It is straightforward to assume that this aspect contributes to the particular expressiveness of the tone. Tones 8 and 13 are notable in that the pitch glissando consists of two parts that are clearly visible in the displacement and velocity curves. The change in this glissando is deliberate. It affects the expressive character of the glissando, making it lighter.

The main conclusion of this analysis is that *guqin* tones are generated by a complex interplay of very efficient corporeal articulations. They consist of preparatory (counter)movements and effective (control) movements which together define an action that leads to the production of a tone. Important and time-critical articulations are clearly anticipated and are prepared for by a movement in the opposite direction and of almost equal duration. Ineffective or ancillary movements are rarely noticed. Repetition of sequences of movements is very accurate, which is reflected in the velocity curves.

In this context, the characterization of music as moving sonic forms is useful. It captures the idea that the sound structure encodes aspects of the player's actions. The sound structure reveals the encoding of the biomechanical energy as sound energy. Behind this sound energy are movements aimed at producing tones. These tones are intended to function in tone configurations or musical phrases. From the listener's point of view, the sound defines the proximal cues, while the player's actions define the distal cues. Clearly, not all aspects of the player's movements are encoded; preparatory, anticipated, and ancillary gestures remain hidden. Only some of the gestural controls are effective in the sense that they are reflected in the sound structure. All this suggests that the moving sonic forms are intentional and functional. The next step, then, is to investigate how well the listener is able to capture these aspects of moving forms.

### 6.2.4    Monitoring the Listener's Movements

In this case study, I focus on two listeners. The first listener knew the musical fragment very well but was not an expert in Chinese music. The second listener was entirely new to the music and the piece.

Their corporeal articulations were monitored with the help of a joystick (figure 6.6). The listeners were standing, and while listening to *guqin* fragments through headphones, they were requested to move a stick in accord with the music. Thus, the corporeal articulations were reduced to movement in two dimensions. The listeners listened to the *guqin* piece twice. Figure 6.7 shows the movements of two listeners (L1, L2) during two trials (T1, T2) for the second part of the piece, starting at tone 5 (P1).

**Figure 6.6**
The listener's recording equipment.

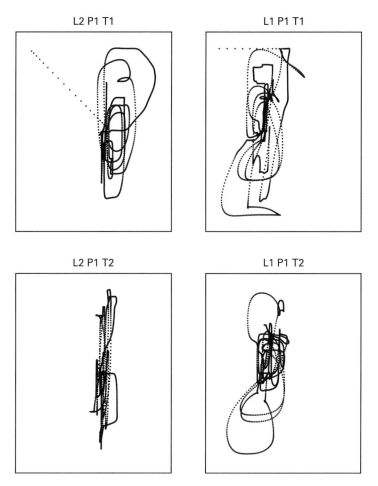

**Figure 6.7**
The listener's movements. L, listener; P, piece; T, trial. The X and Y axis represent horizontal and vertical movement, respectively. (See text for further explanation.) Figure 6.8 shows the corresponding velocity patterns (of the second part of this movement).

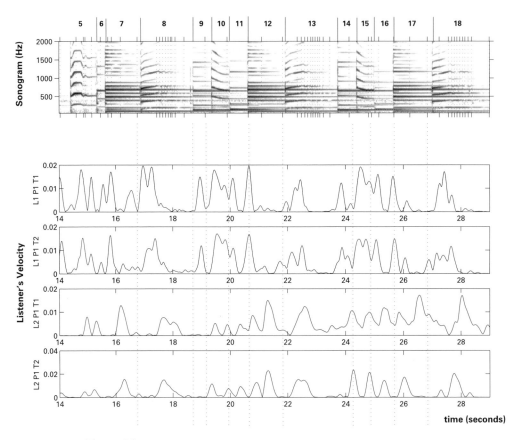

**Figure 6.8**
Sonogram of the second part of the *guqin* fragment and velocity curves of two listeners during two trials. (The velocity curves show the absolute values of the velocity.)

The velocity patterns were derived from these movements and are shown in figure 6.8. The top panel shows the sonogram, with tone labels, tone segmentations, and gesture segmentations marked by the vertical grid on the sonogram.

**Analysis of Listener Behavior**
Several observations can be made concerning consistency, synchronization, resonance, and the induction of ideomotor responses:

•     In this *guqin* fragment, the beat is not prominently present, al-though a beat can be induced by the rhythmic structure in the second part of the piece. Indeed, tones 9, 10, and 11 have the same duration. If we take the length of one of these notes as the unit length, then tone 12 is twice this duration and tone 13 is almost three times this duration. The pitch shift in tone 13, for example, takes about the unit length (similar to tones 8 and 18), which reinforces the rhythmic subdivision of the tones in terms of a unit length. This underlying rhythmic pattern may mark a beat to which listeners respond. The induction of a repetitive pattern in the movement is more clearly present in subject 2 than in subject 1, for example, during tones 10, 11, and 12, and during the repetition at tones 15, 16, and 17.

• Subjects seem to be rather consistent in their movements over the two trials, in the sense that they tend to replicate their movement speed when listening to the music in subsequent trials. However, over different trials, subjects tend to make different movements, as can be inferred from the movement patterns shown in figure 6.7. Thus, what is invariant here is not the displacement as such, but the speed of the movement. In addition, subjects differ in terms of the types of movements they make, as well as in terms of timing. What constitutes the start of a movement (low velocity) for subject 1 may correspond to a point of maximum velocity for subject 2. Although corporeal articulations may differ greatly from one subject to the other, the subject can replicate its own speed very accurately. This suggests that the velocity of the movement is an invariant feature of embodied perception.

• Synchronization of the movement with the characteristics of a sound is an expression of resonance behavior with musical energy. In this example, two types of synchronization can be observed: (1) synchronization related to the onset of a tone and (2) synchronization related to the characteristics inside the tone (typically, effects of sliding).

—First, concerning the onset, it can be observed that the start of a(n elementary) movement is not always in agreement with the actual start of the sound. In fact, the movement may start earlier, and it may happen that the start of a tone falls exactly on the maximum speed of the movement. This can be observed at tone 12, where the onset of the tone falls exactly on the point where the movement of subject 1 has the highest speed. For subject 2, this point corresponds to the start of an elementary movement. A similar observation can be made with respect to tones 10 and 15. Note that at tone 10, both subjects have their maximum speed on the beat, while at tone 15, only subject 1 does. Consider also tone 17, where this aspect of synchronization is salient.

The corporeal articulations of the listeners thus have an anticipatory character which is more pronounced in the experienced listener than in the nonexperienced one. The anticipation is characterized by the fact that the elementary movement may start before the tone onset and reach its maximum velocity at the tone onset.

Remarkably, such anticipated movements sometimes tend to synchronize with the movements of the player. For subject 1, this can be noticed at tone 8 (first trial), where the movement starts at the same moment as the movement of the player (indicated by the dotted vertical lines that connect with the sonogram). Also, for tones 9, 10, 11, 13, 14, and 15, the onset of the elementary movements corresponds to the onset of the player's elementary movements.

—Second, there is a clear effect of pitch-sliding on the synchronization. For example, at tone 13, the maximum speed in all trials is reached at the moment when the pitch shift becomes stable and is transformed into a vibrato. This effect can also be observed at tone 8 for subject 1, whereas subject 2 shows the opposite response, in that the movement starts during the vibrato. A similar trend can be observed in tone 18. In tones 10 and 15, the velocity of the movement tends to slow down in both subjects, while in note 13, the velocity tends to rise in synchrony with the velocity of the pitch shift. This illustrates that the corporeal articulation can be in resonance with pitch effects.

The above observations suggest that listeners are able to attune their elementary movements to characteristics of the sound energy, such as onset and pitch change. In the experienced listener, the corporeal resonance behavior has a more pronounced predictive character. The onset of the listener's elementary movement often agrees with the onset of the player's elementary movement. The speed of the movement can be influenced by the speed of the pitch change. Whether pitch goes down or up seems to affect the decrease or increase of the listener's movement velocity in this example.

The data provide evidence for the hypothesis that the listener's perception is predictive at short term. The accurate synchronization of the anticipatory character of the movements suggests that they are intentional. It is tempting to assume that aspects of this corporeal intentionality may relate to the performer's corporeal intentionality. Indeed, anticipation of the sonic moving forms seems to synchronize with the player's corporeal articulations. Whether such a close relationship between the players' articulations and the listener's articulations can be assumed, remains to be seen on the basis of more studies.

What these data suggest, however, is that the listener is capable of grasping music as an intended moving form. This can be explained by the fact that the listener's movements translate sound energy to the listener's action-based ontology. In doing this, the movements take on the character of an action (goal-directed movement) whose intentionality is in turn projected onto the sound energy and, by extension, onto the movements of the listener. Thus, player and listener are able to establish a relationship of mutual information exchange at the level of action.

Alternatively, one may consider music as a proximal cue in which the listener perceives (or forms the hypothesis of) the distal cue, that is, the action which gives rise to the proximal cue. Through corporeal attuning, the listener can express the perceived intentionality which, as shown here, can be measured and studied. This projection of human motion onto music is facilitated when the cause of that motion is itself a human actor, and thus the motion is human (Juslin et al., 2002). This mechanism is similar to the human ability to decode human action patterns from point-light displays in the visual domain (see, e.g., Pollick et al., 2001; Pollick, 2004; Troje et al., 2005).

Obviously, the movements of the listener are not (and perhaps cannot be) exactly the same as the movements of the player. What is more or less the same in both the listener and the player is the motor system that encodes and decodes moving sonic forms. The above data suggest that music perception involves a motor attuning component through which an intentional character can be attributed to music and, by extension, to the composer and performer. Motor-attuning helps the listener to read the minds of the composer and the performer, and thus to understand the music as an embodied mental phenomenon. According to Wilson and Knoblich (2005), the predictive behavior that is made possible by motor attuning (called emulation) would in turn facilitate perception. It is indeed straightforward to assume that this facilitation helps listeners to experience music as a peak experience. The predictive character of corporeal attuning is likely to be the expression of fundamental and automated patterns of communication (Bargh and Chartrand, 1999). Hawkins and Blakeslee (2004) state that predictive behavior is the essence of human intelligence.

To summarize, the case study supports the theory that the musician encodes gestures in sound, and the listener can decode particular aspects

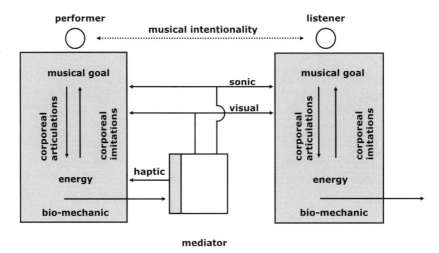

Figure 6.9
Model of musical communication between performer and listener (see text for explanation).

of them through corporeal imitation (see also Leman et al., submitted). The mechanism enables the communication of intended motion, which provides a basis for an embodied perception and mind-reading of music. This type of perception and understanding is assumed to play a key role in the listener's focus on peak experiences and the understanding of structure, emotion, and cultural significance.

### 6.2.5   A Model of Musical Communication

The above case study supports a model of musical communication in which the encoding and decoding of biomechanical energy allows the communication of intentions. Figure 6.9 is a schematic summary of this musical communication model in which a performer and a listener are involved, in addition to a mediator.

The starting point is the performer, who has in mind a musical goal or idea (possibly provided by a composer). This goal is realized as sound energy, using the human body and a mediation technology. More specifically, the musical goal is realized through corporeal articulations, whose biomechanical energy is transferred to the music mediation technology (the music instrument). This device in turn translates part of the biomechanical energy of the performer into sound energy, while another part of the biomechanical energy is bounced back as haptic energy (energy related to the sense of touch). The control of the musical instrument is realized in a closed loop with haptic, sonic, and perhaps visual feedback. In the mind of the performer, this physical interaction can be enhanced by corporeal imitation processes that translate the sensed energy back into the action-oriented ontology, giving meaning to the interaction. Thus, haptic energy may largely contribute to the perceptual disambiguation of the particular relationship between gestural control and sonic output.

Next, the mediator transmits the sonic and visual energy to the listener, who, through mirror processes, can make sense of it. Corporeal resonance (or imitation) thereby forms the basis of musical involvement which ultimately leads to an understanding, both corporeal and cerebral, of the music's underlying intended articulations (expressions of moving forms at local and more global levels). Obviously, the listener's understanding of the music's intentions need not necessarily be the same as the performer's. It is sufficient that the listener can relate the moving sonic forms to his or her own action-relevant ontology in order to make sense of the perceived physical energy. The listener's processing of musical information is likely to be reflected in corporeal articulations, which can be seen by other listeners.

There is a further important aspect of this model. That the mediator—for example, an acoustic instrument such as a Chinese *guqin*—can be conceived of as an extension of the performer's body. Obviously, for the performer this is an illusion, albeit a very natural one. It is generally believed that haptic feedback may largely contribute to the creation of this illusion of non-mediation. In fact, experiments show that self-attribution of body parts is based on multisensory perceptual correlations of which action-related sensing forms an important aspect (van den Bos and Jeannerod, 2002).

The model suggests a musical signification practice that is based on the encoding and decoding of patterns of corporeal articulations. Music encodes corporeal articulations in sound (moving sonic forms) which can be decoded, predicted, and understood because they rely on movements which appeal to the action-based ontology of human subjects. Although these movements may be culturally learned, they can be imitated and related to a common framework of the composer/performer and the listener. Since this framework is neurally encoded, it can be stated that musical communication is based on the sharing of neural structures that pertain to movement. This forms the power of music as universal language. However, one should always keep in mind that any signification practice may also call upon a cerebral approach to music as a meaningful cultural phenomenon. In this practice, corporeal perception and understanding seem to be fundamental because they are based on moving forms and the resonant structures of the human body. It does not require knowledge of the cultural background of music, although such knowledge may be of great help in setting appropriate motor structures ready for action. In addition, the perceived movement may be an incentive for the activation of other processes—for example, those related to arousal and emotion. The communication of music is fundamentally based on multimodal sensing, using a motor model for encoding and decoding.

## 6.3   Constraints of Interactive Communication

The above model of musical communication can be extended to interactive music systems, and in particular to electronic musical instruments and digital virtual musical environments. In using interactive music systems for artistic purposes, one of the key problems is the configuration of a proper mediation technology. This configuration can be considered from four viewpoints: (1) biomechanical control and haptic feedback, (2) constraints of electronic music mediation, (3) group effects of musical communication, and (4) motivation. Taking the above model of musical communication as the base, these viewpoints define a framework for interactivity in which musical communication is embedded. The framework is complicated because it involves different aspects of action and perception, from sensorimotor interaction to intentional behavior. The primary interest in relating the theory of corporeal articulation and resonance to interactive music systems is that it offers a straightforward grounding of multimodal experience in a context of multimedia technology. The above model of musical communication can be of help in understanding the relevant issues.

### 6.3.1   Biomechanical Control and Haptic Feedback

As shown in the case study of *guqin* music, acoustic musical instruments draw upon the fact that the movements of the performer are tightly connected with a mechanical-energetic interface that produces sound. This connection implies that part of the performer's biomechanical energy is used to shape the microstructures of the sound energy. A smaller part of this energy is bounced back as haptic energy, which the performer can feel by the sense of touch. Sound energy and haptic energy are basic sources of feedback on which the performer can rely for fine gestural control of the instrument and subsequently, fine control over musical expression (Winold et al., 1994).

Haptic feedback is believed to be important for the prediction, self-adaptation, and modification of sound control at the millisecond level. Recall the asymmetric shape of figure 6.2. The first part of the movement is typically unconstrained by sensory feedback, while the second part is based on sonic and haptic feedback (after touching the string). Haptic feedback to the performer is important in that it allows a disambiguation of the control unit, and thus of the perceived effects (proximal cues) of the mediator (Ernst and Bülthoff, 2004). Haptic feedback contributes to a more reliable estimate of the sonic output of the mediator. In many ways, it is a multimodal prerequisite for musical expressiveness. Indeed, research on haptic feedback is often linked with research on musical expression and performer nuances.

Of particular relevance for mediation technologies is the idea that the performance nuances subsume a layer of communication that runs in parallel with sensorimotor processing and higher-level couplings of action and perception (Sheridan, 2004). From the viewpoint of the performer, this level is more focused on the expression of a particular sensitivity or affect, while from the viewpoint of the listener, this level is more focused on the understanding of action-relevant characteristics induced by kinesthetic involvement. Much of the research on performer nuances is on the clarification of the relationship between local and global aspects of musical expressiveness.

### 6.3.2   Constraints of Electronic Music Mediation

Overall, haptic feedback is a natural characteristic of acoustic instruments. By their design, these instruments allow the transformation of biomechanical energy directly into sound energy. In contrast, electronic instruments have no mechanical-energetic interface that mediates between corporeal articulation and sound. In electronic music systems the energy for making sound (electricity) is independent from the haptic biomechanical energy exerted by the musician. Consequently, the interfaces and gestural control devices are decoupled from the sound production device. A consequence of a lack of haptic feedback may be that the mediator is not really experienced as part of the human body and, consequently, that corporeal articulations are badly reflected in the microstructure of the sound energy, which in turn may be problematic for the listener.

In view of the musical communication model, this decoupling has a number of consequences for the design of effective mediators. The problem should be considered with respect to haptic feedback, mappings of control parameters, and characteristics of musical action and perception.

**Simulating Haptic Feedback**

The lack of haptic feedback in electronic musical instruments has been acknowledged as a central problem in their design (e.g., Rovan and Hayward, 2000; Gunther and O'Modhrain, 2003; Howard and Rimell, 2004). In recent years, much attention has been devoted to the possibility of simulating haptic and tactile feedback using electronic devices (see, e.g., Wanderley and Battier, 2000; Paradiso and O'Modhrain, 2003; Camurri and Rikakis, 2004; Johannsen, 2004). In addition to haptic feedback, visual feedback cues have been investigated (Camurri, Lagerlöf, et al., 2003; Kapur et al., 2003). This work has just begun, and needs much more elaboration in the future. It is related to a number of other problems, in particular mediator mappings and issues of music perception.

**Mediator Mappings**

Clearly, electronic music systems allow much more freedom for the performer, because mappings between gestural control units, on the one hand, and sound production units, on the other hand, are not constrained by any biomechanical regularities. This type of freedom has attracted the interest of many artists and researchers (Tarabella and Bertini, 2004; Karjalainen et al., 2004; Ng, 2004). It allows the playing of a complicated scale on the piano or guitar by a simple wave of the hand. The movement of the hand may be captured by a video camera and used as a trigger for playing the scale. However, as most electronic music performers know, it is exactly this freedom of mapping that may disturb the sense of contact and of non-mediation.

To better understand the problem of mapping in electronic musical instruments, figure 6.10 distinguishes among the gestural controller unit, the mapping unit, and the production unit (Wanderley and Depalle, 2004). The components in the dotted box can be seen as parts of the mediator that is depicted in the musical communication model of figure 6.9. The gestural controller is defined as the part where physical interaction with the performer takes place. It contains sensors and software for

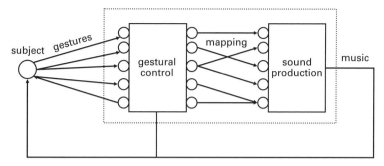

**Figure 6.10**
Conceptual model of an interactive system consisting of gestural controller, mapping, and production unit.

feature extraction. The gestural controller can also give feedback to the performer, for example, by means of a computer screen or simulated (electronic-based) haptic feedback. Next to the gestural controller is a mapping unit which translates gestural controls into parameters for the production of sound or other types of energy. The sound production block can be considered a sound synthesizer whose output is controlled by a number of parameters that vary in time.

In this model, the mapping unit forms an important part of the mediator in that it connects human corporeal articulations with the production of music and possibly with associated multimedia events. The mapping allows a lot of freedom, but this freedom has an obverse side: performers often feel that the information flow cannot be accurately controlled in its fine details. If this happens, it is likely that the information flow is experienced as unpredictable. As a result, it can be hard to create the illusion of non-mediation.

**Mediating Musical Sound**
The lack of haptic feedback may have a significant effect on the effectiveness of the mediator and, consequently, on the chain of musical communication. However, this lack is not the only problem. It is part of a set of problems that define the delicate balance between unlimited freedom in sound control, on the one hand, and constraints that limit human action and perception, on the other. After all, the purpose of a musical instrument is to allow music to be made by retaining the interest of the performer and the listener. This interest depends on the performer's ability to control the mediator in a precise way, but it also involves the listener's

ability to make sense of the situation. Mediation technology cannot be seen independently from the fact that biological organisms have a natural bias toward action-relevant cues in the environment. In music, things become even more complicated because cultural constraints have to be taken into consideration.

Therefore, an appropriate design of the mediation technology should cope with a diverse set of natural as well as culturally relevant aspects in order to keep the interest of the performer and the listener. At least four different aspects of interaction can be taken into account, related to (1) the listener's natural bias toward sonic sources, (2) structural similarities, (3) gestures, and (4) learned conventions.

**Mediating sonic sources (the ecological approach)**   First, consider the bias toward the perception of action-relevant cues (affordances). This aspect was mentioned in the earlier discussion of the Gibsonian model of perception. The bias means that in natural environments, perception is oriented toward the action-relevant cues of the physical energy that give rise to the perception. In recent studies on ecological psychoacoustics (Rocchesso and Fontana, 2003; Neuhoff, 2004), it was shown that listeners have an impressive ability to identify very specific action-relevant characteristics of the mechanics that cause the sounds. Listeners detect the width of struck bars; the length of dropped rods; the hardness of struck mallets; the size, material, and shape of struck plates; vessels with different levels of fluid; determination of gender from footsteps; the ascending or descending of staircases; and anticipate the trajectory of approaching sound sources (Rosenblum, 2004). Listeners seem to have a natural bias for the perception of the source mechanics. This provides a basis for source-related understanding of the interactive musical instrument.

When the subject perceives the sound as being produced by a physical mechanism, it may form the impression that the sound is real; hence, that the environment in which it has been produced is real; and hence, that this environment has a high degree of presence, which in turn may facilitate the experience of being immersed. From the perspective of the performer, multisensory (sonic, visual, tactile, haptic) feedback may contribute largely to the perception of action-relevant sources and the illusion of biomechanically based control. It can be assumed, therefore, that mediators that account for action-relevant cues may yield a high degree of presence, and therefore have the potential to be more effective in engendering a higher musical involvement for the performer and the listener.

**Mediating structures and similarities (the gestalt-based or cognitive approach)**  There are many cases where the perceptual system of a listener may not be able to make sense of the action-relevant source. For example, in newly composed artificial sounds, often the source mechanics cannot be retraced and the perceptual system has to look for an alternative solution. In that case, the cognitive approach assumes that attention is directed toward the structural properties of musical audio, such as the relationship among intensity, pitch, timbre, and so on.

It is characteristic of music perception that the focus of attention may not be so much directed at the mechanical source of the sounds as at higher-level structural musical qualities of melodic lines, rhythm patterns, harmony, and timbre. Thus, in cases where source mechanics cannot be retraced, or where the musical context is such that the emphasis is on sonic forms rather than on the sources that produce these sounds, attention may shift toward structural characteristics. After all, these characteristics are an emerging aspect of the processing of multisensory information. Principles of perceptual organization, such as integration and segregation, will transform sound energy into musical objects as a function of disambiguation (Bregman, 1990). If action-related cues are not strong, or are put in an unusual context, the signification process may turn to the meaningful relationships between structural features. It may be assumed that the perceptual system is predisposed to organize stimuli into such structures of gestalts, independent of whether source-relevant cues are available or not. Thus mediators may be constructed so that they produce gestalt-based meaningful relationships between structures in sound energy.

**Mediating gestures (the embodied cognition approach)**  In addition to the ecological approach and the gestalt approach, the embodied cognition approach assumes that listeners seek to give meaning to musical sounds in terms of emulated actions, that is, of corporeal articulations (grounded in the subjective action-oriented ontology) in response to sonic energy. This aspect should be distinguished from the recognition of the mechanical sound source, as well as from the cognitive involvement with sound structures (proximal cues). The sound source concerns the mechanical cause of the sound, something that is external to the human subject. This can be called the mechanical distal cue. Instead, the gesture is about the human cause which is behind the mechanical cause of things, which is internal to the human subject. This can be called the intentional distal cue. In that sense, sounds of a symphonic orchestra, for example, even if they cannot be related to a particular external mechanical cause, can be related to intended gestures when they appeal to corporeal articulations and imitations by the listener. Therefore, mediators that take this aspect of human-related movements into account may be of interest in the context of electronic music mediation.

**Mediating conventions (the cultural approach)**    Finally, it should be noted that listeners are sensitive to learned patterns and cultural conventions. These find their way into the articulations that are typical for a particular musical style (Hatten, 2003). Musical communication may draw on the knowledge of these patterns, which may relate to different types of conventions, including symbolic or narrative conventions such as the heralding of spring using the characteristic pitch interval of a cuckoo, or rhythmic patterns that refer to secret messages, as in Mozart's Masonic opera *Die Zauberflöte*. Therefore, conventions should be taken into account in mediation, even in electronic music performances.

To sum up, mediators for electronic interactive environments should take into account principles related to natural and cultural constraints of human action and perception. These principles range from sensorimotor processes, such as haptic feedback, to ecological and embodied aspects of perception and conventions. Human perception is rich, and it is likely that all these aspects should be taken into account in developing electronic devices that mediate between mind and matter. The above considerations clearly show that mediation is a matter not only of sensorimotor interactions but also of careful design that takes into account global constraints of musical communication.

### 6.3.3   Motivation

The above considerations are also related to motivation, the reasons why a subject would be interested in a human–technology interaction. Motivation brings in a number of factors, which may be external or intrinsic. For example, social group pressure is an external drive which may force a subject to attend a concert dressed in a particular way, to move and behave in particular ways, to pay attention to particular aspects of the performance, and to use particular music mediation technologies (e.g., iPods rather than mp3-players). External motivations may also partly drive intrinsic motivations.

Csikszentmihalyi and Csikszentmihalyi (1988) relate intrinsic motivations to intrinsically rewarding (or autotelic) experiences, which bring the subject to a state of experience that is self-motivating. They state that this state of intrinsically rewarding experience is a kind of psychic negentropy which is obtained when the contents of consciousness are in harmony with each other and with the goals that contribute to the development of the subject's self, or what I call the subject's action-oriented ontology. It is the collection of mental entities (beliefs, values, valences, motivations) by which the subject structures and anticipates its actions in the physical environment.

Music may provide an excellent context for intrinsically rewarding experiences. Through learning, challenges may be set at gradually higher levels and skills can be adapted to them. Thus, an optimal balance can be found and interest can be maintained. In that respect, self-motivation is something dynamic. If skills develop and challenges remain the same, challenges may become boring and the subject may lose interest and abandon the task. On the other hand, if the challenges are too high, the subject may become frustrated and unmotivated. According to Csikszentmihalyi and Csikszentmihalyi, it is only when challenges and skills are in balance that the subject is able to engage in an autotelic experience.

The mechanism of intrinsically rewarding experience is of particular relevance for the development of music mediation technologies. Indeed, if gestural control and sound generation are physically decoupled, skills and challenges may become decoupled and interest may be quickly lost if the subject has the impression that improvement of skills has no apparent effect on feedback from the interactive system. A major challenge for the development of a mediator is to keep track of the balance between challenges and skills.

The following example illustrates the role of intrinsic motivation in the development of a music mediation device. The device was presented at the Accenta exhibition at Ghent in 2005 (figure 6.11). Visitors to the booth heard a pure tone in a headphone and were requested to imitate the pitch of that tone by singing. This is an action that offers little apparent return, except for those interested in singing. A digital mirror showed a deformed reflection of the subject's face. It was only by repeating the sung tone correctly that the deformed image became a clearly visible mirror image. After a very brief learning period, subjects rapidly become

**Figure 6.11**
Interactive game called *Spiegeltje aan de wand* (Accenta exhibition, Ghent, 2005). You can see yourself in the digital mirror when you correctly imitate the tone you hear in the headphone. Otherwise, the image is deformed.

experts in imitation. Most subjects, especially children, enjoyed the game because of the intrinsic motivation to see themselves in the mirror. Low-level musical involvement was thus mediated by means of a visual feedback which stimulated self-motivation.

Recent designs of interactive music systems show that mediators can be constrained such that mirroring becomes an integrated part of the interaction. For example, Pachet (2003) developed an experimental system that interacts with a human performer by means of style imitations. The gestural controller and the sound production system are traditional keyboards with piano tones, but the system is able to learn features of the musical style of the human performer. It can reproduce responses that imitate the style. Experiments with this system support the idea that performers interact with the system at a high mental level of stylistic content exchange. This approach opens new ways to conceive the mediator technology in terms of interacting agents capable of mirror-

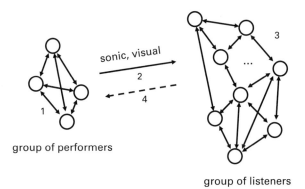

group of performers

group of listeners

**Figure 6.12**
Model of social music communication, with interaction (1) among performers,
(2) from performers to listeners (music-driven interaction), (3) among listeners,
and (4) from listeners to performers.

ing the subject's intentionality. These initial experiments show that
mirroring supports the motivation for being involved in an interaction
process.

### 6.3.4    Group Effects in Musical Communication

In addition to the previous issues, there is another aspect of communication (figure 6.9) that is likely to be very important in music: group behavior and, more particularly, entrainment or mutual adaptive behavioral
resonance. Although this aspect will not be discussed in detail in this
book, it is relevant to mediation technologies and interactive multimedia
systems.[10]
    A model for social music communication is depicted in figure 6.12.
Performers and listeners are represented by circles, and the arrows between circles suggest exchange of energy patterns through sonic, visual,
olfactory, and tactile information channels. The actions of the performers (interaction type 1) generate music (sonic/visual energy). Listeners capture sonic energy and see the gestures of the performers. This
sonic and visual scene may drive the movements of the listener in response to music (interaction type 2). In addition, listeners perceive each
other, and in response to that (interaction type 3), they may start exert-
ing an influence on each other. Corporeal resonance in a listener may
thus result from the musical/sonic and visual energy as well as from the

multimodal energy coming from neighboring listeners. The latter may be called the social entrainment energy. In a similar way, the performers are influenced by musical/sonic energy, haptic feedback, and social entrainment energy coming from the audience (interaction type 4). This type of interaction also may entrain the action of performers. Indeed, performers report that the audience tends to be perceived as a gestalt whose action is likely to have an effect on their playing. As can be seen, the social interactions are quite complex.

The hypothesis is that in a context where groups of people are together, corporeal imitation can lead to emergent behavior, as in concert halls where masses of people start waving their hands in the air at the same time, or when, after a concert, the applause becomes synchronized (Neda et al., 2000). In both cases, the emerging behavior of the audience results from the fact that subjects are imitating their neighbors (see section 5.1.2). This phenomenon has been observed and studied in populations of insects, fish, birds, and other animals (see, e.g., Theraulaz and Spitz, 1997; Bonabeau and Theraulaz, 1997), as well as in humans (Grammer et al., 1998, 2000; Bargh and Chartrand, 1999; Lakin et al., 2003; Niedenthal et al., 2005).

It can be assumed that group imitation behavior has an enormous effect on the participants' individual experiences during this applause. Arousal, attention, and the feeling of presence may be enhanced through this type of group resonance effect. Performers, too, seem to appreciate the effects of allelo-mimetism in an audience, which they perceive through auditory, visual, and tactile channels. They perceive this effect as a global emerging effect of the audience, which can be very stimulating for their performance.

Entrainment thus forms the dynamic multimodal framework from which musical magic, a peak experience of a group of people, may emerge. Given the widespread phenomenon of this so-called magic, it must be that humans are particularly sensitive to it. Although the dynamic primitives that account for entrainment are not completely understood, it may be assumed that the exchange of corporeal articulations through different energy channels and its subsequent mirroring is a key component of this behavior. It is also likely that this magic is related to empathy, which is strongly associated with feelings of social connectedness.

Because of the social aspect involved in entrainment, I consider the development of interactive music systems that can deal with group effects of social musical cognition to be one of the major challenges of future music research. Is it possible to design a proper mediation technology that deals with this social aspect of musical involvement? Interactive music systems could be designed to enhance this type of social resonance communication, in contexts where many subjects are confronted with many machines. In this approach, machines become social agents with which it becomes possible to exchange intentions.

To conclude this section on musical communication, it can be stated that electronic systems offer many new possibilities in human–technology interactions. Of particular interest is the idea that musical communication is situated at the level of intentions, while the primitives for that level of communication are based on the encoding, transmission, and decoding of energy. Low-level sensorimotor interactions play an important role in the encoding and decoding processes, but they stand as a function of higher-level forms of action and perception. Sounds may have a strong appeal to corporeal articulations and they may involve the subject in mirroring aspects of moving forms in sound. These corporeal articulations provide a basis for an immersing involvement with music. Consequently, beyond source-related feedback and haptic feedback, interactive music systems offer the possibility of interacting with machines at higher mental levels. The realization of those levels of interaction is based on corporeal articulations that transform physical energy into mental representations that are related to the action-oriented ontology. Mirror processes form a basic part of this kind of corporeal articulation, and mediators that incorporate mirror processes are of great potential interest for interactive music systems.

## 6.4   Multimedia Environments

The model of musical communication discussed so far has assumed that a musical instrument is a technology for the mediation between (1) the performer's intended corporeal articulations and (2) sound energy (sounding music). Electronic musical instruments aim at extending this paradigm to the electronic and digital domains. As suggested above, this framework should be further expanded to autonomous multimedia technology and virtual social agents. After a brief sketch of what I mean by this and how it connects with multimedia technology, I turn to a concrete example of a system that implements autonomous interactive behavior.

### 6.4.1  Autonomous Social Agents

In the acoustic musical instrument, the corporeal articulations of the performer are translated into sound energy using a mediator based on biomechanical energy. In the electronic musical instrument, corporeal articulations are mapped to sound production parameters using an electronic mapping device. The next step is an electronic music environment which behaves as an autonomous virtual social agent with which it is possible to communicate via the exchange of physical energies.

Such an agent is typically equipped with capabilities of synthesis and analysis, conceived in terms of artificial composer/performer modules and listening modules. These modules typically simulate the behavior of a real human musician and a real listener because this may allow interaction at the level of intentions. Clearly, this concept implies a paradigm of music production that is rather different from that of a musical instrument, even from an electronic musical instrument.

The main purpose of a musical instrument is to transmit the performer's musical actions to a listener. In contrast, the main purpose of the music environment is to establish an interaction between a human agent and a technological agent. The technology no longer forwards the musical actions of a performer. Instead, it interprets and generates actions on its own. Accordingly, the mediation is no longer based on a one-way transmission of information, but on dialogue between humans and machines. In this concept, packages of physical energy, transmitted between humans and machines, form the primitives on top of which humans can develop communication patterns at the intentional level.

This concept fits rather well with the concept of open structure in the avant-garde art and music of the twentieth century (see, e.g., Sabbe, 1987a, 1987b). Open structure in art draws upon the principle of logical and chronological indifference of the components that make up the art piece. Sabbe argues that in music, such structures were first explored by Beethoven, and later by Schoenberg, Stockhausen, and Cage. Interaction with musical environments, or artificial musicians, fits well with this tradition of open structure in art. Indeed, interactions follow no organizational hierarchy or logical preferences for structural units. Instead, the artistic result emerges from a trajectory of constrained interactions, without any need for logical foundation or for positional precedence of the multimedia objects involved. The interactions may include randomness but also imitation, and adaptation (entrainment). In my view, these interactions should allow the exchange of intentions from the actors/

performers, as well as the perception of intentional communication from the audience. Indeed, the real challenge is to build machines that cope with this high level of human communication. Such machines should be strong in anticipating human actions. In accord with the above model of musical communication, this entails that they should be equipped with a humanlike memory and prediction framework (Hawkins and Blakeslee, 2004).

### 6.4.2   Connection with Multimedia Technology

Multimodal interactions with musical environments or artificial musicians allow a subdivision of the problem into different steps: sensing, feature extraction, classification, and anticipation. I briefly treat these points, but I do not intend to go deeper into the involved technical aspects.

**Sensing**
First of all, music environments use all kinds of currently available sensor technology, such as audio and video capture, infrared, ultrasound sensing, and other techniques. Most of these techniques focus on the detection of change in energy. Given that human perception has a biological bias to human movements, it is likely to assume that sensing should focus on movements of the human body. But of course body movement is not the only form of information that may be expressive. In musical ecosystems, for example, there is no human interaction besides the potential resonances of material objects in a concert hall filled with people (e.g., Di Scipio, 2003).

**Feature Extraction**
Whatever the energy that is captured, it is turned into an electric and digital signal. From that signal, particular features are extracted for further processing. The extracted features may closely reflect the properties of the energy, or they may be processed to higher levels of description. The designer of a system may draw upon a whole arsenal of multimedia techniques and approaches.

**Classification**
Once features have been extracted, the next step is to employ them in a meaningful way. This typically involves the reduction of the dimensionality of the detected features. Given the fact that features represent

signals related to motion, most music environments will have to deal with the description of motion at more abstract levels (so-called reduced parameter spaces). Ultimately, these description levels will allow the exchange of information between multiple modalities of information-processing, allowing the transition from the visual or haptic domain to the audio domain and vice versa.

**Anticipation of Action**

Anticipation of human action may be based on a statistics of learned patterns (e.g., as in hidden Markov models) or a motor model that emulates the perceived action through a virtual physical simulation. Anticipation would imply that human movements can be accurately predicted at the millisecond level. However, this is something that is beyond the capacity of most existing interactive music systems that I am aware of.

### 6.4.3   A Platform for Musical Expressiveness

In what follows, an example is given of a platform that allows the design of music environments using modules that do sensing, feature extraction, and classification by means of multimedia technology. The platform aimed at providing a set of tools from which an artist could assemble an instrument or an environment for the processing of music-related expressiveness. The main objectives were (a) to have a better understanding of the primitives of nonverbal communication that underlie expressiveness in art; (b) to develop computational modules for sensing, feature extraction, and classification of expressiveness in real time; and (c) to exploit this understanding in artistic multimodal interactive music/dance/video applications. All this had to work in the context of a music theater, such as an opera house or cultural center, and with the potential active participation of the audience.[11]

In a context where multiple media (music, video, computer animation) were used, the focus was on the transmission of expressiveness from one domain to another, such as from music to computer animation, or from dance to music. For example, in music-to-computer animation applications, the task was to extract the expressiveness from the sonic energy and use that information to control an avatar or graphical scene that expressed sadness to a similar degree. In dance-to-music applications, the task was to extract expressiveness-related features from body movement and use them to control the expressive character of the music.

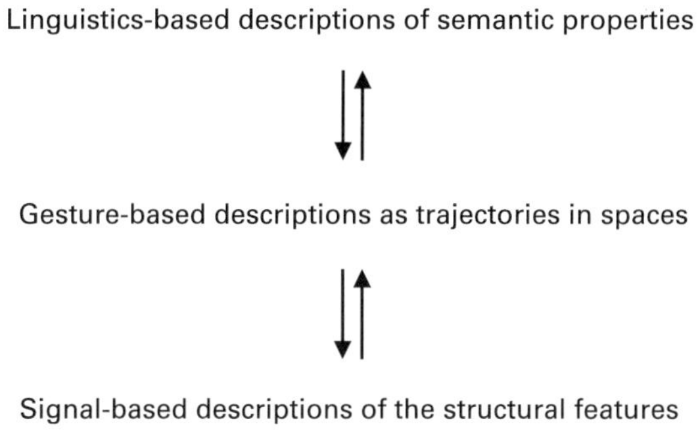

Linguistics-based descriptions of semantic properties

Gesture-based descriptions as trajectories in spaces

Signal-based descriptions of the structural features

**Figure 6.13**
Conceptual framework for the multimodal processing of expressiveness.

## Layered Conceptual Framework

Figure 6.13 sketches the conceptual framework for the platform. It aims at clarifying the possible connections among three different levels of processing: a sensory level, a gestural level, and a semantic level. The gestural level is a key component in this concept, in that it can be seen as the mediator between sensory-based descriptions and semantic descriptions. It typically contains trajectories of features which reflect aspects corporeal articulations.

Before going deeper into the nature of these layers, it is of interest to have a look at the information flow between these levels. This flow takes into account aspects related to hierarchical processing (bottom-up and top-down), as well as cross-modal processing (horizontal). In the bottom-up direction, sensory properties of physical energy are extracted and mapped into gesture trajectories, using techniques of classification. At the next higher level, these trajectories are related to semantic descriptions. In the top-down direction, a particular semantic description will be associated with a gesture trajectory. This trajectory may then be connected with parameters that control the synthesis of a particular energetic modality. In other words, the upward and downward directions of figure 6.13 represent the hierarchical analysis and synthesis of expressiveness.

The three levels comprise horizontal relationships as well, which allow the cross-modal transitions. These transitions may happen at the three levels, depending on the degree of hierarchical processing. For example, at the sensory level, it is possible to translate features from one modality directly into another. For instance, the quantity of body movement (extracted from a video recording of a dancer) is correlated with sound intensity. Therefore, without the mediation of a gesture space, the analyzed body movement can be translated into synthesized sound intensity. The effects of this translation will be direct and will resemble the mappings used in electronic musical instruments. However, it is also possible to make this kind of cross-modal translation at a higher level of the hierarchy. For example, energy and velocity trajectories extracted from sound can be used to control the movements of an avatar. Or, at the semantic level, semantic terms extracted from dance movements can be translated to related semantic terms that control the synthesis of sound. In short, the upward and downward directions represent analysis and synthesis, whereas the horizontal directions typically represent the mappings, relationships, and correlations of patterns.

The design of this layered conceptual framework (Camurri et al., 2001; Camurri, Volpe, et al., 2005; Camurri, De Poli, et al., 2005) shows some global similarity with the memory-prediction framework for intelligent systems, as proposed by Hawkins and Blakeslee (2004). The latter framework contains a similar hierarchical as well as cross-modal processing. Yet Hawkins and Blakeslee's model is inspired by the architecture of the human brain, and it puts more emphasis on anticipation and prediction, paving the way for a fine-grained and thorough probabilistic processing. The layered framework for musical expressiveness is not that far developed in terms of a brain architecture, nor is it very apt to anticipate and predict. Yet it does offer some working modules which give a crude idea of what could be possible in a future intelligent system that allows expressive interaction with an autonomous environment. Below, I briefly summarize some of the characteristics of the different processing levels.

### Sensory Level

The sensory level focused on features that were supposed to be relevant for expressiveness in music. They were extracted from various manifestations of physical energy.

In sound, for example, low-level features were related to onset, tempo (number of beats per minute), tempo variability, sound level (measured in dB), sound level variability, spectral shape (which is related to the timbre characteristics of the sound), articulation (features such as legato, staccato), articulation variability, attack velocity (which is related to the onset characteristics, which can be fast or slow), pitch, pitch density, degree of accent on structurally important notes, periodicity (related to repetition in the energy of the signal), dynamics (intensity), roughness (sensory dissonance), noisiness, tonal tension (the correlation between local pitch patterns and global or contextual pitch patterns), and so on (Leman et al., 2005). Most of these features are based on the processing of local energy. Thus, they reflect local aspects of musical expressiveness.

When more context information is involved (typically in musical sequences that are longer than three seconds), sequences of features can be considered as trajectories representing aspects of corporeal articulations. These aspects may be related to melody, harmony, rhythm, source, and dynamics.

Whether all these features and trajectories are relevant to expressiveness is another matter, and research is needed to determine the precise relationship between features and components of expressiveness. Yet several of these features are known to work well in applications that envision the musical synthesis of basic expressions such as sad, happy, heavy, or light (Bresin and Friberg, 2000; Canazza et al., 2000). In analysis, it was possible to relate several acoustic cues to affect adjectives (Leman et al., 2005; Lesaffre, 2005) and use these in artistic applications.

In the domain of dance analysis, a similar approach has been envisaged that draws on a distinction between features calculated on different time scales (see Camurri et al., 2004a, 2004b). An example of a low-level feature is the amount of contraction/expansion that can be calculated on just one video frame or picture. The contraction index is a measure of how the dancer uses the surrounding space. This feature can be related to Laban's notion of personal space (Laban and Lawrence, 1947; see also table 7.6). Other examples of low-level features are the detected amount of movement, and the silhouette and orientation (figure 6.14). The amount of movement is based on variations in the silhouette shape. It can be considered an overall measure of the amount of detected motion, involving velocity and force. The silhouette shape and the orientation of this shape provide information about the orientation of the dancer.

Examples of descriptors of the overall direction of a movement are upward or downward movement, its directness (i.e., how much the movement followed direct paths), motion impulsiveness, and fluency. It is possible to segment a movement in terms of a sequence of elementary movements (characterizing the beginning and ending times). Then a collection of descriptors may be applied to these elementary movements, which may give statistical summaries of particular features related

**Figure 6.14**
Motion descriptors extracted from expressive gestures in a dance performance.
(a) Some subregions are identified as corresponding to arms and trunk. (b) Trajectories of points on the body are collected. (c) The global amount of detected movement (corresponding to the dark region around the dancer) is measured. (d) Body orientation and shape are computed starting from an ellipse approximating the body (Camurri et al., 2005). (Reprinted with permission.)

to the elementary movement, such as the average body contraction/expansion during the stroke, and so on.

## Gestural Level
Often, features correlate with each other and form trajectories of values that change over time. Often these sensory-based trajectories can be reduced to trajectories in low-dimensional spaces. Different types of reduction are possible and different types of spaces can be considered (for a recent overview, see De Poli, 2004).

Kinematic tempo and energy (related to staccato/legato and intensity) were explored as representational frameworks for expressiveness (Canazza et al., 2000, 2003, 2004). In a similar context, affect spaces, based on valence and activity, have been related to sensory features (related to legato/staccato and tempo) (Leman et al., 2005). The spaces can be derived from perceptual evaluations of different expressive music performances, using data-reduction methods (e.g., principal component analysis).

The robustness of these spaces was confirmed in the expressive synthesis of musical scores, in which the machine played the score in a sad or happy way, depending, for example, on the expression in the posture of a dancer (e.g., Bresin and Friberg, 2000). The basic idea is that expressive performance can be captured in terms of a weighted set of control parameters that influence loudness and duration, such as double duration (decrease of the interonset interval contrast for two adjacent notes having the nominal interonset interval ratio 2:1), duration contrast (long notes are played longer; short notes, shorter); faster uphill (decrease the interonset interval of notes in uphill motion of the melody), and so on. In several studies (e.g., Friberg et al., 1998; Sundberg et al., 2003), attempts were made to learn these rules by imitation of actual artistic performances. The extracted rule parameters can be mapped onto a two-dimensional space for intuitive control. The interactive platform can be used as a rapid prototyping environment for experimental setups, and the results can be used for artistic applications (Friberg, 2006).

### Semantic Level

Semantic maps aim at relating kinesthetic/synesthetic and affective/emotive spaces to semantic descriptors. For example, fast tempo can be associated with semantic descriptors related to activity/excitement, happiness, potency, anger, and fear. Slow tempo can be matched with sadness, calmness, dignity, and solemnity. Loud music may determine the perception of power, anger, solemnity, and joy, whereas soft music may be associated with tenderness, sadness, and fear. High pitch may be associated with happiness, grace, excitement, and anger, fear, and activity, and low pitch may suggest sadness, dignity, and excitement, as well as boredom and pleasantness. And so on.

Semantic spaces will be discussed in more detail in chapter 7, where linguistic descriptors of music are considered in the context of music search and retrieval. It suffices here to mention that semantic spaces form a link with underlying gestural spaces and sensory spaces. Consider the semantic space that is defined by descriptors which relate to valence and activity. Valence is about positively or negatively valued affects, while activity is about the force of these affects. Recent research seems to indicate that aspects related to the activity dimension can be more easily predicted than aspects related to the valence (pleasantness) dimension. Leman et al. (2005) addressed this question using combinations of a limited number of structural cues extracted from musical audio. It was shown that valence adjectives such as "carefree," "gay," and "hopeful" can be partly accounted for by sensory-based cues such as tempo and musical consonance, which enhance the perception of positive qualities. Activity adjectives such as "bold," "restless," and "powerful" are related to sensory-based cues such as centroid/width, pitch prominence, and loudness. The higher the loudness, the more the music is perceived as bold, restless, and powerful. The study shows that an intersubjective semantics of musical expressiveness can be partly grounded on sensory-based cues, but that activity could be better predicted than valence.[12]

To sum up, the platform for the study of musical expressiveness is grounded in a layered conceptual framework that supports both hierarchical and horizontal processing. Up and down the hierarchy corresponds with analysis and synthesis, respectively, while horizontal processing is needed for cross-modal transitions. Based on this framework, it is possible to develop a mediation technology that deals with musical expressiveness. The grounding for this is based on scientific research and correlation studies that aim at finding the relationships between measured features (third-person descriptions) and experienced, articulated, and annotated features (second-person descriptions). This correlation study takes into account the multimodal foundations of human/machine interactions. Thus far, less attention has been devoted to the anticipation and prediction of human actions. A probabilistic and brain-based architecture such as Hawkins and Blakeslee's (2004) may be helpful in transforming the present framework into a memory-predictive one that would account for the anticipation of human action. The latter may provide a key to establishing a convincing human/machine interaction.

## 6.5    Conclusion

Interactive music systems offer a new dimension for the classical forms of opera and music theater. They allow the microinteraction of different modalities of human expressiveness based on body movement (dance), playing music, image projections, changes of scenes, video projections, computer animation, lighting effects, visual effects, and perhaps olfactory effects. Such interactions, if well designed, open a new world of expressive possibilities in art. At the same time, they open challenging research questions related to music mediation, multimodal perception, and multimedia technologies.

The development of interactive music systems, from musical instruments to music environments, engages music research in a number of challenging problems related to mediation technology. A basic problem concerns the adaptation of electronic equipment to the action-oriented ontology of the human subject, so that technology-based mediation can create an illusion of non-mediation. This illusion may form the basis of an interaction between minds (real and/or artificial), which is the ultimate goal of musical communication.

The relationship between physical energy and mental processing makes the study of interactive music systems challenging and places it at the edge of many new developments in science and technology. Moreover, the systems have an enormous potential for the production of art, and they can also be used for multimodal scientific research and programs in human education and therapy.

# 7 Search for and Retrieval of Music

This chapter considers the description of music in a context of search and retrieval. Finding ways to retrieve music from a database is one of the hot topics of music research today. Conventional systems use the name of the composer or the title of the song as search fields, whereas content-based systems allow search and retrieval on the basis of a description of intrinsic musical qualities or what these qualities mean for a subject. Examples are descriptions of what music is like, how music has been appreciated, and what music means or signifies, such as "music with a clear melody and a strong beat," "beautiful music," or "music with a melancholic character, which consoles me."

A major problem of content-based querying is the way in which users state a query—how they transform an idea into a query which a machine can understand. I argue that querying can be conceived of in terms of embodied cognition. This approach highlights the role of second-person descriptions and music information retrieval in terms of mediation technology.

The chapter consists of two parts. In the first part, corporeal and verbal second-person descriptions are studied in detail. The second part explores how these descriptions can be processed by mediation technologies.

## 7.1 Conceptual Architecture

The conceptual architecture of a standard search-and-retrieval scenario is sketched in figure 7.1. The right side is the query side, and the left side is the target side. The query side processes questions from the user, and the target side contains the musical database (as audio). In this scenario, the task is to provide a proper description of a target, so that the machine can search for and retrieve the intended target (or similar

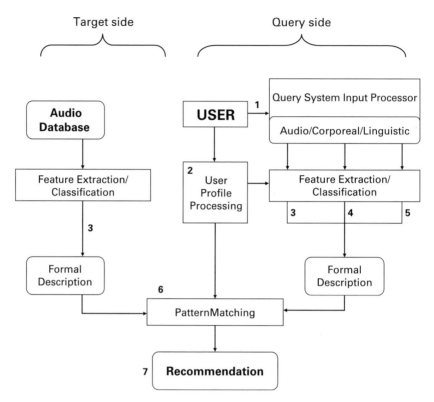

**Figure 7.1**
General schema of a music information retrieval system.

targets) and recommend it (them) to the user. This recommendation will provide access to the intended target.[1]

The user's task is to formulate a question which will be input to the system (figure 7.1, 1).[2] The question is a description of the required information, which may be formulated, for instance, by providing audio examples, by singing or moving, or by generating linguistic descriptions.

The system's task is to encode the query, using feature extraction and classification, into a formal description (figure 7.1, 3, 4, 5). These formal descriptions allow matching of patterns with formal descriptions of target files. Since target files are involved, audio feature extraction and classification may apply to both query and target. In this scenario, targets are basically audio files, and queries can be posed in several description formats, including audio (3), text (4), and motor movements (5). This involves multimodal processing at the query side.

The left side of the figure, the target side, contains a database of audio files and a preprocessed set of formal descriptions extracted from the audio files (figure 7.1, 3). Physical energies cannot be compared directly with each other, nor can linguistic descriptions (words) be compared directly with physical energies. What is needed is a more abstract level of description suitable for query–target comparisons. This comparison is called pattern-matching (figure 7.1, 6). It involves the calculation of distances or cost functions which penalize the changes needed in order to make a given formal description of the query similar to a formal description of the target. Finally, when a good match between a query and targets is found, a recommendation can be formulated (figure 7.1, 7). This recommendation typically consists of a pointer or a list of pointers to musical audio files in the database. The user can then choose the preferred suggestion and retrieve the audio.

Clearly, the above description reveals some critical issues in music information retrieval:

• Musical querying: What are the different ways of querying, and how accurately do users describe what they are looking for?

• Mediation technology: What technology can mediate between the user's intention and the search-and-retrieval application? What features should be extracted, and at what level of abstraction should they be classified and formally described?

• Machine-processing: How can query and targets be compared? How can a similarity measurement be defined? How can pattern-matching be made efficient in large databases?

These questions involve advanced issues in psychology (human perception, categorization, memory, experience, and imagery), engineering (audio feature extraction, classification and statistical information-processing, formal techniques of pattern-matching and data-mining), and musicology (study of user behavior, content description, annotation).[3]

This chapter focuses on the first two questions: musical querying and mediation technology. Machine-processing is more technical in that it concerns comparing formal descriptions. This topic, although important, will not be discussed.[4]

## 7.2  Musical Querying

Content-based querying of music is the act of describing music for a search-and-retrieval task. This may involve a description of the intrinsic qualities of the music as well as of subjective experiences of the music. Obviously, the two types of description may be related.

Querying implies the reverse of a perception-based signification process. While perception implies a transfer from physical energy to a subjective action-oriented ontology, querying implies that a mental representation has to be described and connected with encodings of physical energy. In other words, ideas have to be turned into matter (or better, energy) in order to be recognized by machines. This process assumes some creativity on the part of the human subject, who is assumed to produce musical content. Given that this creative act is a function of consumption, subjects may tend to use the most cost-effective method, that is, the method which is least demanding in terms of turning an idea into reality.

Table 7.1 provides a taxonomy of different query types which are considered important in music search and retrieval. This taxonomy is based on a distinction among three types of querying: audio, corporeal, and symbolic/linguistic. Audio querying is based on audio recordings. Querying based on corporeal movement is subdivided into making music, music navigation, and body movement. Querying based on symbolic/linguistic descriptions is based on extramusical and intramusical descriptions. The extramusical descriptions pertain to metadata, lyrics, and context specifications and significations; the intramusical descriptions pertain to structural descriptions, semantic descriptions, graphic sym-

**Table 7.1**
Overview of query types

| Audio | Corporeal | Symbolic/linguistic |
|---|---|---|
| Recordings | Making music (singing, playing,...) Navigation (visual, tactile,...) Body movement | Extramusical    Metadata (title, name, geography,...)    Lyrics (song texts, topic,...)    Signification (historical, cultural,      review,...) |
| | | Intramusical    Structural (melody, rhythm, timbre,      texture,...)    Graphic/symbolic (score, icons,...)    Semantic (genre, style,...)    Corporeal      Synesthetic (brightness, color,...)      Kinesthetic (fast, up, down,...)      Affect/emotion (gay, sad,...) |

bols, and corporeal descriptions. The latter are further subdivided into descriptions related to synesthesia, kinesthesia, and affect/emotion. Even though this taxonomy may not be exhaustive, it covers an important part of possible content-based querying methods. Not all items of this taxonomy will be handled in this chapter.[5] In what follows, I briefly consider querying based on audio examples, then go deeper into corporeal querying, followed by symbolic/linguistic querying.

### 7.2.1  Querying Based on Audio Examples

From the user's point of view, using audio examples may be the easiest way of querying because turning an idea into a descriptive act is then reduced to finding a proper audio example. All that is needed is a recorded fragment of music. It is likely that querying with audio examples will become a popular search method of music retrieval systems.

A more advanced method of search based on audio examples involves content specifications. For example, one can search for a particular rhythm of which an example is given in an audio fragment. Only the rhythm is important, not the melody or the harmony. In addition, the user may want to have the rhythm in the audio example slightly faster or slightly more swinging, which may be indicated with movements of the arm.

Audio-based querying and its extension with verbal descriptions and movements offers a number of possibilities. Yet, its multimodal nature raises questions: How feasible is it? What types of descriptions can be distinguished? How do these descriptions relate to encodings of musical physical energy? The sections that follow aim to clarify these questions in more detail.

Querying by audio is not very difficult. Audio examples can be plucked from the air, so to speak, and provide genuine articulations of the search intention. For that reason, querying by example can be considered a subcategory of the second-person description in the sense that pointing to an object is a me-to-you activity which typically involves the attention of a second subject. In this case, the second person is a machine.

### 7.2.2  Corporeal-Based Querying

In previous chapters, I have argued that the human body can express aspects of musical physical energy via corporeal articulations that blur the traditional distinction between experience and description (see section 1.4.2). Can these articulations be used as search intentions? It is straightforward to consider singing, navigation, and movement as examples of corporeal-based querying.

**Querying by Singing or Playing**

The rationale behind querying by singing is that a verbal description of a melody may be very difficult, if not impossible, while articulating the melody in a song may be easy. Singing is probably one of the more important forms of music description. It uses an instrument (the human voice) as mediator to transform an idea into sound energy. For subjects who like to express themselves this way, it may be a very natural means to present a search intention. Alternatively, a musical instrument may be used instead of the human voice, but this requires more learned skills. Like querying by audio example, the query consists of sound energy, and it is the task of the query processor to extract the appropriate level of formal description for music retrieval.

Recent studies point out that singing and playing may be feasible in the context of musical information retrieval, provided the user sings more or less accurately (De Mulder et al., 2006). Lesaffre et al. (2003) addressed how users tend to express themselves in a semispontaneous music retrieval context. In this study a large set of vocal-related queries was collected and analyzed.[6] The study revealed that subjects rely on different querying techniques, as shown in table 7.2.

About 38 percent of the time, queries consist of singing the lyrics (text); 40 percent, of singing syllables; 17 percent, of whispering; and about 5 percent, other methods, such as humming (4 percent), performing percussive acts (0.5 percent), and giving verbal comments (0.4 percent). The 40 percent of time devoted to syllables indicates that many subjects forgot the exact lyrics, but could remember the melodic mime, and therefore used syllables as an alternative to words. Subjects tended to change to syllabic singing or whispering when the text of the title was exhausted.

**Table 7.2**
The percentage of total time that users took to adopt a particular query technique

| Vocal query methods | % |
| --- | --- |
| Singing lyrics | 38 |
| Singing syllables | 40 |
| Whispering | 17 |
| Humming + other | 5 |

Further analysis of syllabic singing showed that *na*, *da*, and *ta* were most often used. A good 75 percent of the vocal queries could be characterized as melodic, and only a small fraction were rhythmic. The rest, about 20 percent, were neither melodic nor purely rhythm-based singing. Of further interest was the fact that the mean duration of a query was about fourteen seconds. Other remarkable observations were that for older age groups, queries were less similar to the targets. Musicians tended to use less text and more syllabic and whistled time. Overall, they made longer queries than non-musicians (for more details, see Lesaffre, Moelants, et al., 2004; Lesaffre, 2005).

The study pointed out that subjects were quite successful in turning an idea into a song. Not only did they recollect pitch contour sequences similar to the original, but quite a number of subjects also seemed to be able to reproduce sequences in a way that structural features of the original music, such as tone color and pitch inflections, were reproduced. Imitation sometimes appears to be related to corporeal and acoustic gestures of the performer. This finding suggests that subjects may remember music through association with corporeal gestures in addition to the purely melodic cues (as represented in a score), but further research is needed to identify the relationship between imitation and corporeal behavior of the original.

Unfortunately, a quantitative account of how well subjects were able to replicate an original is not a trivial matter, because it requires the definition of a similarity measure between imitation and original. Subjects do not imitate in the sense of *exact* replication. They start a melody with lyrics, then change to syllables, humming, or whispering. Often they start with the right notes of the melody (albeit sometimes in a different key), but if the melody reproduction takes too long, they may confuse the melody with other melodic fragments of the same song, thereby displaying considerable variation and formation of new combinations. All this puts heavy constraints on how to measure similarity. Typically, techniques have to take into account variations in pitch contour, issues of time-warping, and, perhaps more difficult, concatenation of melodic segments which were not concatenated in the original.

The study shows that certain melodies can be recollected more easily. This is reflected in the fact that subjects tend to sing the same fragments rather than different fragments of the original. In gestalt theory, this compact good form is known as the *Prägnanz* (terseness or precision) of a melody. It would be highly interesting, therefore, to know what part of a melody has such compact good form and why it can be recollected more easily than other forms.

Recent experimental work which addresses this question has pointed out that a melody is conceived to be a good melody if an underlying harmonic schema can be applied to it (Jansen and Povel, 2004). This finding, although based on artificial stimuli with a focus on tonal structure, assumes that cognitive processing is the underlying factor determining compact good form. A good melody is one in which subjects can imagine an underlying harmonic structure as a tonal cadence (e.g., chord degrees of I–IV–V–I). This harmonic structure is assumed to be built up in memory as the most common or most stable harmonic structure, and hence it would be used to disambiguate the melody.

Whether this hypothesis is true in a natural context has not been investigated thus far, but our query-by-voice study suggests that good form may indeed be an important factor in the expression of melodies. Yet what is considered to be a good melody may be defined not only by underlying harmonic structure but also by its capacity for being imitated. It may be that harmonic structures are helpful in performing this imitation, but other aspects, related to embodiment, should be taken into account as well, such as pitch inclinations, coloring, ornamentation, and other aspects related to style and gesture. My hypothesis is that apart from harmonic structure, a good melody contains many expressive components which allow corporeal attuning. To what extent this is the case, and whether this information can be of use in the retrieval process, is a matter for further study.

To sum up, querying by singing or playing music can accurately transform an idea into sound energy. This transformation draws upon memory structures involving motor behavior. Moreover, querying by singing or playing music is very creative, and therefore very challenging for this property. The drawback is that not all people are equally creative or equally willing to engage in active vocal querying. Not all people are capable of singing a melody in tune or according to the original melody contour. In addition, some people may be reluctant to sing to a computer in order to find a piece of music in a database if anyone else can hear them. Therefore, its application may be limited and alternative methods should be explored.

## Querying by Graphical Navigation
One alternative is querying by navigation, which is based on the idea that navigation within data can be based on spaces. Similarities between data can be visualized as distances between data points. Using virtual tools, users can navigate from one data point to another. Three-

dimensional navigation in virtual space is an option for the future, and most research so far has focused on more down-to-earth applications which draw on spatial organization of data (Tzanetakis and Cook, 2001; Pampalk et al., 2004; van Gulik et al. 2004). Synesthetic associations such as colors, textures, distances, perspectives, and sonifications have been used as markers of virtual objects as well. These markers can be linked with structural or verbal semantic features, so that navigation in combination with symbolic meanings can become a powerful tool for search and retrieval in very large databases.

Research on navigation and the related issue of data visualization draws strongly on similarities among musical pieces. The main idea is that similar pieces of music can be represented as close together, while dissimilar pieces can be represented as far apart. Thus similarity is visualized as distance in a space. For that reason, studies on similarity relationships form a central part of the research on data navigation.

Clearly, the objective is that similarity relationships among musical data would reflect the human perception of similarity among these data. However, global similarity between musical pieces is very difficult to define. Instead, it is much easier, and perhaps also useful, to deal with local similarity because it can be better estimated. For example, music can be compared according to one or two structural parameters, such as melody and rhythm, rather than a number of structural parameters, such as melody, rhythm, harmony, texture, and timbre. Different visualizations can then be generated, depending on the chosen structural cue.

Pampalk et al. (2004), for example, explore visualization and navigation using similarity measures based on rhythmic aspects and timbre, in combination with meta-information such as artist or genre. Van Gulik et al. (2004) focused on visualization of musical information for retrieval on small music mediation devices such as portable hard disk players. Navigation through music collections is traditionally accomplished by using folder-based hierarchical structures based on genre/artist/album, but the visual scale of current user interfaces is not adapted to the hierarchical search in a large database. A visualization is based on commonalities between artists and other types of description related to structural and contextual descriptions (such as tempo, year, mood, genre) (figure 7.2).

In these applications, users can select their preferred visualization from a combination of coloring and attribute magnets (e.g., mood and tempo) which provides them with complete control of the

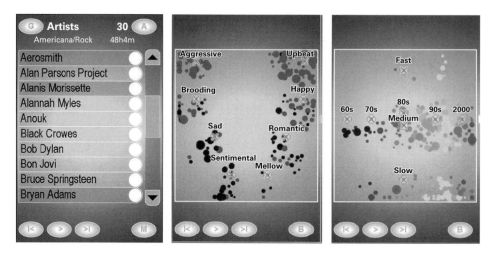

**Figure 7.2**
Large databases are difficult to navigate by using the traditional hierarchical structures (left). Graphical spaces can be based on visualizations of similarities between data, such as mood maps (middle) and year-tempo maps (right) (Van Gulik et al., 2004). (Reprinted with permission.)

visualization and navigation of their music collection. The example shows that querying can be based on human communication capabilities that greatly extend the traditional focus on symbolic descriptions. It shows that corporeal and symbolic/linguistic content specification are not mutually exclusive. Navigation is a typical example in which both approaches can be brought together.

## Querying by Gestures

It may be asked whether bodily movements can be used as expressions of search intentions. This question is highly intriguing in view of the assumption that sensory perception is reflected in corporeal articulations. Can pure corporeal articulations be used for querying? Are gestural expressions sufficiently accurate to serve as a query? Not much is known about the possibilities of querying by mime. As a first approximation, it seems straightforward that a distinction should be made between intentional and unintentional movements.

In intentional movements, users have in mind a particular goal for corporeal expression. They may rely on knowledge of overt motor resonance or corporeal articulations for the retrieval of music, based on previously experienced forms of synchronization, attuning, imitation, and empathy. These experiences can be used to express an intention in a mime.

An example is conducting. Many people conduct—that is, move hand, arm, and posture like a conductor—when listening to music. They tend to indicate tempo and expressiveness. The movements can be picked up by a machine equipped with a video camera. From that signal the tempo can be extracted and compared with the tempi stored in a database. Obviously, the success of such a query depends on the accuracy of the memory for tempo. Levitin and Cook (1996) suggest that memory preserves the absolute tempo of the musical performance, but more studies are needed to confirm this finding (see Moelants et al., 2006). It can be assumed that models can be developed for individual users and their level of accuracy for remembering tempo.

In addition, expressive content can be extracted from the movements, using parameters such as amount of movement (little, much), movement articulation (jerky, smooth), and movement speed (slow, fast) (Camurri et al., 2004b). Given the known relationship of these features to loudness (soft, hard), articulation (staccato, legato), and tempo (slow, fast), it is possible to use information from expressive gestures in a search-and-retrieval task. As a matter of fact, it may be assumed that expressive gestures will preferably be used in combination with other query tools. The multimodal nature of expressiveness may allow the transfer from one modality to another. Apparently, subjects are quite successful in identifying expressive intent in piano or violin performances, regardless of whether they were allowed only to listen, only to watch, or both to watch and listen (Krumhansl and Schenk, 1997; Mitchell and Gallaher, 2001; Dahl and Friberg, in press).

In unintentional movements, little or no mental control of corporeal responses is assumed, yet these corporeal utterances may serve as indicators of internal states of the subject. If these internal states can be measured, it is likely that they can play an important role in querying. Sensors may be used that capture physiological markers of corporeal utterance and apply this information to music search and retrieval. A straightforward application comes from sports; the measurement of speed, respiration, and other physiological cues may be used to find pieces with a musical beat which fits the movements of the subject (Styns et al., in press).

Gómez and Danuser (2004) found that respiratory patterns may reflect general dimensions of emotional response. Breathing accelerated, minute ventilation was augmented with increases both in rated valence

Table 7.3
Physiological markers relate to valence and activity (arousal)

|  | Valence | | Activity | |
|---|---|---|---|---|
|  | Positive | Negative | High | Low |
| Breath time | Fast | Slow | Fast | Slow |
| Breath volume | High | Low | High | Low |
| Skin conductance |  |  | High | Low |
| Heart rate |  |  |  |  |
| Chills |  |  | Many | Few |

and arousal, and skin conductance level increased with arousal ratings. Such differences are also reflected in brain activity. Schmidt and Trainor (2001) found that the frontal brain electrical activity (EEG) distinguishes between valence and activity of musical emotions. See also research by Panksepp and Bernazky (2002) and the early work of Berlyne (1971).

Table 7.3[7] shows physiological markers such as breath time, breath volume, skin conduction, heart rate, and chills in relation to valence and arousal. Gómez and Danuser (2004) found that strong relations between affective judgments and structural cues relating to time very likely reflect the synchronizing effect of music on respiration. Breath accelerates, and flows augment, with increase of tempo. Skin conductance seems to be unrelated to valence, but it can measure the difference between intense and less intense emotional involvement (Rickard, 2004). Chills are correlated with high arousal. Results for heart rate are less conclusive, especially if subjects don't move while listening. Clearly, heart rate is highly dependent on physical movement of the human body.

To sum up, corporeal articulations and utterances are candidates for querying a music database. Singing, navigation, and body movement are useful for that purpose. They assume the translation of a mental representation into energy, using the body as mediator. In the case of singing, sonic energy is mediated by the vocal system, while in the cases of navigation and body movement, it is motor energy and/or optic energy, mediated by the movement of the body. From a technological point of view, recorders and sensors are needed to capture the biomechanical energy and transform it into an appropriate encoding for further search and retrieval. The next section looks at how this information can be processed in a meaningful way.

### 7.2.3   Symbolic/Linguistic Querying

Queries based on symbolic or linguistic descriptions can be divided into two important subgroups. One group is concerned with description of properties that are external to music (or extramusical); the other group is concerned with descriptions of properties that are internal to music (or intramusical). In both cases, however, one could say that the descriptions are semantic because they relate to meanings.

Extramusical querying is based on metadata descriptions, such as composers' names, titles, groups, orchestras, geographical regions, ethnic origin, or even genre or style. These descriptions will not be discussed here. Instead, I focus on intramusical querying, which is based on verbal (linguistic) descriptions of intrinsic musical qualities, and what these qualities mean for a subject.

**Intramusic Queries**
Intramusic queries can be divided into structural descriptions, corporeal-based descriptions, and contextual descriptions. There is a fundamental difference in how these descriptions involve the participation of the subject.

First, structural descriptions of music are concerned with perceptual categories, such as pitch, rhythm, timbre, articulation, melody, and harmony. In fact, these categories are often related to third-person descriptions. However, they are not genuine third-person descriptions because they involve a subjective component. They rely on a personal experience, but they focus on properties of an external object (the music). Descriptions of musical structure can be considered more objective (or more intersubjective) than any other type of verbal description because they address properties on which subjects of a particular population and culture may agree in many respects.

Second, (verbal) corporeal-based descriptions are genuine second-person descriptions because they aim at revealing aspects of intimate experiences. As mentioned earlier (section 4.1), second-person descriptions function in the context of diagnosis, which requires that self-observed corporeal articulations be reported as accurately as possible, and preferably detached from any social and cultural interpretation. The latter could contaminate the diagnostic purpose of the communication. Important corporeal-based descriptions are related to synesthesia and kinesthesia, and affect and emotion.

Finally, contextual descriptions are about stylistic semantic content and subjective interpretations involving social and cultural contexts. They can be associated with first-person descriptions.

In what follows, I deal with these different types of intrinsic semantic descriptions in more detail.

### Queries Based on Structural Descriptions

Structural descriptions of music are about perceivable intrinsic musical properties such as configurations of melody, harmony, tonality, rhythm, loudness, texture, and timbre. These descriptions are assumed to be closely related to the description of audio structures, and therefore they are thought to be very useful for the specification of musical content.

A melody, for example, may be characterized as ascending, descending, gap-filling, U-shaped, inverted U-shaped, pseudo-polyphonic, centrifugal, or centripetal. These descriptions can also be applied to patterns in fundamental frequency. Thus, it is possible to establish a relationship between features of the melody (as perceived) and features of the frequency pattern (as physical energy). Similarly, a rhythm pattern may have a particular structure which refers to the structure of the acoustic signal. Timbre also may be taken into account. For example, a sound may be called bright when the spectral energy is in the high register. There seems to be reason to say that structural descriptions provide a direct connection with objective measurements of physical energy.

**Problems with structural descriptions**  The relationship between perceived structural descriptions and measured structural descriptions may seem evident, but it turns out that measured structural descriptors often have a problematic operational definition which may disagree with the action-oriented bias of human perception.

Consider an apparently simple concept such as loudness. Even if loudness is correctly interpreted in terms of its psychoacoustic definition (e.g., Stevens' method of loudness measurement), there can be problems with understanding what subjects actually mean when using this term in a musical context. For example, when two fragments of music are played at the same loudness level, will users describe them in terms of psychoacoustic loudness? Imagine a fragment of *guqin* music and a fragment of steel drum music. Most listeners will probably characterize the *guqin* as soft, and the steel drum as hard, and for that reason, they may claim that the *guqin* is less loud than the steel drum. The reason is that the characterization of the sound as being soft or hard may be based on knowledge of the musical instrument. The *guqin* cannot produce a loud sound, and this knowledge is independent from the loudness level at which the sound is played through the loudspeakers. In contrast, a steel drum cannot (almost) produce a soft sound. Again, knowledge independent from the loudness level is used in the description. Moreover, in the characterization of soft and loud, other factors, related to onset and spectrum, may play a role. In other words, it may be hard to apply an operational definition of loudness to real-life circumstances. The main issue is that in natural contexts, subjects tend to perceive properties of objects in terms of their functioning sources rather than in terms of their stimulus properties. Therefore, from the subjective point of view, the impact of a *guqin* is soft, whereas the impact of a steel drum is loud.

In much the same way, the notion of sensory dissonance, or roughness, can be given a well-defined psychoacoustic meaning in terms of beat frequencies (Sethares, 1998). However, when subjects are asked to describe roughness in a musical passage, it is not clear whether they rely on beat frequencies or whether other issues related to texture are involved (Leman et al., 2005). Subjects tend to associate roughness with other features such as staccato, loudness, and temporal granulation. Since musical sound often varies in time, the perception of a passage of music may be influenced by these additional contextual factors. This shows that context may be a determining factor in subjective descriptions of roughness.

In short, the use of structural descriptors may not be as straightforward as it might seem. There is a discrepancy between the widespread use of structural descriptors for music, on the one hand, and the lack of clarity and uniformity of their meaning, on the other hand. Clearly, structural descriptions most often pertain to objects of the subject's action-oriented ontology rather than to forms of physical energy. They may be used at different levels of musical complexity, and their meaning may be based on a complex network of relationships, with reference to traditions and musical styles. Moreover, embodied perception is source-related rather than stimulus-related, and context-related rather than context-free. While the use of ill-defined terms may not be a problem in common communications about music, it may become a significant problem when the communication connects with technology that mediates physical energy. Therefore, the user-related definition of structural descriptors and the relationship between subjective and objective structural descriptors pose a serious problem that must be solved.

**A taxonomy of structural descriptors**   In order to capture the multitude of descriptors, and to have a better idea of the meaning of terms that can be used for search and retrieval of music, it is often useful to develop taxonomies for structural description of music. In doing this, however, it should be kept in mind that taxonomies merely classify terms and put them in an ordered framework. They do not specify the semantic relationships among terms.

Table 7.4 presents an example of a general taxonomy of structural descriptors that has proven to be useful in music information retrieval.[8] The different levels of description pertain to physical, sensory, perceptual, and formal descriptions. Physical and sensory descriptions are typically situated on a time scale that is less than about three seconds. They are defined as being noncontextual. The physical level contains descriptors for frequency, intensity, duration, and spectrum, while the sensory level contains descriptors for pitch, time, loudness, and timbre/texture. In contrast, perceptual and formal descriptions are situated on a time scale that is generally longer than three seconds. The descriptors are defined as musically context-dependent. That is, their content is defined by the musical context in which they appear. For example, the function of a chord is defined by the tonal context in which it appears, and a beat is characterized by a context of onsets and accents. Major divisions are melody, harmony/tonality, rhythm, articulation, and source (see table).

In this taxonomy, higher levels of description are based on the assumption that information-processing capabilities of the human brain are involved in more context-based and abstract forms of representation. In that sense, the taxonomy reflects a hierarchical structure of information-processing from periphery to center, that is, from sensory to perceptual to more formal symbolic categories. Frequency, for example, is related to the perception of pitch and, higher up, to melodic contour and chord functions. Duration is related to aspects of timing and, higher up, to tempo, beat, and rhythm. Intensity is connected with loudness and articulation, and spectrum with timbre, texture, and instrument type. Generally speaking, features subsume hierarchies but hierarchies may in turn determine lower levels of features. The example of a chord function clearly shows that a higher-level descriptor such as tonality has an effect on a lower-level descriptor.

Accordingly, taxonomies should be used with great care. Often they are merely intended as general schemes which can be expanded in several directions. While a taxonomy can be refined and described in

**Table 7.4**
Taxonomy of structural cues

| | Structural Features of Music | | | | | |
|---|---|---|---|---|---|---|
| Concept Level | Melody | Harmony/Tonality | Rhythm | Articulation | Source |
| **Contextual (>3 sec)** | | | | | |
| *Formal* | contour (up, down, centripetal,...) character (ornament, kernel,...) | chord related (names, function,...) key related (names, tension,...) | rhythm patterns tempo tempo changes | gestural cue (up, down,...) staccato-legato sound level | instrument type voice |
| *Perceptual* | successive intervallic patterns | simultaneous intervallic patterns | beat inter-onset interval | dynamic range | |
| | Pitch | Time | Loudness | Timbre/Texture | |
| **Noncontextual (<3 sec)** | | | | | |
| *Sensory* | Perceived pitch Pitch deviation Fundamental frequency | Note duration Offset Onset | Sone Decibels | Roughness Flux Centroid | |
| *Physical* | Frequency | Duration | Intensity | Spectrum | |

Based on the taxonomy in Lesaffre et al. (2003).

more detail, it does not contain real definitions of terms, nor descriptions of interrelationships between terms.

**Empirical solutions**  In search-and-retrieval applications, discussions about the meaning of terms can be partly overcome by adopting a more pragmatic approach. An example may clarify how this could work. In an annotation experiment (Leman et al., 2004, 2005), twenty-five musicologists rated sixty musical fragments for different structural features. The musical excerpts represented genres such as pop and rock, heavy metal and punk, African American pop, dance, classical music, jazz, folk, chanson, and ethnic music. The structural features which musicologists had to rate were tempo, on a scale from slow to fast; roughness, on a scale from consonant to dissonant; brightness, from dull to sharp; articulation, from staccato to legato; loudness, from soft to loud; melody, from lack of melody to clear melody; ambitus (spread of energy), from small to big; and register, from low to high. This is summarized in table 7.5. The leftmost column shows the structural features evaluated on different scales (indicated in the columns).

Afterward, a statistical analysis based on principal component analysis was applied to the data. This analysis revealed a clustering in three groups: melody-related (clear or diffuse), articulation-related (bounded or punctuated), and timbre-related (dark or bright) (see table 7.5). A clear melody was associated with consonance, soft sound, defined brightness, pronounced melody, and defined register. A diffuse melody was associated with dissonance, loud sound, undefined brightness, unpronounced melody, and undefined register. Slow tempo and legato went together in bounded articulation; punctuated articulation was defined by fast tempo and staccato playing. Dull brightness, small *ambitus*, and low register often went together and defined dark timbre, while bright timbre resulted from sharp brightness, large *ambitus*, and high register. *Defined* and *undefined* mean that subjects agree and do not agree about the cue assignment, respectively. For example, register can be low or high in relation to timbre, but in relation to melody, it is a matter of subjective agreement or disagreement. In short, when the subjects tended to agree on register (low, middle, or high), melody was often clear. When subjects tended to disagree on register, melody was often diffused.

The analysis reveals that for a given database of music, structural descriptions may be correlated, and therefore certain terms may be used in correlation with other terms. This is an interesting finding which is

Table 7.5
Structural cues are interdependent and group into three clusters

| | Melody-related | | Articulation-related | | Timbre-related | |
| --- | --- | --- | --- | --- | --- | --- |
| | Clear | Diffuse | Bounded | Punc-tuated | Dark | Bright |
| Tempo | | | Slow | Fast | | |
| Roughness | Consonant | Dissonant | | | | |
| Loudness | Soft | Loud | | | | |
| Articulation | | | Legato | Staccato | | |
| Brightness | | | | | Dull | Sharp |
| Brightness* | *Defined* | *Undefined* | | | | |
| Melody | Pronounced | Unpronounced | | | | |
| Ambitus | | | | | Small | Big |
| Register | | | | | Low | High |
| Register* | *Defined* | *Undefined* | | | | |

Based on data from Leman et al. (2005).
* Whether the feature is defined or undefined.

certainly useful for practical search-and-retrieval applications but which has more general musicological implications as well. In fact, this example shows that only three structural cues (melody, articulation, and timbre) may be sufficient for describing music. It is suggested that the problem of the definition of terms can be given a pragmatic solution based on empirical observations.

To sum up, queries based on descriptions of musical structure have a grounding in perceptual categorizations that pertain to the subject's action-oriented ontology. For that reason, descriptions of musical structure are subjective and their meaning may not always be straightforwardly related to descriptions of physical structures of musical audio. Consequently, they cannot be considered as genuine third-person descriptions. More precise definitions are needed, even of apparently straightforward structural descriptions such as loudness and roughness. Taxonomies can be very helpful in clarifying the meaning of such structural descriptors, but empirical studies are also useful. Empirical studies may reveal unexpected correlations between structural descriptions, for example, that pronounced melody correlates with soft loudness. However, these correlations may depend on the nature of the database as well as on the population of the subjects involved in setting up the statistics. Therefore, structural descriptions should be used with care in the context of musical querying because they could be application-dependent. Interdependencies between structural descriptors as well as relationships with physical structures of musical audio need a much more elaborate and careful study.

It is wise to conceive of descriptions of musical structure as second-person descriptions. They focus on music qualities rather than on subjective experiences. For that reason, they may provide a bridge to genuine third-person descriptions.

### Queries Based on Synesthetic–Kinesthetic Descriptions

The next category of queries deals with synesthetic and kinesthetic descriptions. They pertain to verbal (second-person) descriptions of an experienced multimodal corporeal involvement with music.

Synesthetic terms are often used in the description of structural features. Think about terms such as high and low pitch, bright and dark timbre, and rough or flat, or hard or soft, sounds. These terms relate to spatial (high, low), color (bright, dark), or tactile properties (rough, flat, soft, hard). Kinesthetic descriptions concern the perception of movement of objects or persons in space (outer movement) or the perception of movement of the body of the subject (inner movement). In what follows, two questions are important. First, what kind of synesthetic and kinesthetic terms make sense? Second, how can these terms be related to structural cues in music? The latter question can be seen as a step toward the connection with the physical energy of music.

**Perception of inner movement and effort shapes**   In choreography, Laban and Lawrence (1947) distinguished different types of sensing of movement, such as gliding, dabbing, floating, flicking, pressing, punching, wringing, and slashing. These were called effort shapes because they pertain to the efforts of corporeal articulations. Effort shapes have been defined in terms of weight or exertion (force), space (displacement), and time (velocity) (table 7.6). For example, gliding is based on light force, direct displacement, and sustained velocity, while slashing is based on strong force, flexible displacement, and quick velocity.

In chapter 6, it was argued that music may communicate intended actions, which can be encoded and decoded using corporeal articulations. These intended actions may be revealed in terms of their effort shapes. Listeners may be able to understand the effort shapes in the acoustic energy of music on the basis of their own subjective motor imitation (or simulation). Through mirroring, musical physical energy is

Table 7.6
Taxonomy of Laban's theory of effort

| Exertion (Force) | Space (Displacement) | Time (Velocity) | Effort Shape |
|---|---|---|---|
| Light | Direct | Sustained | Gliding (smoothing, smearing, smudging) |
| | | Quick | Dabbing (patting, tapping, shaking) |
| | Flexible | Sustained | Floating (strewing, stirring, stroking) |
| | | Quick | Flicking (flipping, flapping, jerking) |
| Strong | Direct | Sustained | Pressing (crushing, cutting, squeezing) |
| | | Quick | Punching (thrusting, poking, pressing) |
| | Flexible | Sustained | Wringing (pulling, plucking, stretching) |
| | | Quick | Slashing (beating, throwing, whipping) |

Table 7.7
Relationships between body movement and musical structural features

| Body Movement | | | Structural Features | | |
|---|---|---|---|---|---|
| Amount of movement | Few | Much | Loudness | Soft | Hard |
| Movement articulation | Jerky | Smooth | Articulation | Staccato | Legato |
| Movement speed | Slow | Fast | Tempo | Slow | Fast |

transferred into a motor activity that appeals to the action-oriented ontology.[9]

For example, a connection can be made between speed and amount and articulation of movement, on the one hand, and tempo, loudness, and articulation of sound, on the other. Table 7.7 overviews this extrapolation, showing tendencies toward correspondence between few movements and soft sounds, much movement and loud or hard sounds, jerky movements and staccato in sounds, smooth movements and legato in sounds, slow movement and slow tempo, and fast movement and fast tempo.

This schema should be tested in more detail because it provides an interesting basis for understanding the relationship between movement and sound. Nevertheless, the schema is useful. For example, table 7.7 can be related to Laban's categories of force, displacement, and velocity in corporeal articulations (table 7.6). Force can be related to the amount of movement, while displacement has something to do with the articulation of the movement, and velocity with speed. Therefore it is tempting to make translations from corporeal descriptions to structural descriptions of music in the following way. For example, a movement which is described as *gliding* corresponds to light force, direct displacement, and sustained velocity. This corresponds to few, smooth, and slow movements, and thus to soft loudness, legato articulation, and slow tempo. In contrast, *slashing* is based on strong force, flexible displacement, and quick velocity, which corresponds to many, jerky, and fast movements, and thus to much loudness, staccato articulation, and fast tempo.

What this shows, so far, is that verbal descriptions of corporeal articulations (perceived in the behavior of other subjects or in the involved subject) may be related to verbal descriptions of musical structural cues. This relationship suggests that further links can be made with (bottom-up) measured structural cues (see section 7.4.4). In search-and-retrieval applications, the prospect is that kinesthetic descriptions of music may be translated into perceived and measured structural cues, which makes it easier for a machine to relate this to encoded physical energy.

**Perception of outer movement**   Though little information is available about empirical studies that fully address kinesthesia in relation to outer movement perception, it is of interest to refer to the work of Broeckx (1981), who proposed a theory of expressive meaning formation which draws upon the sensing of external space. In many ways, the viewpoint adopted by Broeckx may be conceived as complementary to Laban's theory of effort. While Laban focuses on body movement, Broeckx focuses on the sensing of tactile properties of surrounding time-space.

Table 7.8 summarizes Broeckx's intuition in defining spatiotemporal properties such as extension, boundary, and compactness in terms of musical structural cues and associated expressive meanings. For example, the perception of spatial extension as broad/narrow or faraway/nearby is defined in terms of big/small intervals, soft/hard loudness, and the use of extreme (low, high) or middle register. An open space boundary is defined in terms of extremes in loudness and dark timbre, while a closed space boundary is related to middle register and sharp timbre. Compact space is associated with hard loudness, high register, and sharp timbre, while empty space is associated with soft loudness, low register, and dark timbre.

In Broeckx's approach, these properties are related to expressive meanings. For example, a broad, open, and full space, defined by big

**Table 7.8**
Categories of tactile perception (extension, boundary, compactness) are related to musical structural cues (intervals, loudness, register, brightness)

| | Extension | | | | Boundary | | Compactness | |
|---|---|---|---|---|---|---|---|---|
| Character | Broad | Narrow | Faraway | Nearby | Open | Closed | Full | Empty |
| Meaning | Unreal Imagery | Real Presence | Unreal Imagery | Real Presence | Freedom | Intimacy | Real | Unreal |
| Intervals | Big | Small | | | | | | |
| Loudness | | | Soft | Hard | Soft, Hard | Middle | Hard | Soft |
| Register | | | Low, High | Middle | | | High | Low |
| Brightness | | | | | Dark | Sharp | Sharp | Dark |

Based on Broeckx, 1981.

intervals, hard loudness, and high register (including sharp and dark timbres), is assumed to contribute to the impression of freedom and adventure. The impression of expanding space, approaching, increasing depth, and spaces becoming sharper or more diffuse is based on changes in extension, boundary, and compactness.

All this contributes to the idea that musical expression can be understood as a pantomime of features that are subject to tension, attraction, continuity, discontinuity, collaboration, conflict, adaptation, resistance, activity, and passivity. The pantomime can be understood because it can be simulated, imitated, and associated with earlier tactile experiences. These experiences can be traced to musical structural cues. Obviously, the latter are assumed to relate to acoustic structural cues. In short, descriptions of musical expression can be formulated using descriptions of tactile properties of time-space experiences. These descriptions are situated at the level of a subjective action-oriented ontology, but they can be deconstructed to descriptions situated at the level of musical structural cues. This level is assumed to have a straightforward relationship with acoustic structural cues. As with Laban's theory, this theory needs further investigation and empirical testing, but it provides an interesting intuition to start from.[10]

To sum up, queries based on synesthesia and kinesthesia have a grounding in the perception of corporeal articulations, that is, in how the body behaves in response to music. In contrast with the perception of structural cues, where perception was focused on the structural properties of the musical object outside the human body, the focus was now on the subject's own body, and on the body in relation to the entire spatial/temporal environment. While descriptions of musical structure tend to be related to third-person descriptions, descriptions of kinesthesia and synesthesia are typically second-person because they rely on the observation of the subject's own body. In the context of social communication, the description is addressed to a *you* (second person) rather than to a *he* or *she* (third person). Clearly, second-person descriptions are subjective, but it is likely that they can be related to structural properties. Their status is therefore interesting because they mediate between pure subjective involvement and pure objective description.

### Queries Based on Descriptions of Affects/Emotions

Querying based on verbal descriptions of affects and emotions offers another type of high-level subjective description. In fact, these descriptors have attracted much attention in recent years (see, e.g., Juslin and Sloboda, 2001). Emotions are often associated with basic emotions such as fear, anger, love, hate, gaiety, and sadness, and with spontaneous physiological arousal; hence they are based on corporeal articulations. Affects cover a broader range of more subtle descriptions related to feelings, moods, and other types of qualitative descriptions that touch the senses, such as being solemn, vulgar, tender, careless, or exciting.

**Attribution and induction of affect**   It is important to note that the descriptions which are dealt with in the context of search for and retrieval of music often relate to cognitive appraisal of affect in music, and less to subjective emotional involvement or induced emotional arousal. Yet, in talking about affect in music it is often difficult to distinguish between the attributed subjective properties of music and the affective/emotional involvement of the subject: whether the subject is talking about music or about his or her private emotions.

For example, to say that music is boring or interesting tells me something about the subject's personal relationship with music, but not about the music itself. In contrast, to say that music is solemn or vulgar is mainly a matter of cognitive appraisal of musical properties. The description is of the music, not of the subject's personal appreciation. The problem is that sometimes the subject's focus may be more on the cognitive aspect, and sometimes more on affective involvement. Much depends on the context in which affect-processing occurs (Scherer and Zentner, 2001; Dibben, 2004). Therefore, one should be careful in using affect-based queries.[11]

**Affect and musical structure**   In the context of search and retrieval, the important questions are again related to which affect/emotion terms make sense, and how these terms can be related to structural properties of music.

In the past, several studies reported commonalities in the way subjects describe music by using affect adjectives (see, e.g., Hevner, 1936; Rigg, 1939; Watson, 1942; Wedin, 1972; Nielzén and Cesarec, 1982; Leman et al., 2005). Such commonalities refer to a low-dimensional mental representation of affects and emotions based on valence and activity/arousal.

Figure 7.3 shows a valence–activity map and some emotional adjectives randomly taken from a list of 142 terms compiled by Cowie et al. (2001). *Valence* refers to positive adjectives such as joyful or adventurous, or to negative adjectives such as unaffectionate and disappointed, while *activity* refers to low-activity adjectives such as disinterested and gloomy, and to high-activity adjectives such as aggressive and

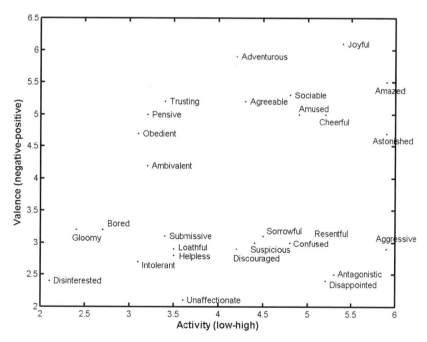

Figure 7.3
Two-dimensional representation of affects on a valence–activity scale. The vertical axis represents valence, from negative to positive, and the horizontal axis represents activity, from low to high. (Based on data from Cowie et al., 2001.)

astonished. Terms close to each other on this map have similar emotional meaning—for example, sociable, amused, and cheerful. Empirical studies show that most emotional adjectives can be cast in terms of these valence and activity coordinates (Faith and Thayer, 2001).

Given such a two-dimensional map, specification of a position on the map would allow users to formulate an affect–emotion query in terms of its valence and activity components. However, in the context of search-and-retrieval technology, such a query makes sense only if the terms can be decomposed and connected with musical structural cues or, ultimately, with structures in the music's physical energy. Given the deconstruction in terms of valence and activity components, one idea is to determine how these components relate to musical structural cues.[12]

One experiment (Leman et al., 2005) showed a clear distinction between interest-related affect descriptors and valence–activity-related affect descriptors. The interest-related descriptions were found to be less consistent among subjects, perhaps because they rely on context-dependent factors (Scherer and Zentner, 2001) that are difficult to control. In that sense, terms such as moving, indifferent, exciting, boring, pleasing, and annoying have to be distinguished from terms such as care-free, anxious, gay, sad, bold, tender, calm, and restless. The latter terms show less variance among subjects. They are applied to describe affective qualities of music, whereas the former are more about the subject's emotional state.

Concerning the relationship with structural cues, several music-related cues can be identified and related to affect-processing (see Gabrielsson and Lindström, 2001). For example, tempo is considered to be an important factor affecting emotional expression in music. Fast tempo is associated with expressions of activity/excitement—happiness, potency, anger, and fear—and slow tempo, with expressions of sadness, calmness, dignity, and solemnity. Loud music may be determinant for the perception of expressions of intensity, power, anger, and joy, whereas soft music may be associated with tenderness, sadness, solemnity, and fear. High pitch may be associated with expressions such as happy, graceful, exciting, angry, fearful, and active; and low pitch may suggest sadness, dignity, and excitement, as well as boredom and pleasure.

Table 7.9 gives an approximate assessment of the possible relationship between musical structural cues and the dimensions of the affect circle (valence and activity). The trends are interesting. For example, positive valence correlates mainly with consonance (36 percent) and with

Table 7.9
Estimated performance of structural descriptors for affect dimensions (expressed in percentages)

| | Valence | | | Activity | | |
|---|---|---|---|---|---|---|
| | Positive | Negative | % | High | Low | % |
| Tempo | Fast | Slow | 10 | Fast | Slow | 13 |
| Roughness | Consonant | Dissonant | 36 | Dissonant | Consonant | 13 |
| Loudness | | | | Loud | Soft | 50 |
| Articulation | Staccato | Legato | 15 | Staccato | Legato | 13 |
| Articulation* | Defined | Undefined | 15 | | | |
| Melody | Pronounced | Unpronounced | 15 | Unpronounced | Pronounced | 10 |
| Ambitus | | | | Big | Small | 2 |
| Register* | Defined | Undefined | 8 | | | |

Based on Leman et al. (2005).
* Whether the feature is defined or undefined.

staccato, defined articulation, and pronounced melody (each 15 percent), fast tempo (10 percent), and defined register (8 percent). The percentages give an indication of the weight or importance of that feature in combination with other features. High activity is related mainly to loud intensity (50 percent), and also to dissonance, fast tempo, and staccato (each 13 percent), and unpronounced melody (10 percent). Big *ambitus* is less relevant. Apart from loudness, the structural features are distributed over both affect dimensions, which makes the deconstruction of affect description into structural features difficult.

It is of interest to compare table 7.9 and figure 7.3.[13] For example, *joyful* has both a positive valence and a high activity. Therefore, we can expect fast tempo, loud sound, and staccato playing to be relevant structural cues. In addition, we are more likely to expect consonance than dissonance. In contrast, *aggressive* has a negative valence and a high activity, which corresponds to dissonance, loud music, and unpronounced melody. *Gloomy* has both a negative valence and a low activity, which corresponds to slow tempo, legato, and likeliness to be dissonant.[14] Through comparison a link is established from a network of related affect descriptors to musical structural descriptors, using deconstruction of affect descriptors in valence/activity components.

To sum up, queries based on descriptions of affects and emotions in music are grounded in the sensing of corporeal articulations. In contrast, with descriptions of musical structure and of synesthesia/kinesthesia, descriptions of affect and emotions rely on layers of the action-oriented system that involve the instinctive assessment of positive and negative reward from the environment, and energetic intensity—in other words, of the impact of an event. Interestingly, the ontology of valence and activity provides a reservoir of terms that can be used to describe perceived objects other than ourselves. This description of music as being the expression of an affect or an emotion is based on a chain of emotional involvement starting with movement simulation and movement action, and progressing to genuine emotional experiences. In considering search for and retrieval of music applications, the most straightforward use of affect adjectives is when subjects can dissociate the description of musical affect from their personal interest, using terms which can be deconstructed in terms of musical structural cues. However, as with all subjective descriptions, individual profiles may be helpful in trying to determine the decomposition of affect descriptions into musical structural cues.

### The Transitivity Hypothesis

The three types of (intramusical) semantic description discussed so far—structural descriptions, synesthetic/kinesthetic descriptions, and affect/emotion descriptions—are connected with each other via a transitivity relationship.

Descriptors of musical structure occupy a special status because they pertain to that part of the subject's action-oriented ontology which is closely related to structure in physical energy. In both cases, it is structure that is considered, from either a more subjective or a more objective point of view, whereas in corporeal-based descriptions the focus is more on subjective experience. Note that structural descriptions focus on music as a proximal stimulus, whereas synesthetic/kinesthetic and affect/emotion descriptors focus on music as a distal stimulus.

For that reason, descriptions of musical structure are often considered to be more objective than the corporeal-based descriptions. This intuition seems to be supported by the finding that the notes of a melody can be easily discerned in a spectrogram, whereas it is much more difficult to discern a gliding movement or solemnity in a spectrogram. Accordingly, in music research it has been common practice to assume that musical structures (e.g., those related to pitch, melody, harmony, onset, rhythm, timbre, and so on) have a close relationship to structural properties of the musical audio (e.g., frequency, intensity, time).

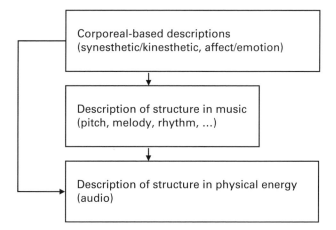

Figure 7.4
The transitivity hypothesis.

Despite the fact that the link between subjective descriptions of structure and the actual structure in physical energy is not at all evident, it has been very useful to relate corporeal-based descriptions and affect-based descriptions to structural descriptions. In doing this, the musical structural descriptions can be seen as forming the bridge to descriptions of physical energy.

Thus the supposition is that descriptions of musical structure can be linked with descriptions of structure in acoustic energy patterns. If descriptions of corporeal and affective involvement can be linked with descriptions of musical structure, then, by transitivity, there can also be a link to descriptions of structure in acoustic energy patterns. I call this the transitivity hypothesis (figure 7.4).[15]

The transitivity hypothesis may be a useful concept in music research, provided that the subtle relationships between structure in sound, perceived structure, and experienced motion and affects are taken into account. These relationships are indeed intricate. Often very subtle issues of semantic description have to be taken into account. There is a whole army of subjective factors that should be considered, including the effects of (distal) source-related and context-related perception. Unfortunately, in studying the relationship between semantic descriptors and descriptors of structure in sound, there is a lack of annotated data, as well as of quantified correlations among semantic descriptors. All this means that in practice, the transitivity hypothesis, despite its popularity, should be handled with great care.

## Queries Based on Contextual Descriptions

A third and final category of semantic descriptions is contextual descriptions. In general, contextual descriptors can be conceived as important for providing information about the role of music in a social and cultural context. Contextual descriptions are related to first-person descriptions because they involve interpretation, and, often, a good knowledge of the context. Examples are musical genre and style descriptors, which provide labels for classifying music into categories. Unfortunately, there is no uniform definition of these labels, and they may address very different aspects of a context.

Many record shops, and even broadcasting facilities, classify music by genre and style descriptors, but they do this in different ways because music can have different social and cultural functions. Consequently, music appeals to different contexts and labels may therefore be misleading. Genre categories such as "Children" and "Soundtrack" are difficult because they may contain classical music as well as pop music. Genre terms are typically based on concepts related to history, particular musical forms, or even musical techniques. They may describe geographical ("African music"), chronological ("Baroque music"), technical ("Free jazz"), and functional contexts ("Dance music"). Yet despite nonuniform definition, genre and style, as well as other contextual descriptors, can be the subject of data-mining. Labels can be related to measured acoustical cues, which make them useful for search-and-retrieval applications (Tzanetakis and Cook, 2002).

To sum up, semantic description of music can be divided into approaches ranging from metadata descriptions, to descriptions of musical structure, kinesthesia/synesthesia, and affects/emotions, to contextual descriptions. Studies reveal that subjects tend to conceptualize music in terms of their action-oriented ontology. This ontology, which is at the same time a memory and a prediction/anticipation framework, involves a number of subjective factors which relate to demography, education, mood, emotions, and so on. Attention should also be paid to the fact that semantic descriptions are goal-oriented and, therefore, constrained by the particularities of a social and cultural context. Nevertheless, one is likely to assume that semantic descriptions, especially those that function in a diagnostic context (i.e., second-person descriptions), can be correlated with third-person descriptions. Unfortunately, there is still a lack of elaborate user-oriented studies which address music description in terms of the application context.

## 7.3    Mediation Technology

In this section, I address the problem of music description in terms of the mediation technology. Once the query has been formulated by a subject, it is the task of the mediating technology to link query and target, that is, a search question and one or more musical excerpts retrieved from a large music library. Such a link can be grounded on a common data representation providing (1) a level which allows the integration of audio, text, and corporeal movements as descriptions of music, and (2) an action-relevant mediation component, so that search for and retrieval of musical information becomes a natural thing to do.

### 7.3.1    A Scenario for Multimodal Querying

Given the rich variety of music descriptions, a mediator should be able to handle different modalities of content specification. For example, a user may specify that the required music "should be similar in melody to the given example (audio excerpt is provided), but with a more gliding dance rhythm than the one contained in the excerpt, like this...(and then an arm movement is shown)." Obviously, this query is a combination of different modalities: acoustical energy (the audio excerpt), linguistic/symbolic input ("similar in melody," "gliding rhythm"), and motor/optic energy (movements). These modalities pose questions about the same object. Therefore, they should be deconstructed and related to a common description of music. A possible way to deal with this problem is to deconstruct the query modalities in terms of a symbolic description of music. For example:

•    The request for "similar melody" requires that a melody can be extracted from the audio excerpt and that the system can search the library for similar melodies. In this scenario, we assume that melodies were already extracted from target audio files, either manually or automatically, and stored in a database as symbolic metadata descriptions (a series of notes). The art is to find target melodies which are similar to the melody that is extracted from the query.[16]

•    The request for "gliding dance rhythm" requires a similar deconstruction into more elementary units of description. However, this modality is linguistic, and a semantic network of concepts may be useful for deconstruction. For example, using the Laban effort-shape theory explained above, the expression "gliding rhythm" can be related to light force, direct displacement, and sustained velocity. This can be further related to soft loudness, legato articulation, and slow tempo (table 7.7). In this scenario, target audio files should have been preprocessed up to a level of acoustic cues and related structural descriptions. The search for a gliding rhythm is then reduced to a search within the structural descriptions that relate to soft loudness, legato articulation, and slow tempo. Alternatively, targets could have been preprocessed in terms of semantic descriptions that refer to the Laban effort shapes, so that search could be based on these high-level descriptions rather than low-level ones.

• Finally, when gestures have been captured—for example, using a video camera or a joystick—they can be further characterized as sequences of elementary movements from which certain parameters can be extracted. These parameters also can be further described in terms of symbolic cues that relate to the physical energy of a movement, such as the amount of movement, movement articulation, and movement speed (see also section 6.4). Some of these cues relate to structural acoustic cues such as loudness, articulation, and tempo. Thus, corporeal articulations can indicate audio content specifications, especially in the domain of musical expressiveness.

In short, the above scenario suggests that machines can deal with different query modalities and translate them into a common structural description of music that is suitable for formal pattern-matching and similarity search.

### 7.3.2   A Model for Multimodal Query Processing

A model for multimodal query processing is summarized in figure 7.5. It shows a subject posing a query using different modalities of expression (audio, motor, and linguistic).[17] The query processors (one for each modality) deconstruct the queries to the middle level or midlevel description. By means of pattern-matching techniques, this description is compared with a similar type of description in the target files, which allows an appropriate recommendation to be made.

It is fairly evident that this multimodal search-and-retrieval schema can be implemented in a number of different ways, depending on the size of the database, the user's requirements, and a number of other factors. One important implementation issue is the degree to which the targets are preprocessed. For example, starting from an audio example and the

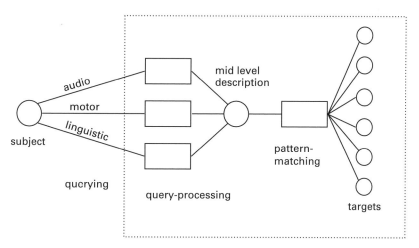

**Figure 7.5**
Multimodal access to musical information. The user enters a query using audio, motor, and linguistic modalities. The query processor has to deal with different query modalities as a function of the search-and-retrieval task. These modalities are processed and related to each other in a midlevel description. If target files have been processed up to a similar kind of description, then pattern-matching techniques can be used to find similarities among query and targets.

verbal request to find something similar in melody but with a gliding rhythm, it may be sufficient to focus on melody and rhythm in two independent search-and-retrieval tracks. If target files have been preprocessed in terms of melody, then candidate melodies may be found by using melody similarity algorithms. If target files have also been preprocessed in terms of the Laban effort-shape descriptions, for example, then the search for a particular gliding rhythm may work on a purely linguistic basis, without having to involve an association matrix. The search results for melody and rhythm may then be aggregated, using logical procedures. In that specific scenario, the linguistic description of the rhythm does not need to be deconstructed to lower levels of the acoustic structural representation because its symbolic description already belongs to a specific processing domain to which search and retrieval can be applied directly.

## Midlevel Description
The midlevel description has a special epistemic status with respect to the mind/body/matter problem, in that it can be seen as a core mediation

component that allows the extension of the human mind into the virtual world of electronic devices.

To clarify the concept of midlevel description a little further, it is instructive to consider traditional music notation from this viewpoint. For example, a melody (as a series of notes) can be said to provide access to a sounding melody, because the score can be reproduced by singing or playing the notes. The score thus provides mental access to sound energy by offering a set of instructions on how to generate the music. The connection can be realized by corporeal articulations, such as singing or playing music. Therefore, the score can be seen as a mediator between mind and sound. In a similar way, a drum pattern (as a score) can be considered a midlevel description because it can be reproduced as a percussion performance. Thus, the midlevel description is action-relevant, because it can be executed and realized through corporeal articulations. In addition, the midlevel description is neither too abstract nor too complex in terms of data representation, nor is it too low-level or too closely related to the structure of acoustical energy.

In the context of search-and-retrieval technology considered here, the midlevel description is linked with electronic processing units, which support a mediation component between the action-oriented ontology of the subject and the physical energy that is encoded in the machine. If the midlevel description is not directly accessible by the user, then action-oriented hooks should be provided. For example, in audio identification (section 7.4.1), the midlevel representation is low-level and barely accessible. However, the action-oriented hook allows users to input audio examples which they want to identify.

### Illusion of Non-mediation

Seen from the perspective of a mediation technology, the midlevel description is most effective when it creates the illusion of non-mediation. Note the parallel with playing a musical instrument (see chapter 6). Mastering the instrument means that the instrument forms part of the human body in such a way that attention can be focused on the musical goal rather than on the technicalities of handling the instrument. Search-and-retrieval technology also should allow users to focus on the goal—to retrieve what they want—rather than on the mediator (how to retrieve what they want). However, in contrast with musical instruments, users may not be prepared to spend too much of their time mastering the technology for music search and retrieval.

## Empirical Modeling

So far, it has been stated that the task of query and target processing is to translate the query and the target into a midlevel description which allows search for and retrieval of music. Clearly, the development of such a midlevel description is complex and demanding, and it involves a number of technical skills as well as psychological and musicological knowledge.

Basically, the idea is that a midlevel description can be developed by considering regularities which can be grasped using probabilistic learning procedures. Empirical modeling complies with the idea that measured features (third-person descriptions) can be related to articulated features (second-person descriptions), as shown in figure 4.2. The empirical modeling approach conceives this relationship between third-person and second-person descriptions as probabilistic. Once the learning has been accomplished, the model should be general enough for new data to be processed.

**Annotation**   In empirical modeling, the most important requirement is good annotated data because annotation defines the nature of the midlevel description, including possible access from the subject's action-oriented ontology. There are many different ways to proceed in this research area, but a straightforward distinction can be made among symbol-based annotation, corporeal-based annotation, and micro-annotation (see, e.g., Lesaffre, Leman, et al., 2004; Tanghe et al., 2005).

•     Symbol/linguistic-based annotation is concerned with the symbolic annotation of music, as in music transcription, where a listener writes down the notes heard in the melody. Annotations of structural cues, or cues related to synesthetic/kinesthetic and affect/emotions, fall under this category. These annotations could be called (intramusical) semantic annotation, in that they focus on the intrinsic meaning of a musical excerpt.

•     Corporeal-based annotation is related to attuning and harmonizing. For example, subjects can listen to a (polyphonic) song and harmonize with the melody in order to obtain the melody pattern that an algorithm should extract from the (polyphonic) audio. Or a percussionist can play on a MIDI-drum pad along with the music heard through headphones. The MIDI sequences provide a symbolic annotation of the drum sounds of the performer in response to music. This type of annotation is continuous in the sense that it is carried out while listening to music, and it draws upon corporeal articulations in response to music.

•     Micro-annotation is concerned with fine-tuning, for example, providing very detailed descriptions of the frequencies and the timing onsets and offsets of the notes that annotate a sung melody. This type of annotation is often based on precise measurement with the help of other tools. The precise annotations of onsets and offsets of the notes in a sung melody could be useful for the training of a pitch-extraction algorithm.

•     Often, annotation is based on a bootstrap method. This method uses existing tools for the development of new tools. For example, in order to be able to extract the melody from polyphonic music, the melody can be recorded by a singer harmonizing to the original melody in its polyphonic context. The resulting monophonic melody can then be automatically translated into a symbolic notation, using an existing tool, and afterward micro-annotation can be done in order to fine-tune the annotation and correct mistakes in it. This melody can then be used as the reference melody which a melody extractor should be able to find.

Clearly, the kind of labeling needed depends largely on the particular task to be modeled, that is, the particular midlevel descriptions required.

**Feature extraction and classification**   Once annotated data are available, the core of a mediation system can be built, typically using a two-step process of feature extraction and classification (see also section 6.4.2). Feature extraction processes audio into descriptions of low-level descriptions, while classification uses these low-level descriptions to obtain midlevel descriptions, which are typically connected with the annotated data. By splitting the annotated data into a training part and a testing part, it is possible to measure the performance capabilities of the feature-extraction and classification model, and thus of the mediation process.

Since the ultimate aim is to provide a connection between aspects of the musical energy (third-person descriptions) and aspects of the subject's action-oriented ontology reflected in the annotations (second-person descriptions), useful results may be obtained with feature-extraction algorithms that simulate the way humans process information. The rationale is that knowledge of the physiological mechanisms of the human auditory system, and in particular the input/output principles which are functionally equivalent to physiological mechanisms, can be implemented in computational models. By doing this, the models can provide information which is "objective" in the sense that it is structurally close to the way the human auditory system processes information.

Auditory-based models of melody transcription are a good example of this approach (see, e.g., De Mulder et al., 2004). Such models transcribe the melody of a given song into a melody score. The output is similar to the output of an expert human transcriber of melodies. In developing such models, knowledge of auditory physiology can be used for the pitch-extraction part. However, mechanisms of temporal segmentation are less well known, and machine learning methods are needed to train a system to do correct segmentations. For that aim, a large number of annotated pitches and segmentations would be needed.

### Schema of the Empirical Modeling Paradigm

Empirical modeling can be considered a core modeling paradigm for the development of mediation technology. Figure 7.6 summarizes the basic concept behind this paradigm.

Pieces of musical audio are represented by the pile of boxes at the right. The upper part shows human perception and annotation, and

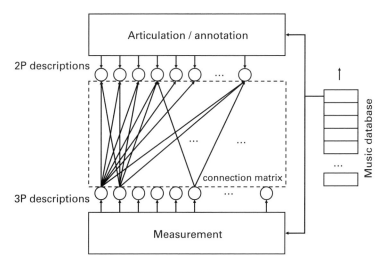

**Figure 7.6**
Empirical modeling of features. Connections can be established between audio features (first-person descriptions) and human annotations (second-person descriptions).

the lower part shows low-level feature extraction. When many examples are processed, it is assumed that the relationship between third-person and second-person descriptions can be partly reconstructed by considering the correlations in large sets of measured data and annotated data.[18] The result is a predictive model which would also work for new music files which did not form part of the training.

Note that the method takes into account three types of regularities among the data. First, acoustical regularities, which pertain to the structural properties of the acoustical signal; second, cultural regularities, which pertain to categorizations of objects that display similar action-relevant characteristics; and third, biological regularities, which pertain to human information-processing capabilities. As argued in chapter 3, these regularities define the framework in which connections emerge that accumulate into progressive steps toward more advanced levels of cultural and technological development. Therefore, the empirical modeling approach can be considered to be embedded within the global ecological framework proposed in that chapter.

### Descriptions of Cultural Issues

A major question of music annotation concerns the nature of the features that could serve as appropriate midlevel descriptors. It has been argued, so far, that second-person descriptions, which express the articulation of action-relevant cues, would be very useful. However, in the empirical modeling approach, it has not been excluded that contextual descriptions involving subjective cultural interpretations (first-person descriptions) may be used as midlevel descriptions.

The only assumption in the empirical modeling paradigm is that there are regularities in the data. Clearly, when culturally bound concepts such as genre descriptions are used, regularities may be limited to particular populations of users, as well as to particular data sets (see, e.g., Whitman and Ellis, 2004), but there may also be regularities, and these regularities may be exploited. Given a sufficient amount of data, such regularities can be explored for individual subjects and models may be developed for particular individual use.

Clearly, if the use of semantic descriptions is based on the instantaneous feelings of a subject, which largely depend on context and factors that otherwise cannot be taken into account because they are by nature unpredictable, then there may be a problem. Descriptions should be accurate in the sense of being stable and consistent. Then it will be possible to build an association matrix that mediates between first-person and third-person description.

In general, however, subjective descriptions may fit with the above schema, provided they are sufficiently regular. It is likely, however, that regularities can be more easily obtained with structural descriptions than with emotion-related descriptions. As mentioned before, structural descriptions are meant to describe perceived structural properties of physical energy. In contrast, descriptions based on emotions require self-interpretation, and this may depend on feelings and context factors which are more difficult to address.

Another aspect of description concerns individual differences between subjects. This has already been mentioned briefly. Up to now, much research in music perception has been based on the behavior of groups of subjects. Accordingly, search-and-retrieval applications have been based on the behavior of a population of users, and less on the behavior of a single individual. It is not excluded, however, that reliable music mediators can be developed that better fit with the profile of individual subjects. After all, search-and-retrieval technology can deal with profiles of individual users. Users could bring their properly trained mediator so that the machine could be adapted to the particular mediator profile of that particular user.

To sum up, the processing of multimodal information requires a kind of data representation that is not too complex and not too simple, is situated at a crossroads of multiple modalities, and provides a link with human action. This kind of data representation is called the midlevel description. It is embedded in a technology that mediates between mind and matter, thus forming the extension of human action in domains where human biomechanics falls short, such as an electronic database. From a subjective point of view, this mediation technology should "disappear" when it functions correctly. In general, it is most effective when it is not noticed and when it gives the illusion of non-mediation. The midlevel description is the workhorse of technology-based music mediation. It provides a level of description that fits or allows hooks with human action-relevant information-processing. Midlevel descriptions can be developed using empirical modeling techniques. The approach is based on the idea that computer tools can be developed that associate measured data with annotated data, or third-person descriptions with second-person descriptions. Once the machine has been trained, new queries and targets can be processed.

## 7.4  Examples of Search-and-Retrieval Systems

The remaining sections give a few examples of systems that allow query-processing in different ways.[19] First, audio identification is briefly discussed, then a query-by-voice system, which allows users to sing a melody and to retrieve similar melodies from a database. Third, the empirical method is briefly illustrated in a system which does drum and melody extraction from polyphonic audio. Finally, a semantic search-and-retrieval system for music is illustrated which allows the use of combined linguistic queries based on genre, expressive movement, affects/emotions, and structural features.

### 7.4.1  Audio Identification Using Fingerprinting

If the task is audio identification (not music identification!), then it suffices to compare a query with targets at a level of encoding which is close to the physical energy. Such a level of encoding is called audio fingerprinting. The audio fingerprint is designed to be invariant against audio quality degradation. Hence, the level of representation should be sufficiently abstract from the waveform representation that differences in audio quality (CD quality, MP3 quality, noisy environments) can be overcome. Moreover, only a short audio sequence of the song should be needed to characterize the audio fingerprint of a piece of music.

The audio fingerprint is a unique piece of information which can be understood as a kind of low-level content summary of a musical audio excerpt.[20] What that means is best understood by giving a brief example from Carl Orff's "O Fortuna" in figure 7.7a. The audio features are represented as a thirty-two-bit black-and-white pattern. One such pattern (depicted on the horizontal axis) is called a subfingerprint. On the vertical axis, from top to bottom, are 256 subfingerprints that correspond to 256 segments of the original musical audio. The whole audio fingerprint thus amounts to about three seconds of music. Figure 7.7b shows the fingerprint from the same music in MP3 audio encoding. Figure 7.7c shows the difference between the original and the MP3 version. The code is robust enough to deal with different qualities of the same musical example (CD quality, MP3 quality).

The extremely compact representation allows a fast search in large databases and a wide field of applications (Haitsma and Kalker, 2003), which is interesting from the point of view of a music mediation technology. No wonder, then, that audio fingerprinting has been the first com-

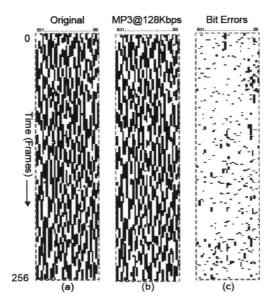

**Figure 7.7**
Audio fingerprint. (a) Original CD quality, (b) MP3 quality, (c) difference between (a) and (b) (Haitsma and Kalker, 2003). (Reprinted with permission.)

mercial content-based application in music information retrieval. Audio identification simply works, even if its capabilities in terms of content extraction are limited.

Furthermore, the technique allows a number of applications that go beyond the paradigm of music information retrieval. For example, audio fingerprinting is valuable for the detection of copyright infringements, and it is perhaps the key technology through which the music industry hopes to be able to regain control of protected music in peer-to-peer networks. The code can also be watermarked and encoded with the physical energy that makes up the music (Gomes et al., 2003).

Audio fingerprinting is based on a statistics of musical audio properties. It is a third-person description of physical characteristics of music without the consideration of any higher-level structural or subjective descriptions. Therefore, in many applications where users want to provide content descriptions, fingerprinting technology is largely insufficient. For example, when using audio fingerprinting it is not possible to identify a piece of music that has been performed by different players or at different performances. This failure clearly shows the differences between identification of musical audio based on descriptions of local energies contained in sonic forms, and identification of music based on sensor-imotor capabilities of human users. The latter is based on previous experiences and specifications of higher-level structural and semantic relationships.

### 7.4.2   Query by Voice

In this application, the query is a sung melody which is translated into an electronic score. The aim is to identify the sung melody and to retrieve the music that contains this melody.

A simple query by the voice system would typically contain three parts. In the first part, a song melody is processed by a melody transcriber into a sequence of note segments with their associated note frequencies. In the second part, this sequence is translated into a more abstract representation so that melody transposition (melodies in a different key) or different timing (slower tempo), and perhaps other small variations, can be taken into account. Such a description resembles a melody/rhythm contour. In the third part, this description is compared with a database of similarly encoded melodies, using pattern similarity techniques.

An example of a melody transcriber is the MAMI melody transcriber, which was developed using an empirical modeling approach (De Mulder et al., 2004). Annotated queries (see figure 7.8) were used to train the melody transcriber to make the correct pitch segmentations. The resulting melody representation contains a sequence of note names with associated beginning and ending time points.[21]

An example of the melodic contour description is the CubyHum description (Pauws, 2002), which uses the encoding schema shown in table 7.10. This encoding schema translates intervals into numbers, leaving room for mistuned melodies, mainly errors introduced by the singer. The result is a melody contour which makes abstraction of the pitch height and considers only intervals. It has been demonstrated that the MAMI melody transcriber, in combination with the CubyHum encoding schema, can work rather well in the context of melody-based search for and retrieval of music (De Mulder et al., 2006).

Clearly, there are different possibilities for describing a melody. And obviously the choice may depend on the application one has in mind. Instead of pitch contour, the description can be based on pitch distributions, for example, using a histogram of the number of pitch occurrences in the melody. The pitch histogram typically reveals the pitch scale

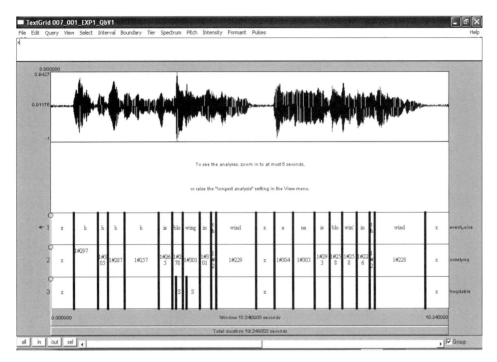

**Figure 7.8**
Annotation of segmented pitch. The upper part shows the waveform of the sound. Below are three layers of annotation, the lyrics of the song, the frequency, and an indication of whether the pitch is stable or not. The vertical lines indicate segmentation. (The analysis environment is Praat.)

**Table 7.10**
Pitch contour representation for the CubyHum music retrieval system

| Interval name | Interval size | Integer code |
|---|---|---|
| Descending perfect fifth and greater | $<-6$ st | $-4$ |
| Descending perfect/augmented fourth | $-5$ or $-6$ st | $-3$ |
| Descending minor/major third | $-3$ or 4 st | $-2$ |
| Descending minor/major second | $-1$ or $-2$ st | $-1$ |
| Unison | 0 st | |
| Ascending minor/major second | 1 or 2 st | 1 |
| Ascending minor/major third | 3 or 4 st | 2 |
| Ascending perfect/augmented fourth | 5 or 6 st | 3 |
| Ascending perfect fifth and greater | $>6$ st | 4 |

Based on Pauws (2002).

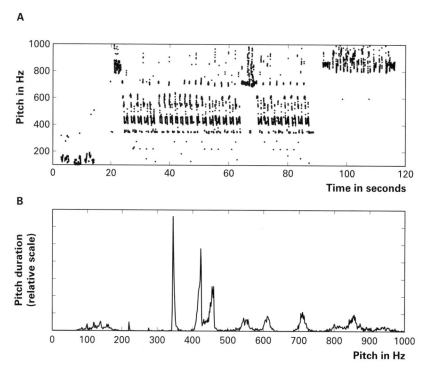

**Figure 7.9**
Pitch contour and histogram of flute music from Burundi. The top panel (a)
shows the pitch contour as extracted by a pitch transcriber (without pitch segmentation). The bottom panel (b) shows the histogram of this contour with the
main pitches played during this recording.

that is used throughout the piece. Figure 7.9 shows the pitch contour and
the pitch histogram of a typical sound file (of about two minutes) taken
from a large collection of music from Burundi.[22] The first seventeen seconds of this file is a fragment spoken by a male voice. This is typical for
field recordings. In principle, the voice could be separated from music by
a dedicated speech/music segregation algorithm. In this example, however, this has not been done. Figure 7.9a shows the pitch contour (in
Hz) of the voice and the music. Only pitch detection is done, without
time segmentation of pitches. Figure 7.9b shows the histogram, which
represents the sum of the durations of all pitches during the recording. This histogram gives an indication of the pitch scale used in the
piece. Clearly, the pitch of the spoken voice is but a small part of
the whole, and it can be considered as a noise component of the pitch

scale. For search-and-retrieval purposes, the pitch scale can be further processed and then compared with a database of similar encoded pitch distributions.

### 7.4.3    Midlevel Descriptions for Polyphonic Music

Recent work in music engineering aims at extracting midlevel representations from polyphonic music. This is done for structural features such as melody, onset, tempo, rhythm, texture, and timbre. The following examples briefly mention some approaches in melody and drum extraction.

**Melody Extraction**

Melody extraction concerns the extraction of pitch patterns from a polyphonic musical audio file (Gómez et al., 2003; Klapuri, 2003, 2004). The melody can be considered as the structural feature of music which listeners would be inclined to imitate when requested to sing the main melodic lines of the music.

The problem of melody extraction from polyphonic audio is typically split into subproblems, and each subproblem may be based on empirical modeling techniques. Pitch detection would typically be based on knowledge of the human auditory system. State-of-the-art auditory models provide pitch patterns from which probabilities for fundamental frequencies can be estimated. These fundamental frequencies are estimates within local time frames. Salient peaks over time should then be connected in order to form segmented pitch objects. This process delivers a set of tones with frequency, start time, duration, and evidence per frame. Tone-filtering may then provide the most prominent tones. Finally, melody detection may connect tones by size of pitch interval, and aims at constructing the most evident path. This gives a set of candidate melodies of which the most salient can be considered the melody. At different levels of this schema, parameters may be trained and optimized so that the melody extraction from an audio file fits with the annotated melody.

**Drum Extraction**

The extraction of drum patterns from musical audio leads to a description of timing and type of drum instrument, like a score for percussion instruments (Degroeve et al., 2005; Tanghe et al., 2005). These descriptions are assumed to provide what is perceived in music in terms of percussion patterns. Presumably they can be imitated by a singer or by a percussionist.

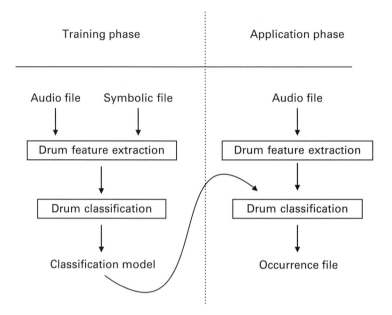

**Figure 7.10**
Empirical method with training phase and application phase. Results of the training are used in the application phase (based on Tanghe, Degroeve, & De Baets, 2004).

In the context of an empirical modeling methodology, a model for drum pattern detection would be based an algorithm that is first trained with annotated drum patterns. Once trained, the algorithm would be used in an application. The general schema is shown in figure 7.10.

In the training phase, the user supplies an audio file and a corresponding file which contains a symbolic representation of the drum events on the sound file. For each relevant drum event in the audio file, then, there is an indication of a time moment and of the drum types. The latter represent categories of percussion instruments such as bass drums, snare drums, and high hats.

The actual detection of drum events from an audio file consists of three steps: onset detection, feature extraction, and classification. The onset detection locates moments in time where drum events might be present. The feature extraction extracts low-level features from the audio around the detected onsets. And the classification stage makes a decision for each onset (based on the extracted audio features) about which type of event is present at that location (drum event or not; and if drum event, which type). The end result is a drum occurrence file which can be used for further processing or evaluation. Further information can then be extracted, such as beat, tempo, rhythm patterns, types of percussion instruments, and so on.

For this application, the subjective description or annotation of the occurrence of a drum event should be very accurate. Two strategies have been used to obtain accurate annotations: corporeal annotation and micro-annotation. Corporeal annotation is based on drum imitations by musicians (percussionists) using MIDI drum pads. In addition, micro-annotation is used to refine the obtained annotations. The latter is less based on imitation behavior but can draw upon it to a certain degree. In figure 7.14 annotated drum events are in the symbolic file (Tanghe et al., 2005).

### 7.4.4  User Profiling and Semantic Description

The final example is an application of a music search-and-retrieval system based on (intramusical) semantic description. The three types that were discussed in the previous section—structural descriptions, synesthetic/kinesthetic descriptions, and affect/emotion descriptions—are taken into consideration.

The application uses knowledge from a large experiment in which subjects were asked to annotate 160 different musical excerpts labeled according to the genre, structural descriptors, kinesthetic descriptors, and affect/emotion descriptors (Lesaffre, 2005). Using an approach similar to the one explored in Leman et al. (2005), it was possible to set up an application where users could search in the database, using combinations of descriptors in order to retrieve music. The database has a good spread in demographics and background. This allows the specification of a particular user profile, so that the correlations between descriptors can be adapted to the specific profile of the user.

Figure 7.11 shows a screen of the semantic music retrieval system. Users can choose descriptors related to genre, structural cues, kinesthetic cues, and affect/emotion cues. The figure shows the search screen on top and a recommendation list below. The recommendation list is the result for a female expert searching the database for classical music, using the emotion descriptor "sad," the sound descriptor "soft," and the movement descriptors "dynamic" and "slow." The user can listen to any recommended music excerpt. The score (in percentages) reflects the global degree of agreement among subjects on the features entered in the query.

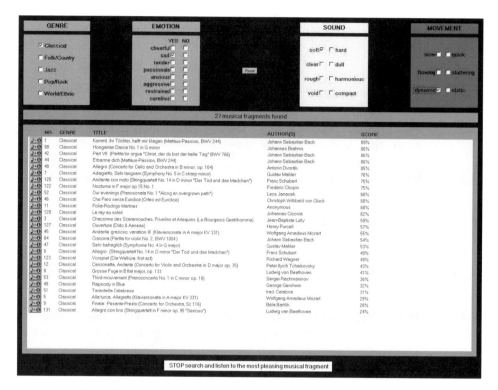

**Figure 7.11**
Search engine which allows the search for and retrieval of music using semantic descriptors relating to genre, structural cues, kinesthetic cues, and affect/emotion cues (Lesaffre, 2005).

All titles are shown up to a threshold of 20 percent of intersubjective agreement. While the user selects search options by means of check boxes, the list adapts itself according to the query input.

## 7.5   Conclusion

Search for and retrieval of music is a very active field of research. The main goal of this chapter was to show that technologies can be built which bridge the gap between mind and matter, and which extend human action into a domain of virtual reality, the domain of electronic music libraries, in which search for and retrieval of music is a concrete application.

Given the theoretical background put forward in the previous chapters, it was argued that descriptions can be based on different categories of human involvement with music, related to different types of corporeal and cerebral involvement. Although up to now, there has been little knowledge available about how users tend to use these content-based search-and-retrieval engines, it is generally believed that content description of music can greatly enhance access to music.

Content-based search for and retrieval of musical audio implies the translation of ideas and intentions into a format that storage systems can deal with. This translation implies that users have some content in mind, and that they know how to express it. This is a difficult issue because users may have ill-defined goals or they may fail to translate ideas to specific content descriptions.

In that perspective, the chapter focused on the human task of posing a music-related search question (querying) and the subsequent machine task of query-processing. It has been argued that queries may be multimodal and that midlevel descriptions of information may provide a suitable level for multimodal integration and access to the subject's action-oriented ontology. These midlevel descriptions can be obtained by a research approach that is based on annotation and subsequent empirical modeling.

The hypothesis put forward is that querying by audio examples may offer many possibilities, provided that additional specifications, using keywords for structural and subjective descriptions, can be added. These search options require knowledge of how linguistic descriptions and corporeal behavior can be connected with the properties of the musical audio. The combined querying based on audio, corporeal, and linguistic descriptions is probably one of the most useful types of querying because it allows users to exploit the most straightforward description options.

Empirical modeling assumes that algorithms have to be trained to extract features from musical audio that are relevant from the viewpoint of human description. Making this connection is not always easy, either from the viewpoint of bottom-up algorithm development or from the viewpoint of top-down human annotation. The bottom-up approach may profit from knowledge of human physiology, and the top-down approach may profit from computational tools for the description of content, both of musical structural and of subjective experiences with music. Empirical modeling then assumes that these two levels can be connected, using training by examples.

The midlevel description should be conceived of as the level where bottom-up algorithmic and top-down human annotation meet.

However, the step from algorithm-based descriptions of musical audio to human descriptions of musical audio is still huge, and the mechanism by which descriptions of physical energy are translated into action-based description ontology is a largely unsolved problem. Since these associations depend on cultural conditions as well as subjective personalities, they should be learned, possibly on an individual basis. Until recently, research in musical audio encoding focused on structural features such as melody extraction and rhythm extraction. Since descriptions of subjective experience can be decomposed in terms of subjective structural descriptions, it is generally believed that descriptions of subjective experience can be connected with musical audio. However, the large variance in descriptions of subjective experience may drive this research in the direction of individual modeling. In other words, it is not excluded that a subjective fingerprint may be developed for each individual subject. This fingerprint would contain the association matrix which connects bottom-up feature descriptions with the subjective midlevel descriptions proper to the individual subject. This approach is feasible because music mediation technology is based on a concept that allows individual subjective interactions with machines.

Research in content-based musical querying aims at providing a proper analysis of the different possibilities of turning an idea into a music description. This is not an easy task because the intentions of the user may not be known beforehand. Intentional search may range from "being interested in recommendations and global indications for further searching" to "I have a specific piece of music in mind and I want to find more music of that kind" to "here is an audio example and I am searching for music which is similar in certain respects." Not all query formats will be equally effective, and the effectiveness may depend on the conditions of the search action. Furthermore, query interfaces have to handle a smooth transition from human intentionality to machine encodings of information. This aspect is sometimes forgotten.

This chapter also showed that more research is needed in order to better understand the different types of descriptions and how they relate to one another. Indeed, the whole problem of musical querying and encoding cannot be dissociated from several other aspects, including human memory capacity, feature extraction, pattern-matching, access technology, user interfaces, recommendation, and cultural and social goals. In this chapter these aspects have not been dealt with because they require interdisciplinary solutions which far exceed the purpose of the book.

# Conclusion

Embodied music cognition entails a view on mind, matter, and the human body. It conceives the musical mind as embodied, that is, as mediated by the human body. Mediation technology aims at extending the natural mediation of the human body so that access to sound energy in digital environments becomes possible. If the human body and mediation technology are hooked into each other, then it is possible to conceive the digital domain as a natural extension of the physical domain. The human mind will then extend its activity range to this digital environment in a natural way. This book offers a concept and a framework for developing such an embodied music mediation technology.

Human action and, more particularly, social interaction provide the basis for understanding how music relates to mind, body, and matter. In that respect, I have suggested that subjects tend to behave with music in the same way that they tend to behave with other subjects. That is, they aim at understanding each other's intentional actions.

Music may have intentional actions encoded in moving sonic forms, that is, patterns in physical energy, and subjects can decode these patterns into something that appeals to their action-oriented ontology. The ontology relates to the subject's self, the mind, or the memory that is built up through long-term experience. The subjective action-oriented ontology is biologically designed to predict and anticipate the sources in the environment that provide energy. This bias provides a suitable basis for interaction and intentional understanding of music. Music is thus seen as something with particular appeal to interaction and intentional understanding. The underlying process which makes this understanding possible is called behavioral resonance, and its markers or embodied expressions have been called corporeal articulations.

Several forms of corporeal articulations have been distinguished: from mere passive resonance (response to loud sound), to synchronization (tapping the beat), to attuning (to melody, harmony, or tonality), to empathy (behaving as if feelings engendered by the music are shared), to entrainment (mutual adaptation of subjects' behavior while involved with music). This list is perhaps not exhaustive, but the idea is that different forms of behavioral resonance, such as attuning and imitation, mediate the moving sonic forms to the musical mind, where they fit with an action-oriented ontology. In that sense, the notion of action-oriented ontology can also be understood in terms of beliefs, values, goals, and truths about the things that exist for a subject, from the viewpoint of action.

At several places in this book, I have pointed out that an embodied music cognition approach may open up a number of new possibilities for music research, in particular with respect to the study of subjective experiences, communication, and technology.

## Subjective Experiences of Music

The embodied cognition approach has some important consequences. First of all, the subject is now seen as an active contributor rather than a passive receiver. Experiments should aim at engaging subjects in musical actions rather than preventing them from being active. Embodiment assumes that subjective experiences are expressed in bodily changes which can be monitored, measured, and explored in mediation applications. Therefore, new techniques based on attuning and imitation need more attention in music research. Second, corporeal articulations are fully subjective in the sense that they may be unique for each individual. Yet it can be expected that aspects of these expressions, which relate to second-person descriptions, subsume regularities (a) among each other and (b) with structures in physical energy. In my opinion, subjectivist skepticism on this matter may be unjustified.

## Musical Communication

In this book, perception has been approached from an ecological viewpoint. In particular, I have stressed the action-relevant aspects of perception in view of the energetic sources that come from an environment. In many respects this view agrees with the idea that listening focuses on the moving source of a sound rather than on the sound itself. My focus on sources relates to the role of action in perception. It embraces the idea that the moving source of a sound is often related to the action-relevant ontology of the listener, and not necessarily to the real cause that generates the sound. This point of view may differ from gestalt-based approaches that tend to consider music perception basically in terms of cognitive structures. Reference can be made to attuning experiments which show that core aspects of tonality can be captured fairly well by an embodied cognition approach.

The hypothesis that musical communication is based on the encoding, transmission, and decoding of intended actions is, I believe, an attractive one. However, at this moment it is more a working hypothesis than an established fact. I would consider its proof by hard empirical evidence a major achievement of embodied music cognition research. It would certainly be a step toward a better understanding of social music cognition.

## Technology

Finally, in this book technology has come into the picture because, in our society, music is often available as an encoded physical energy in a particular device. To access music in that device, we depend on mediation technology. I have argued that mediation technology should be conceived as an extension of the human body and that the mediation technology should focus on the connection between human intentions and the physically encoded energy. The background for that type of technology-oriented research can be provided by embodied music cognition research in which attention is focused on aspects of presence and non-mediation. Indeed, in many cases music mediation technology is effective when it becomes invisible (or, better, when it becomes an extension of the natural mediator which is the human body). This aspect is very challenging in core areas of modern music research: music information retrieval and interactive music systems.

Finally, in this book I have distinguished between corporeal and cerebral understanding of music. The precise relationship between both types of understanding may need further attention and investigation as well. Corporeal understanding is assumed to be based on mimetic processes originating in motor resonance processes, whereas cerebral understanding is assumed to be based on a cognitive interpretation of subjective experiences and on the projection of these experiences onto cultural contexts. In music signification practices, both aspects should be taken into account and a cerebral interpretation of music should be regarded as no less important than corporeal involvement. In fact, the focus on corporeal understanding or cerebral understanding may largely depend on the social context in which music is dealt with. However, there are reasons to believe that an embodied involvement with music relies on fundamental gestural and mimetic forms of communication which, phylogenetically speaking, precede language and linguistic communication. What it means to understand music corporeally has been largely neglected in the past. A deeper scientific understanding of its mediating role in music may reshape the landscape of modern music research.

# Notes

## Chapter 1

1.   Obviously, music is not the only stimulus which can engage humans in such a state of immersion. Paintings, statues, cinema, and natural environments have the power to engage humans in experiences of behavioral resonance. Other stimuli may come from social engagements such as mass demonstrations, sports, and religious rituals. In general, ritualized activities seem to have a strong power to engage a human being in a state of behavioral resonance with energies from the environment. Energies come from other human beings or other physical entities which the human body can sense in auditory, visual, tactile, and olfactory modalities.

2.   A mental representation is here defined as a model of the environment in the mind of a subject. A description makes such a model explicit or encodes it in a material medium so that it functions as an exchange of information between subjects.

3.   Even the imitation of a cuckoo that signifies the heralding of spring, or the *lamento* theme, signifying sadness, or goal-oriented temporality, signifying the progressive time of Revolution, or "musical endings," signifying male behavior, could be taken into account (Monelle, 2000).

4.   Reference can be made to structuralist and formalist accounts of music analysis (e.g., of the 1960s and 1970s), where subjective interpretation was confined to the structural properties of music. The focus at that time was more on the principles of composition than on the listening experience. Because of this liberation, musicologists nowadays experience this method as the "emancipation of the sign" (Tarasti, 1997).

5.   The symbols of a linguistic description, such as the words *pastorale*, *authoritative*, and *heroic*, are socially shared with other persons. In that sense, linguistic narration draws on the rationalization of experiences of intentionality in domains related to our common sensory perception, motor activity, and feelings. Sender and receiver encode and decode the information on the basis of more or less common processing capabilities, common cultural contexts, and common experiences of direct involvement with music. This is why linguistic descriptions

of music might work in a technology-mediation access to music, provided that the common understanding of tacit knowledge is sufficiently reliable.

6.     In music research, the term *affect* may be preferred over the term *emotion* because it allows more subtle subjective descriptions related to subjective sensitivity.

7.     The leading musician indicated melodic curves and ornaments by means of hand movements in the air. Later on, in ninth-century western European culture, the widespread tendency to move hands with music was transformed into the neumatic notation using stylized graphs of the outlines of such movements. A few centuries later it was turned into solmization (by Guido), using single phalanges of the fingers as the seats of melodic intervals. The transition from gesture to notation shows that symbolic music description can be closely linked to corporeal movements in space and time.

8.     Oberholzer and Strumpf (2004) estimated the largest distribution system, FastTrack/Kazaa, to have on the order of 3.5 million simultaneous users in December 2002. On FastTrack/Kazaa there were typically more than 500 million files holding five petabytes of data available at any time. Each week there were more than one billion downloads of music files.

9.     It may, furthermore, change the public's willingness to pay for music, although Oberholzer and Strumpf (2004) found no significant effect of file-sharing on purchases of music albums.

## Chapter 2

1.     The concept of soul can be interpreted in terms of a self or a phenomenal self-model (Metzinger, 2003, p. 504). If this is allowed, Aristotle's viewpoint comes close to modern views on embodied cognition.

2.     Much of the older literature on systematic musicology is summarized in Wellek (1963) and in Elschek (1992). The latter contains a comprehensive catalog of the early achievements of systematic musicology.

3.     The work of the composer I. Xenakis drew upon this idea, and he extended it with tools that allowed more detailed descriptions of the formal structure of musical content, such as note and rhythm distributions and densities. Probability theory and logics were taken as models for the definition and mathematical control of musical pitch and duration parameters (Xenakis, 1963).

4.     It is important to take into account the societal context in which music research came to the foreground in the second half of the twentieth century. Although it is not my intention to give a detailed overview of the history of the development of music research, some important milestones should nevertheless be mentioned. One such milestone is the emergence of an industry for media technology; another is the creation of a research environment for content-based music research. Both industry and research have created a prerequisite for the development of modern music research (Leman, 2005).

5.     The free market provided the conditions for the development of media technology, the technology which allows the processing of music in terms of encoded physical energy. For a history of audio recording technology, see, for example, http://history.acusd.edu/gen/recording/notes.html. The government provided the conditions for the development of music mediation research and artistic music production. Clearly, government support was on a much smaller scale than the free market support, and it came later. Nevertheless, government support has been crucial for the emergence of content-based music research and its application in media technologies.

6.     Similar ideas about the self are found in the theory of optimal experience of Csikszentmihalyi (1990). Any expression of the self, or anything that contributes to its ordering, gives pleasure.

7.     In 2004, for example, the ConGAS COST-287 action (http://www.cost287.org), supported by the European Union, established a network of laboratories that focus on issues related to gesture and music.

# Chapter 3

1.     Strictly speaking, of course, making a musical instrument is not really a musical activity. It is not like playing an instrument or listening to music. Nevertheless, it involves a range of skills which occur in many other activities. The skills which involve production of sound, listening to sound, evaluation of sounds, and making decisions are mainly a function of making music. Such skills have an elementary appeal to music, and they are likely to be at work in technology-mediated access to music as well—for example, while dealing with interactive systems that generate music for artistic purposes.

2.     The steps in making a bell are very well documented in Lehr (1971, 2000a, 2000b), and need not be repeated in the present context. The history of bellmaking provides an excellent example of the impact of skill and tradition. The specific shapes and differences in thickness at the crown, shoulder, waist, and ring of the bell are necessary in order to avoid the highly inharmonic resonances produced by flat bronze plates. The carillon bells made by the Hemony brothers in the second half of the seventeenth century and by Georges Duméry in the first half of the eighteenth century, for example, attest to highly developed skills in bell-founding.

3.     This letter was found in May 2001 in the archives of the University of Ghent library, in a collection of uncataloged manuscripts. A similar letter is available in the archives of the city of Bruges. The carillon of Bruges, one of the most famous in the world, was made by Duméry in the 1740s, after a fire destroyed the previous instrument. Following is a transcription in Old flemish and English translation by the author: *Den onderschreven presenteert aan/d'edel heeren van Brugge, om/een carrillion te ghieten ten dienste/der selver stadt in alle hunne/perfexie ende al egael van/gheluijt, soo goet alser een sal/te luiden wesen, vermits ick mij/verobligiere de selve clocken te doen/hebben alle hunne juste qualitey—/ten bestaende in eenen forcighen/bordon, de juste octave, de kleine/*

*tierce ende quinte ende ene just/super octave, soo danigh dat het/gheel carilion onverbeterlijck sal/sijn, omme dus d'ene clocke soo goet/van delicates, moet sijn als d'ander,/presenterende het selve te voltrecken,/ter keure van alle experte van de/weirelt, welck werck mij verbinde/te maeken binnen dese stadt Brugge/binnen den tijdt van drije jaeren/ende dat voor een prijs van vijf/stuijvers courant gelt.* (The undersigned proposes to the noble sirs of Bruges to found a carillon to the service of the same city in all their perfection and all equal in sound, so good as one shall ever be sounded. Since I obligate myself that these clocks will have all their just qualities, consisting of a strong bourdon, the just octave, the small third, and the fifth, and a just superoctave, so that the entire carillon will be incorrigible, and thus one clock as good as the other one, I will proceed by myself, under review of all experts of the world. I commit myself to make the work in this city of Bruges within a time span of three years and for a price of five [*stuivers*] normal money....)

4.    Manuscripts at the University of Ghent library and the archives of Bruges document that Duméry had to remake some bells after they were judged to be of insufficient quality. The new bells had used material from the old bells, which, due to the fire, contained too much lead (see also Lehr, 1971).

5.    The technique of bell-tuning provides an example of such a skill. Bell-tuning consists of slightly adapting the form of the bell by removing small amounts of bronze at particular places inside the bell that correspond to the mistuned partial tones. This technique was based on a good practical knowledge of the acoustic principles of partial tones. The invention of this technique is attributed to Jacob van Eyck (see Lehr, 1971).

6.    As known, however, even the best carillon bells could not attain the ideal of the harmonic tone. The best approximations have a partial at a minor third of the prime partial which is one octave above the hum or lowest partial—as specified in the assessment letter of Georges Duméry. Although these bells are relatively stable, the minor third is still considered a deviation from the harmonic ideal. The quest for a harmonic bell has recently been solved with the help of computer-aided bell design and optimization. It is now possible to design bells with a major third (Schoofs et al., 1987). More recently, a new type of bell with harmonic properties was designed by McLachlan and Nigjeh (2003).

7.    The idea that stability in music reflected the stability of the universe was known in medieval times as *musica mundana*. It almost certainly had its origin in mythic cultures where the principle of harmony allowed unification of dualistic thinking about natural and supranatural phenomena. This trace is found, for example, in Greek mythology and early Western music theory (cf. Boethius).

8.    Harmonic tones are perceived as pure and stable. The tone structure does not cause amplitude fluctuations. In contrast, inharmonic tones have partial tones which are not integer multiples of a fundamental. These tones produce amplitude fluctuations. They are perceived as impure and unstable.

9.    This example is relevant in terms of the carillon bell. Thus far, the action–reaction cycling has been considered in terms of making a single bell. However, playing the bells imposes further constraints, such as the melodic and harmonic

sounding of multiple bells. This musical application subsumes the use of a pitch scale (a system of fixed intervals between pitches). In Western music, pitches divide the octave into twelve chromatic steps. It accounts for the intervallic distances between the tones played on the instrument.

10.    Purves and Lotto (2003) argue that invariance in perception is based on a statistics of proper relationships between the stimulus and the source that produces the stimulus. Their viewpoint is largely influenced by recent studies in visual perception. Instead of dealing with feature extraction and object reconstruction on the basis of properties of single stimuli, they argue that the brain is a statistical processor which constructs its perceptions by relating the stimulus to previous knowledge about stimulus–source relationships. Such a statistics, however, assumes that aspects related to human action should be taken into account because the source cannot be known except through action. In that respect, this approach differs from previous studies in empirical modeling, which addressed perception regardless of action-related issues. Therefore, the emphasis of empirical modeling on properties of the stimulus should be extended with studies that focus on the relationship between stimulus and source, and between perception and action.

11.    In the tradition of von Helmholtz, roughness is defined as dissonance, which in turn is defined as the energy of beating frequencies around 70 Hz. These beating frequencies can be produced by two tone complexes, one of which is kept constant over time, and the other is gradually shifted at different intervals along the octave. The two tone complexes sound together, and at each point in time the roughness can be calculated.

12.    In humans, evolution has allowed the capacity for fine-tuning after birth as well. Different stages can be distinguished in the ontogenesis of a person. For example, children are born with phylogenetically determined global functions that are refined during their lifetime. Vision and hearing in particular are tuned in the first months after birth. By the age of nine months, however, children are capable of social interaction. They "tune in" to the attention and behavior of adults toward outside entities. Over a period of about seventeen to eighteen years the human brain is fine-tuned to specific cultural habits and conventions, including the learning of advanced skills and adapted behavior (W. Singer, 2002).

# Chapter 4

1.    Ontology is here defined as the set of things that exist for a subject. The ontology is a memory framework, or repertoire, that functions as an action-based anticipatory and predictive model of physical reality. Henceforth, I call it an action-oriented ontology.

2.    From a historical point of view, they appeal to, for example, von Uexküll's (1909) notions of *Umwelt* and *Innenwelt*.

3.    In this framework, action is defined as an intended movement or sequence of elementary movements.

4.    This statement should be read with caution. There are indeed efferent processes operative in our sensory organs. In the human ear, for example, the outer hair cells are mechanical filters, acting as small muscles, that modify the sensitivity of our hearing (Dallos and Evans, 1995). But obviously this motility is not what we could call an action.

5.    I owe much to the insights of Jan L. Broeckx, my former teacher and mentor, especially the theory of expressive meaning formation, which he formulated in his book on musical ratio and affect in 1981. The full impact of that work was never so clear to me as during the writing of this book. Cast in the language of today, the theory leans close to a sensorimotor theory of musical expressiveness, although the focus on conceptualization (and thus verbal description) remains quite strong. Broeckx's book was published in Flemish; a colloquium on it, held in 1983, was published in Sabbe et al. (1986).

6.    The cenesthetic process is related to Damasio's (1999) notion of feeling, as well as to the notion of somatognosis. It is based on a kind of awareness that gives bodily experiences a basis for expression and linguistic description. If properly encoded by the sender, it can be properly decoded by the receiver, on the assumption that some of these multimodal and kinesthetic experiences are shared.

## Chapter 5

1.    Mirroring and imitation are related but separate concepts. Imitation involves the activation of both a mirroring system (motor resonance) and a goal-planning and motor execution system (Leslie et al., 2004).

2.    In this reference, the *Poetics* is translated by I. Bywater.

3.    Visalberghi and Fragaszy (2002) studied capuchin monkeys but concluded that for that species there is no evidence of imitative learning: the potential learners did not behave as if they regarded the observed actions as relevant to their own activities (p. 476). Overall, it seems that chimpanzees are better than capuchin monkeys at noticing and reproducing human actions and movements of objects. Herman (2002) provides evidence that dolphins have a highly flexible capability for imitative acts that extend over a broad range of behaviors and contexts.

4.    For more than thirty years, my parents-in-law had a parrot called Frits. One of his sentences in the local dialect of West Flanders was "k'e no heen nootje hed" (literally, "I didn't got a nut yet"). When he said this, I was quite convinced that he wanted a nut, and he often got one. But obviously, he would not have changed the grammatical structure of the sentence in order to achieve his goal! Nor would he have exchanged the word "nut" for "apple." See Pepperberg (2002) for studies on parrots.

5.    Aristotle says that learning gives the liveliest pleasure "not only to philosophers but to men in general, whose capacity, however, of learning is more limited."

6.     Mirroring is a central given of the imitation mechanism, and obviously it plays an important role in music education. Dr. Z. Juhash of the Hungarian Academy (personal communication, summer 2004) told me that a blind person who learned to play folk music on the flute had experienced difficulties in reproducing certain timbres because they depend on a particular position of the flute in the mouth. When you see the gesture, imitation is straightforward, but it is very difficult to grasp the technique when you just hear the sound or when you have to verbally explain what is happening.

7.     See the example of Beethoven's music in figure 1.2, where the motif of the right hand is imitated with delay in the left hand (first four measures of the motif).

8.     This can be seen in singing contests (e.g., *Pop Idol 2004*) produced by many European television stations.

9.     If possible, examples will be given from ongoing research in my own laboratory.

10.     A beat is defined as the subjective tapping to the musical pulse, and is part of a larger sequential structure. Meter refers to a level at which beats are structured, for example, into groups of two or three. Tempo is expressed as the number of beats per minute. A rhythm, then, can be defined as a pattern that evokes a sense of pulse. As in pitch perception, rhythm perception involves the induction of subjective responses to certain acoustical properties of the music.

11.     In a survey carried out at IPEM, more than 95 percent of 750 subjects reported moving along with music when they listened (Lesaffre, 2005).

12.     However, see Epstein (1995).

13.     For a critique of the probe-tone technique, see Auhagen and Vos (2000) and Leman (2000).

14.     Janata et al. (2002) introduced a methodology for continuous measurement of tonality, although that method was designed for measuring brain activity.

15.     These models were provided by B. Catteau, and T. De Mulder (Ghent University).

16.     The correlation with the profiles of Krumhansl and Kessler (shown in figure 5.2) is 0.94 for major, and 0.89 for minor.

17.     This contour was extracted using the MAMI melody transcriber, and then low-pass filtered.

18.     Data from Leman et al. (2005) were taken as reference.

19.     Empathy is different from sympathy, which is more a matter of agreement with the emotions of the other. Empathy would assume that the subject has an understanding of the emotions of the other.

20.     Both types of pleasure have an obvious appeal to music, but the *aha* experience is clearly more cerebral and symbol-oriented. The recognition of a

particular musical style, say "the musette-like sixteenth-note swirls" as an exemplification of "the pastoral style," may give pleasure to a listener who is focused on cerebral symbolic signification practices. The *aha* experience would be based on the sudden insight that "the musette-like sixteenth-note swirls" stand for "the pastoral style." The *aha* experience in music is probably similar to the *aha* which is experienced upon finding a solution to a mathematical problem. It has a cognitive basis and is linked with symbolic signification. However, the identification of the subject's self with the music's moving sonic forms, through corporeal attuning, can be seen as a far more musical—and physical—process. It pertains to the act of putting oneself in place of the other—like mind-reading, but with corporeal means; like being engaged with another human, but instead of a human, the subject attunes to moving sonic forms.

21.    See also section 6.2.4, and figures 6.6 and 6.8.

22.    Associated with this theory, Aristotle introduces a more restricted theory saying that musical modes such as the Mixolydian, Dorian, and Phrygian, give rise to the perception of a particular affect. In much the same way, a rhythm can have a character of rest; others, of motion; still others can be vulgar or noble. The connection of musical modes with affects or character is more abstract, however, in that it limits imitation to standard forms.

23.    See, e.g., Baker and Scruton (1995) and Gerhard and De la Motte-Haber (1994) for a brief historical overview and introduction to musical expression.

24.    The cent scale divides the octave into 1200 equal intervals. One semitone is then exactly 100 cents (see Loy, 2006, p. 45).

# Chapter 6

1.    Todd and Cody (2000) explain this phenomenon by linking it to human physiology. More particularly, they found evidence for the hypothesis that sound intensity has a direct physical and pleasurable effect on vestibular responses, especially when sound intensities are above 90 dBA SPL. A pleasurable feeling in response to loud music is mediated by mechanisms that induce sensations of self-motion in a primitive central pathway in the brain. In other words, there may be a physiological explanation for the fact that sound intensity has more impact on the listener, and that this physiological explanation is clearly related to pleasurable effects on self-movement.

2.    The distinction between acoustic musical instruments, electronic musical instruments, and multimedia environments and platforms may need further explanation. A platform is a set of system components that can be configured in a particular way, resulting in a particular music interaction system, such as an instrument or an environment. An electronic musical instrument can be conceived of as an extension of the ergonomics of an acoustic musical instrument in the electronic domain. Sometimes these instruments are called hyperinstruments because they enhance acoustic instruments using electronic technology (e.g., Machover and Chung, 1989; Paradiso, 1999). An electronic musical environment draws upon concepts of autonomous processing. Here, the focus is more

on the development of independent agents that interact with humans, giving rise to virtual music environments or *mixed-reality* environments for music (Camurri and Leman, 1997a, 1997b; Camurri and Ferrentino, 1999; Ungvary and Vertegaal, 2000; Arfib, 2002; Paradiso and O'Modhrain, 2003; Johannsen, 2004).

3.    In these approaches, expressive performances have often been measured with respect to purely structural configuration, the so-called neutral level, with flat (or quantized) timing, articulation, and loudness. For measurement purposes, performers were asked to play a score with different expressive qualities, such as neutral, happy, sad, anger, tender, hard, light, or heavy. Then the different cues (e.g., related to timing, pitch, articulation, and timbre) were extracted from the recorded stimuli. For each expressive quality, cues were compared with the neutral level and a set of deviations was calculated.

4.    The Chinese tradition contains eight basic techniques for plucking the string, and four basic techniques for manipulating the pitch. The plucking techniques largely define the gestures related to attack and timbre, while the sliding techniques largely define the gestures related to pitch. In addition, it has been pointed out that the playing indications for the right hand follow mainly visual and motor cues, while the playing indications for the left hand are mainly tactile and auditory.

5.    The kinematic data of the player were recorded by means of a seven-camera infrared motion capture system (Qualysis, Sweden) at a sampling frequency of 100 Hz. I thank my colleagues M. Lenoir and P. Van Cleven at the Laboratory for Movement Studies at Ghent University for their assistance in recording, as well as H. Li for playing the *guqin*.

6.    In Chinese, this finger is called *ming* finger.

7.    At points where the velocity is zero, the marker is not moving and it can be assumed that these points mark the beginning (point A) or ending (point B) of an elementary movement.

8.    The last two notes (19, 20) are not taken into account because they were played to end the musical fragment in a proper way. They do not form part of the original piece.

9.    It may be straightforward to link the movements of *guqin* playing with the movements of tai chi, as well as movements of Chinese calligraphy.

10.    See also section 5.2.3, where music-driven embodied attuning is related to issues in social music cognition.

11.    Reference is made to the Multisensory Expressive Gesture Applications (MEGA) project. In this project, EyesWeb was developed as a software platform to which different hardware and software modules could be connected. (See http://www.eyesweb.org.) Public demonstrations have been given at Genoa, Venice, Padua, Vicenza, Stockholm, Ghent, Bruges, Amsterdam, Zurich, Neufchatel, London, and other places in Europe. (See http://www.megaproject.org.)

12.    Also, Pollick et al. (2001) conclude that activity is more easily predicted than valence. They analyzed the recognition of emotion in human movement

and found significant correlations between motion kinematics (particularly velocity) and the activation axis (greater velocity goes with more activation).

## Chapter 7

1.     Note that metadata search (based on title, composer, year, and so on) is
omitted from this picture. This is mainly for reasons of clarity, because content-
based music retrieval systems obviously include metadata searches. In the present
chapter, metadata will not be dealt with in much detail.

2.     The numbers refer to the parts of figure 7.1.

3.     It is assumed that musicology may play a important role here. As shown
later on, musicology may provide the annotations that are necessary for building
connections between subjective descriptions and physical energy. The rationale is
that humans de facto are able to connect physical energy with their subjective
ontology. This connection should be mapped out and the knowledge should be
implemented in a machine, using empirical and advanced statistical modeling
techniques.

4.     For technical and mathematical details concerning the design and implementation of music search-and-retrieval systems, as well as pattern-matching
techniques, see the proceedings of the ISMIR conferences at http://www.ismir.net.

5.     Less attention will be devoted to extramusical symbolic/linguistic descriptions and to graphic/symbolic descriptions, as well as to genre and style
descriptions.

6.     This set was collected in the following way. Subjects sat in front of a computer monitor on which a list of titles of popular music was displayed. Subjects
were asked to indicate whether they knew the song, and, if they knew it, whether
they would be able to replicate the song or recall its musical content. If they were
able to recall the song, the response was recorded and stored. If the subject could
not recall the song, he or she was first requested to listen to the entire piece. Then
the subject was asked whether the song was known and, if known, to imitate it.
In short, the first study probed long-term delayed imitation of melodies, while the
second study probed the short-term delayed imitation of melodies. The imitation
task drew on skills that involve voluntary music production. The imitation was
evoked on a quasi-spontaneous basis. That is, subjects were presented with a list
of titles and were given the task of formulating queries for those titles they knew.
In this study, 72 subjects were involved and produced 1148 vocal queries related
to 30 titles of pieces.

7.     This figure can be combined with other graphical representations related to
valence and activity, such as those in table 7.9 and figure 7.3.

8.     This taxonomy is based on the taxonomy used in the IPEM Toolbox (see
www.ipem.ugent.be/Toolbox). See also Lesaffre et al. (2003) and Lesaffre (2005).

9.     Friberg and Sundberg (1999) compared the anatomy of the final *ritardando* in classical music with the stopping or running of a human body. The re-

sult revealed a striking similarity between musical tempo curve and locomotion. The slowing of the tempo in final *ritardando* and decrease of velocity in aesthetically pleasing stopping of running followed almost exactly the same curve. Other studies have extended this idea by comparing tone sequences and walking or dancing (Friberg et al., 2000). In addition, evidence has been provided to show that emotional intentions can be conveyed through visual perception of the musicians' movements (Dahl and Friberg, in press); hence there are cues in expressive movements that strongly resemble the audio cues.

10.    Reference can be made to the work of Eitan and Granot (2004), who investigated whether changes in a structural parameter agree with changes in a synesthetic/kinesthetic parameter. More specifically, they investigated whether changes in interonset intervals (tempo), in pitch height, and in loudness would correspond to changes in speed, spatial vertical direction, impression of motion, and distance and energy. The underlying hypothesis was that if the human body attunes to music, then changing the parameters to which it attunes should have an effect on the attuning itself. For example, increase of intensity in interonset intervals should be reflected by an increase in some parameter of the corporeal articulation, which would be sensed and translated into motion-related terms. It was found that the mapping of musical syntax with motion description may be far more complex than was hitherto assumed. Listeners who associate a musical stimulus with a particular kinetic quality often do not associate the inverse stimulus with the opposite kinetic quality. Instead, opposite structural features seem to correspond to different parameters of motion perception. For example, diminuendo gives the impression of descending, and crescendo gives the impression of speeding up. While this might be an unexpected result at first hearing, it shows that more empirical research on the relationship between structural descriptions and synesthetic/kinesthetic descriptions is needed. Such research not only fits the paradigm of corporeal articulations, as explained in chapter 6, it also contributes to the specification of constraints of querying systems for content-based search for and retrieval of music.

11.    While this distinction is prominent in emotion research, it is also relevant to the discussion of motor movement. Also there, the distinction can be made between motor experience as such and description of this experience. The motor system has the ability to simulate because processing of movement can take place until a late stage at which the output is inhibited. According to the above theory, motor activity is a pre-stage of emotional involvement. But emotional involvement also involves physiological arousal. Emotional simulation would imply that the emotional system is not involved, but that the motor system, which normally connects to the emotive system, is active.

12.    See also the discussion in section 6.4.3.

13.    See Juslin (2001) for a similar attempt.

14.    As mentioned before, many terms (such as *bored*) shown in figure 7.3 are more difficult to interpret as descriptors of music because they focus fundamentally on the interest of the subject.

15.    This is clearly a type of transitivity different from the one discussed in section 5.3.

16.    In music information-retrieval systems, the similarity among melodies is often based on string editing. A string is here understood as a series of notes. In string editing, one string is adapted to another string, using editing operations. Each editing operation on the string, such as the addition or deletion of a note, is associated with a cost function. The literature on melodic similarity is quite elaborate (see, e.g., Hewlett and Selfridge-Field, 1998; Meredith et al., 2002; Wiering et al., 2004; Müllensiefen and Frieler, 2004).

17.    It is very unlikely that the waveform of a given audio query would ever match the waveform of a target audio file in the database exactly. Even if the target audio file were an exact replica of the query, such a calculation would quickly become too time-consuming and impractical. Linguistic queries, on the other hand, are not connected to audio targets, and without proper processing of both the linguistic terms and the audio, it will never be possible to match the two types of description. Similarly, motor behavior traced as a signal needs further processing in order to be useful. Clearly, to some extent the content of target files can be preprocessed in the sense that they can be tagged with audio-structural descriptors, motor cues, and even linguistic descriptors. It should be taken into account that many aspects of query-processing depend on whether target audio files have been preprocessed or not. If they have been preprocessed, several cues are already stored in the database, so that search and retrieval may be based on standard database retrieval techniques. However, if target files have not been preprocessed in detail, then the burden is in the available data-mining techniques of query-processing.

18.    In practice, this schema involves advanced methods based on probabilistic theory and statistics (e.g., hidden Markov models, Bayesian models, and support vector machines; Duda et al., 2001).

19.    Further examples of music information retrieval systems can be found at http://www.ismir.net/all-papers.html. Apart from the part on audio identification, I restrict myself here basically to work that has been done at my laboratory. See also Klapuri and Davy (2006).

20.    Fingerprinting works on the basis of extracting low-level acoustical features from musical audio (Gomes et al., 2003; Haitsma and Kalker, 2003). Most techniques use Mel-Frequency Cepstral Coefficients (MFCCs), but additional features based, for example, on sharpness or spectral flatness, can be used. Derived quantities such as derivatives, means, and variances of audio features also are used. Generally the extracted features are mapped into a more compact representation by using classification algorithms (Allamanche et al., 2001).

21.    The vocal queries were recorded during a musical querying experiment (see section 7.2.2).

22.    This example is taken from the collection of the Africa Museum, Tervuren, Belgium.

# References

Allamanche, E., Herre, J., Helmuth, O., Fröba, B., Kasten, T., & Cremer, M. (2001). Content-based identification of audio material using MPEG-7 low level description. In *Proceedings of the ISMIR 2001*. Bloomington: Indiana University Press.

Allanbrook, W. J. (1983). *Rhythmic Gesture in Mozart: Le Nozze di Figaro and Don Giovanni*. Chicago: University of Chicago Press.

Altenmüller, E. (2003). Focal dystonia: Advances in brain imaging and understanding of fine motor control in musicians. *Hand Clinics, 19*(3), 523–538.

Ames, C. (1992). AI and music. In *Encyclopedia of Artificial Intelligence*. New York: Wiley.

Anisfeld, M. (1996). Only tongue protrusion modeling is matched by neonates. *Developmental Review, 16*(2), 149–161.

Arfib, D. (Ed.). (2002). *Digital Audio Effects*. Special issue of *Journal of New Music Research, 31*. Lisse, The Netherlands: Swets & Zeitlinger.

Aristotle. (2001). *The Basic Works of Aristotle*, R. P. McKeon (Ed.). New York: Modern Library.

Auhagen, W., & Vos, P. G. (2000). Experimental methods in tonality induction research: A review. *Music Perception, 17*(4), 417–436.

Bader, R. (2005). *Computational Mechanics of the Classical Guitar*. Berlin: Springer.

Baker, N. K., & Scruton, R. (1995). Expression. In S. Sadie (Ed.), *The New Grove Dictionary of Music and Musicians* (vol. 6, pp. 324–332). London: Macmillan.

Balaban, M., Ebcioğlu, K., & Laske, O. E. (Eds.). (1992). *Understanding Music with AI: Perspectives on Music Cognition*. Cambridge, MA: AAAI Press/MIT Press.

Balkwill, L.-L., & Thompson, W. F. (1999). A cross-cultural investigation of the perception of emotion in music: Psychophysical and cultural cues. *Music Perception, 17*, 43–64.

Bargh, J. A., & Chartrand, T. L. (1999). The unbearable automaticity of being. *American Psychologist*, *54*(7), 462–479.

Barker, A. (Ed.). (1984–1989). *Greek Musical Writings*. 2 vols. Cambridge: Cambridge University Press.

Baroni, M., & Callegari, L. (Eds.). (1984). *Musical Grammars and Computer Analysis*. Florence: Olschki.

Becking, G. (1928). *Der musikalische Rhythmus als Erkenntnisquelle*. Augsburg: Filser.

Bekkering, H., Wohlschläger, A., & Gattis, M. (2000). Imitation of gestures in children is goal-directed. *Quarterly Journal of Experimental Psychology, A: Human Experimental Psychology*, *53*(1), 153–164.

Bengtsson, I. (1973). Verstehen: Prolegomena zu einem semiotisch-hermeneutischen Ansatz. In P. Faltin & H.-P. Reinecke (Eds.), *Musik und Verstehen: Aufsätze zur semiotischen Theorie, Ästhetik und Soziologie der musikalischen Rezeption*. Cologne: Volk.

Berenzweig, A., Logan, B., Ellis, D. P. W., & Whitman, B. (2004). A large-scale evaluation of acoustic and subjective music-similarity measures. *Computer Music Journal*, *28*(2), 63–76.

Berlyne, D. E. (1971). *Aesthetics and Psychobiology*. New York: Appleton-Century-Crofts.

Berthoz, A. (1997). *Le Sens du mouvement*. Paris: O. Jacob.

Berthoz, A., & Jorland, G. (Eds.). (2004). *L'Empathie*. Paris: Jacob.

Bigand, E. (2003). Tonal pitch space. *Musicae Scientiae*, *7*(1), 121–140.

Bigand, E., Poulin, B., Tillmann, B., Madurell, F., & D'Adamo, D. A. (2003). Sensory versus cognitive components in harmonic priming. *Journal of Experimental Psychology: Human Perception and Performance*, *29*(1), 159–171.

Blakemore, S. J., Bristow, D., Bird, G., Frith, C., & Ward, J. (2005). Somatosensory activations during the observation of touch and a case of vision–touch synaesthesia. *Brain*, *128*, 1571–1583.

Bonabeau, E., & Theraulaz, G. (1997). Auto-organisation et comportements collectifs: La Modélisation des sociétés d'insectes. In G. Theraulaz & F. Spitz (Eds.), *Auto-organisation et comportement* (pp. 91–104). Paris: Hermès.

Bonnel, A., Mottron, L., Peretz, I., Trudel, M., Gallun, E., & Bonnel, A. M. (2003). Enhanced pitch sensitivity in individuals with autism: A signal detection analysis. *Journal of Cognitive Neuroscience*, *15*(2), 226–235.

Bregman, A. S. (1990). *Auditory Scene Analysis: The Perceptual Organization of Sound*. Cambridge, MA: MIT Press.

Brentano, F. (1874/1955). *Psychologie vom empirischen Standpunkt*. Hamburg: Meiner.

Bresin, R. (1998). Artificial neural networks-based models for automatic performance of musical scores. *Journal of New Music Research*, 27(3), 239–270.

Bresin, R., & Battel, G. U. (2000). Articulation strategies in expressive piano performance: Analysis of legato, staccato, and repeated notes in performances of the andante movement of Mozart's Sonata in G major (K. 545). *Journal of New Music Research*, 29(3), 211–224.

Bresin, R., & Friberg, A. (2000). Emotional coloring of computer-controlled music performances. *Computer Music Journal*, 24(4), 44–63.

Broeckx, J. L. (1981). *Muziek, ratio en affect: Over de wisselwerking van rationeel denken en affectief beleven bij voortbrengst en ontvangst van muziek*. Antwerp: Metropolis.

Brunswik, E. (1956). *Perception and the Representative Design of Psychological Experiments* (2nd ed., rev. and enl.). Berkeley: University of California Press.

Buccino, G., Vogt, S., Ritzl, A., Fink, G. R., Zilles, K., Freund, H. J., et al. (2004). Neural circuits underlying imitation learning of hand actions: An event-related fMRI study. *Neuron*, 42(2), 323–334.

Budd, M. (1992). *Music and the Emotions: The Philosophical Theories*. London: Routledge.

Byrd, D., & Crawford, T. (2002). Problems of music information retrieval in the real world. *Information Processing & Management*, 38(2), 249–272.

Byrne, R. W., & Russon, A. E. (1998). Learning by imitation: A hierarchical approach. *Behavioral and Brain Sciences*, 21(5), 667–684.

Calvo-Merino, B., Glaser, D., Grèzes, J., Passingham, R., & Haggard, P. (2005). Action observation and acquired motor skills: An fMRI study with expert dancers. *Cerebral Cortex*, 15, 1243–1249.

Camurri, A., Coletta, P., Ricchetti, M., & Volpe, G. (2000). Expressiveness and physicality in interaction. *Journal of New Music Research*, 29(3), 187–198.

Camurri, A., De Poli, G., Friberg, A., Leman, M., & Volpe, G. (2005). The MEGA project: Analysis and synthesis of multisensory expressive gesture in performing art applications. *Journal of New Music Research*, 34(1), 5–21.

Camurri, A., De Poli, G., Leman, M., & Volpe, G. (2001). A multi-layered conceptual framework for expressive gesture applications. In C. Buyoli & R. Loureiro, *Proceedings Workshop on Current Research Directions in Computer Music*. Barcelona: Audiovisual Institute, Univ Pompeu Fabra.

Camurri, A., & Ferrentino, P. (1999). Interactive environments for music and multimedia. *Multimedia Systems*, 7(1), 32–47.

Camurri, A., Lagerlöf, I., & Volpe, G. (2003). Recognizing emotion from dance movement: Comparison of spectator recognition and automated techniques. *International Journal of Human–Computer Studies*, 59(1–2), 213–225.

Camurri, A., & Leman, M. (1997a). AI-based music signal applications. In C. Roads, G. De Poli, S. Pope, & A. Piccialli (Eds.), *Musical Signal Processing.* Lisse, The Netherlands: Swets & Zeitlinger.

Camurri, A., & Leman, M. (1997b). Gestalt-based composition and performance in multimodal environments. In M. Leman (Ed.), *Music, Gestalt, and Computing: Studies in Cognitive and Systematic Musicology* (pp. 495–508). Berlin: Springer.

Camurri, A., Mazzarino, B., Ricchetti, M., Timmers, R., & Volpe, G. (2004a). Multimodal analysis of expressive gesture in music and dance performances. In A. Camurri & G. Volpe (Eds.), *Gesture-Based Communication in Human–Computer Interaction* (pp. 20–39). Berlin: Springer.

Camurri, A., Mazzarino, B., & Volpe, G. (2004b). Analysis of expressive gesture: The EyesWeb expressive gesture processing library. In A. Camurri & G. Volpe (Eds.), *Gesture-Based Communication in Human–Computer Interaction* (pp. 460–467). Berlin: Springer.

Camurri, A., Mazzarino, B., Volpe, G., Morasso, P., Priano, F., & Re, C. (2003). Application of multimedia techniques in the physical rehabilitation of Parkinson's patients. *Journal of Visualization and Computer Animation, 14*(5), 269–278.

Camurri, A., & Rikakis, T. (2004). Multisensory communication and experience through multimedia. *IEEE Multimedia, 11*(3), 17–19.

Camurri, A., & Volpe, G. (Eds.). (2004). *Gesture-Based Communication in Human–Computer Interaction.* Berlin: Springer.

Camurri, A., Volpe, G., De Poli, G., & Leman, M. (2005). Communicating expressiveness and affect in multimodal interactive systems. *IEEE Multimedia, 12*(1), 43–53.

Canazza, S., De Poli, G., Drioli, C., Roda, A., & Vidolin, A. (2000). Audio morphing different expressive intentions for multimedia systems. *IEEE Multimedia, 7*(3), 79–83.

Canazza, S., De Poli, G., Drioli, C., Roda, A., & Vidolin, A. (2004). Modeling and control of expressiveness in music performance. *Proceedings of the IEEE, 92*(4), 686–701.

Canazza, S., De Poli, G., Rinaldin, S., & Vidolin, A. (1997a). Sonological analysis of clarinet expressivity. In M. Leman (Ed.), *Music, Gestalt, and Computing: Studies in Cognitive and Systematic Musicology.* Berlin: Springer.

Canazza, S., De Poli, G., Roda, A., & Vidolin, A. (2003). An abstract control space for communication of sensory expressive intentions in music performance. *Journal of New Music Research, 32*(3), 281–294.

Canazza, S., De Poli, G., & Vidolin, A. (1997b). Perceptual analysis of the musical expressive intention in a clarinet performance. In M. Leman (Ed.), *Music, Gestalt, and Computing: Studies in Cognitive and Systematic Musicology.* Berlin: Springer.

Capps, L., Yirmiya, N., & Sigman, M. (1992). Understanding of simple and complex emotions in nonretarded children with autism. *Journal of Child Psychology and Psychiatry and Allied Disciplines*, *33*(7), 1169–1182.

Carr, L., Iacoboni, M., Dubeau, M. C., Mazziotta, J. C., & Lenzi, G. L. (2003). Neural mechanisms of empathy in humans: A relay from neural systems for imitation to limbic areas. *Proceedings of the National Academy of Sciences of the United States of America*, *100*(9), 5497–5502.

Chalmers, D. (2004). How can we construct a science of consciousness? In M. Gazzaniga (Ed.), *The Cognitive Neurosciences* (3rd ed.). Cambridge, MA: MIT Press.

Chu, L. (1996). Haptic feedback in computer music performance. In *Proceedings of ICMC '96* (pp. 57–58). Hong Kong: ICMA.

Clarke, E. F. (1989). The perception of expressive timing in music. *Psychological Research—Psychologische Forschung*, *51*(1), 2–9.

Clayton, M., Sager, R., & Will, U. (2004). In time with the music: The concept of entrainment and its significance for ethnomusicology. *ESEM CounterPoint*, *1*, 1–82.

Clynes, M. (1977). *Sentics: The Touch of Emotions*. Garden City, NY: Anchor Press.

Clynes, M. (1995). Microstructural musical linguistics: Composers' pulses are liked most by the best musicians. *Cognition*, *55*(3), 269–310.

Cohen, H. F. (1984). *Quantifying Music: The Science of Music at the First Stage of the Scientific Revolution, 1580–1650*. Dordrecht: Reidel.

Cowie, R., Douglas-Cowie, E., Tsapatsoulis, N., Votsis, G., Kollias, S., Fellenz, W., et al. (2001). Emotion recognition in human–computer interaction. *IEEE Signal Processing Magazine*, *18*(1), 32–80.

Csikszentmihalyi, M. (1990). *Flow: The Psychology of Optimal Experience*. New York: Harper & Row.

Csikszentmihalyi, M. (1999). If we are so rich, why aren't we happy? *American Psychologist*, *54*(10), 821–827.

Csikszentmihalyi, M., & Csikszentmihalyi, I. S. (Eds.). (1988). *Optimal Experience: Psychological Studies of Flow in Consciousness*. New York: Cambridge University Press.

Cumming, N. (2000). *The Sonic Self: Musical Subjectivity and Signification*. Bloomington: Indiana University Press.

Cytowic, R. E. (1989). *Synesthesia: A Union of the Senses*. New York: Springer.

Dahl, S., & Friberg, A. (in press). Visual perception of expressiveness in musicians' body movements. *Music Perception*.

Dallos, P., & Evans, B. N. (1995). High-frequency motility of outer hair-cells and the cochlear amplifier. *Science*, *267*(5206), 2006–2009.

Damasio, A. R. (2000). *The Feeling of What Happens: Body and Emotion in the Making of Consciousness*. New York: Harcourt Brace.

Dannenberg, R., & De Poli, G. (Eds.). (1998). *Synthesis of Performance Nuance*. Special issue of *Journal of New Music Research*. The Netherlands: Lisse, Swets & Zeitlinger.

Dautenhahn, K., & Nehaniv, C. L. (Eds.). (2002). *Imitation in Animals and Artifacts*. Cambridge, MA: MIT press.

De Bruyn, L. (2005). Een muziekpsychologische en empirische studie naar muziekempathie bij mensen met een autismespectrumstoornis. Thesis, Ghent University.

De Bruyn, L. and Leman, M. (submitted). Testing musical empathy in subjects with an autism spectrum disorder.

De Mulder, T., Martens, J.-P., Lesaffre, M., Leman, M., De Baets, B., & De Meyer, H. (2004). Recent improvements of an auditory model based front-end for the transcription of vocal queries. In *IEEE International Conference on Speech, Acoustics, and Signal Processing (ICASSP 2004)*. Philadelphia: ICASSP.

De Mulder, T., Martens, J.-P., Pauws, S., Vignoli, F., Lesaffre, M., Leman, M., et al. (2006). Factors affecting the music retrieval in query-by-melody. *IEEE Transactions on Multimedia*, *8*(4), 728–739.

De Poli, G. (2004). Methodologies for expressiveness modelling of and for music performance. *Journal of New Music Research*, *33*(3), 189–202.

Decety, J., & Grèzes, J. (2006). The power of simulation: Imagining one's own and others' behavior. *Brain Research*, *1079*, 4–14.

Decety, J., & Jackson, P. L. (2004). The functional architecture of human empathy. *Behavioral and Cognitive Neuroscience Reviews*, *3*(2), 71–100.

Decety, J., & Jackson, P. L. (2006). A social-neuroscience perspective on empathy. *Current Directions in Psychological Science*, *15*(2), 54–58.

Degroeve, S., Tanghe, K., De Baets, B., Leman, M., & Martens, J.-P. (2005). A simulated annealing optimization of audio features for drum classification. In J. D. Reiss & G. A. Wiggins (Eds.), *Proceedings of the Sixth International Conference on Music Information Retrieval*. London: Queen Mary, University of London.

Desain, P., & Windsor, L. (Eds.). (2000). *Rhythm Perception and Production*. Lisse, The Netherlands: Swets & Zeitlinger.

Di Scipio, A. (2003). Sound is the interface: Sketches of a constructivistic ecosystemic view of interactive signal processing. In *Proceedings of the Colloquium on Musical Informatics, Firenze 8–10 May 2003*. Florence: Centro Tempo Reale.

Dibben, N. (2004). The role of peripheral feedback in emotional experience with music. *Music Perception*, *22*(1), 79–115.

Donald, M. (1991). *Origins of the Modern Mind: Three Stages in the Evolution of Culture and Cognition*. Cambridge, MA: Harvard University Press.

Dourish, P. (2001). *Where the Action Is: The Foundations of Embodied Interaction*. Cambridge, MA: MIT Press.

Downie, J. S. (2003). Music information retrieval. *Annual Review of Information Science and Technology*, 37, 295–340.

Downie, J. S. (2004). The scientific evaluation of music information retrieval systems: Foundations and future. *Computer Music Journal*, 28(2), 12–23.

Duda, R. O., Hart, P. E., & Stork, D. G. (2001). *Pattern Classification* (2nd ed.). New York: Wiley.

Eggebrecht, H. (1973). Über begriffliches und begriffsloses Verstehen von Musik. In P. Faltin & H.-P. Reinecke (Eds.), *Musik und Verstehen: Aufsätze zur semiotischen Theorie, Ästhetik und Soziologie der musikalischen Rezeption*. Cologne: Volk.

Eitan, Z., & Granot, R. Y. (2004). Musical parameters and images of motion. In R. Parncutt, A. Kessler, & F. Zimmer (Eds.), *Proceedings of the Conference on Interdisciplinary Musicology (CIM04)*. Graz, Austria: Graz University.

Elschek, O. (1992). *Die Musikforschung der Gegenwart: Ihre Systematik, Theorie und Entwicklung*. Vienna-Föhrenau: Stiglmayr.

Epstein, D. (1995). *Shaping Time: Music, the Brain, and Performance*. New York: Schirmer Books.

Erneling, C. E., & Johnson, D. M. (Eds.). (2005). *The Mind as a Scientific Object: Between Brain and Culture*. New York: Oxford University Press.

Ernst, M. O., & Bülthoff, H. H. (2004). Merging the senses into a robust percept. *Trends in Cognitive Sciences*, 8(4), 162–169.

Essens, P. J., & Povel, D. J. (1985). Metrical and nonmetrical representations of temporal patterns. *Perception & Psychophysics*, 37(1), 1–7.

Faith, M., & Thayer, J. F. (2001). A dynamical systems interpretation of a dimensional model of emotion. *Scandinavian Journal of Psychology*, 42(2), 121–133.

Faltin, P., & Reinecke, H.-P. (Eds.). (1973). *Musik und Verstehen: Aufsätze zur semiotischen Theorie, Ästhetik und Soziologie der musikalischen Rezeption*. Cologne: Volk.

Fels, S. (2004). Designing for intimacy: Creating new interfaces for musical expression. *Proceedings of the IEEE*, 92(4), 672–685.

Fitch, W. T. (2005). The evolution of language: A comparative review. *Biology & Philosophy*, 20(2–3), 193–230.

Fodor, J. A. (1981). *Representations: Philosophical Essays on the Foundations of Cognitive Science*. Cambridge, MA: MIT Press.

Fraisse, P. (1963). *The Psychology of Time*, Jennifer Leith (Trans.). New York: Harper & Row.

Fraisse, P. (1982). Rhythm and tempo. In D. Deutsch (Ed.), *The Psychology of Music* (pp. 149–180). New York: Academic Press.

Freeman, W. (2000). A neurobiological role of music in social bonding. In N. L. Wallin, B. Merker, & S. Brown (Eds.), *The Origins of Music*. Cambridge, MA: MIT Press.

Friberg, A. (2006). pDM: An expressive sequencer with real-time control of the KTH music-performance rules. *Computer Music Journal, 30*(1), 37–48.

Friberg, A., Bresin, R., Frydén, L., & Sundberg, J. (1998). Musical punctuation on the microlevel: Automatic identification and performance of small melodic units. *Journal of New Music Research, 27*(3), 271–292.

Friberg, A., Colombo, V., Frydén, L., & Sundberg, J. (2000). Generating musical performances with Director Musices. *Computer Music Journal, 24*(3), 23–29.

Friberg, A., & Sundberg, J. (1999). Does music performance allude to locomotion? A model of final ritardandi derived from measurements of stopping runners. *Journal of the Acoustical Society of America, 105*(3), 1469–1484.

Friberg, A., Sundberg, J., & Frydén, L. (2000). Music from motion: Sound level envelopes of tones expressing human locomotion. *Journal of New Music Research, 29*(3), 199–210.

Futrelle, J., & Downie, J. S. (2003). Interdisciplinary research issues in music information retrieval: ISMIR 2000–2002. *Journal of New Music Research, 32*(2), 121–131.

Gabrielsson, A., & Juslin, P. N. (2003). Emotional expression in music. In R. J. Davidson, K. R. Scherer, & H. H. Goldsmith (Eds.), *Handbook of Affective Sciences* (pp. 503–534). New York: Oxford University Press.

Gabrielsson, A., & Lindström, E. (2001). The influence of musical structure on emotional expression. In P. N. Juslin & J. A. Sloboda (Eds.), *Music and Emotion: Theory and Research*. New York: Oxford University Press.

Gallagher, S. (2000). Philosophical conceptions of the self: Implications for cognitive science. *Trends in Cognitive Sciences, 4*(1), 14–21.

Gallese, V. (2003). The roots of empathy: The shared manifold hypothesis and the neural basis of intersubjectivity. *Psychopathology, 36*(4), 171–180.

Gallese, V. (2006). Intentional attunement: A neurophysiological perspective on social cognition and its disruption in autism. *Brain Research, 1079*, 15–24.

Gallese, V., Fadiga, L., Fogassi, L., & Rizzolatti, G. (1996). Action recognition in the premotor cortex. *Brain, 119*, 593–609.

Gallese, V., & Goldman, A. (1998). Mirror neurons and the simulation theory of mind-reading. *Trends in Cognitive Sciences, 2*(12), 493–501.

Gallese, V., & Metzinger, T. (2003). Motor ontology: The representational reality of goals, actions and selves. *Philosophical Psychology, 16*(3), 365–388.

Gerhard, A., & De la Motte-Haber, H. (1994). Ausdruck. In L. Finscher (Ed.), *Die Musik der Geschichte und Gegenwart* (vol. 1, pp. 1043–1051). Kassel: Bärenreiter.

Gerson-Kiwi, E. (1995). Cheironomy. In S. Sadie (Ed.), *Grove Dictionary of Music and Musicians* (vol. 4, pp. 191–196). London: Macmillan.

Gibet, S., Kamp, J. F., & Poirier, F. (2003). Gesture analysis: Invariant laws in movement. In A. Camurri & G. Volpe (Eds.), *Gesture-Based Communication in Human–Computer Interaction* (pp. 1–9). Berlin: Springer.

Gibson, J. J. (1979). *The Ecological Approach to Visual Perception*. Boston: Houghton Mifflin.

Godøy, R. I. (2001). Imagined action, excitation, and resonance. In R. I. Godøy & H. Jørgensen (Eds.), *Musical Imagery* (pp. 237–250). Lisse, The Netherlands: Swets & Zeitlinger.

Godøy, R. I. (2003). Motor-mimetic music cognition. *Leonardo*, *36*(4), 317–319.

Godøy, R. I., Haga, E., & Jensenius, A. R. (2006). Playing "air instruments": Mimicry of sound-producing gestures by novices and experts. *Gesture in Human–Computer Interaction and Simulation*, *3881*, 256–267.

Gomes, L. D. T., Cano, P., Gómez, E., Bonnet, M., & Batlle, E. (2003). Audio watermarking and fingerprinting: For which applications? *Journal of New Music Research*, *32*(1), 65–81.

Gómez, E., & Bonada, J. (2005). Tonality visualization of polyphonic audio. In J. D. Reiss & G. A. Wiggins (Eds.), *Proceedings of the Sixth International Conference on Music Information Retrieval (ISMIR05)*. London: Queen Mary, University of London.

Gómez, E., Klapuri, A., & Meudic, B. (2003). Melody description and extraction in the context of music content processing. *Journal of New Music Research*, *32*(1), 23–40.

Gómez, P., & Danuser, B. (2004). Affective and physiological responses to environmental noises and music. *International Journal of Psychophysiology*, *53*(2), 91–103.

Gowensmith, W. N., & Bloom, L. J. (1997). The effects of heavy metal music on arousal and anger. *Journal of Music Therapy*, *34*(1), 33–45.

Grammer, K., Kruck, K., Juette, A., & Fink, B. (2000). Non-verbal behavior as courtship signals: The role of control and choice in selecting partners. *Evolution and Human Behavior*, *21*(6), 371–390.

Grammer, K., Kruck, K. B., & Magnusson, M. S. (1998). The courtship dance: Patterns of nonverbal synchronization in opposite-sex encounters. *Journal of Nonverbal Behavior*, *22*(1), 3–29.

Gregory, A. H. (1997). The roles of music in society: The ethnomusicological perspective. In D. J. Hargreaves & A. C. North (Eds.), *The Social Psychology of Music* (pp. 123–140). Oxford: Oxford University Press.

Gunther, E., & O'Modhrain, S. (2003). Cutaneous grooves: Composing for the sense of touch. *Journal of New Music Research*, 32(4), 369–381.

Haitsma, J., & Kalker, T. (2003). A highly robust audio fingerprinting system with an efficient search strategy. *Journal of New Music Research*, 32(2), 211–221.

Hanslick, E. (1891). *Vom Musikalisch-Schönen: Ein Beitrag zur Revision der Ästhetik der Tonkunst*. Leipzig: Barth.

Hargreaves, D. J., & North, A. C. (Eds.). (1997). *The Social Psychology of Music*. New York: Oxford University Press.

Hargreaves, D. J., & North, A. C. (1999). The functions of music in everyday life: Redefining the social in music psychology. *Psychology of Music*, 27(1), 71–83.

Haslinger, B., Erhard, P., Altenmüller, E., Schroeder, U., Boecker, H., & Ceballos-Baumann, A. O. (2005). Transmodal sensorimotor networks during action observation in professional pianists. *Journal of Cognitive Neuroscience*, 17(2), 282–293.

Hatten, R. S. (1994). *Musical Meaning in Beethoven: Markedness, Correlation, and Interpretation*. Bloomington: Indiana University Press.

Hatten, R. S. (2003). Thematic gestures, topics, and tropes. In E. Tarasti (Ed.), *Musical Semiotics Revisited* (pp. 80–91). Imatra: International Semiotics Institute.

Hawkins, J., & Blakeslee, S. (2004). *On Intelligence*. New York: Times Books.

Heaton, P., Hermelin, B., & Pring, L. (1998). Autism and pitch processing: A precursor for savant musical ability? *Music Perception*, 15(3), 291–305.

Heaton, P., Hermelin, B., & Pring, L. (1999). Can children with autistic spectrum disorders perceive affect in music? An experimental investigation. *Psychological Medicine*, 29(6), 1405–1410.

Heaton, P., Pring, L., & Hermelin, B. (2001). Musical processing in high functioning children with autism. *Biological Foundations of Music*, 930, 443–444.

Heinitz, W. (1931). *Strukturprobleme in primitiver Musik*. Hamburg: Friederichsen, de Gruyter.

Herman, L. M. (2002). Vocal, social, and self-imitation by bottlenosed dolphins. In K. Dautenhahn & C. L. Nehaniv (Eds.), *Imitation in Animals and Artifacts* (pp. 63–108). Cambridge, MA: MIT Press.

Hevner, K. (1936). Experimental studies of the elements of expression in music. *American Journal of Psychology*, 48, 246–248.

Hewlett, W. B., & Selfridge-Field, E. (Eds.). (1998). *Melodic Similarity: Concepts, Procedures, and Applications*. Cambridge, MA: MIT Press/Stanford, CA: CCARH, Stanford University.

Heylen, E. (2004). Een systematisch muziekwetenschappelijke, methodische en empirische studie naar tonaliteit. Thesis, Ghent University.

Heylen, E., Moelants, D., & Leman, M. (2006). Singing along with music to explore tonality. In M. Baroni, A. R. Addessi, R. Caterina, & M. Costa (Eds.), *9th International Conference on Music Perception and Cognition—6th Triennial Conference of the European Society for the Cognitive Sciences of Music*. Bologna: Alma Mater Studiorum, University of Bologna.

Hickok, G., Buchsbaum, B., Humphries, C., & Muftuler, T. (2003). Auditory–motor interaction revealed by fMRI: Speech, music, and working memory in area Spt. *Journal of Cognitive Neuroscience, 15*(5), 673–682.

Hommel, B., Musseler, J., Aschersleben, G., & Prinz, W. (2001). The theory of event coding (TEC): A framework for perception and action planning. *Behavioral and Brain Sciences, 24*(5), 849–878.

Howard, D. M., & Rimell, S. (2004). Real-time gesture-controlled physical modelling: Music synthesis with tactile feedback. *EURASIP Journal on Applied Signal Processing, 2004*(7), 1001–1006.

Iacoboni, M., Molnar-Szakacs, I., Gallese, V., Buccino, G., Mazziotta, J. C., & Rizzolatti, G. (2005). Grasping the intentions of others with one's own mirror neuron system. *PLoS Biology, 3*(3), 529–535.

Imberty, M. (1976). Signification and meaning in music. In *Monographies de Sémiologie et d'Analyses Musicales*. Montreal: Groupe de Recherches en Sémiologie Musicale, Faculté de Musique, Université de Montréal.

Jackson, P. L., & Decety, J. (2004). Motor cognition: A new paradigm to study self–other interactions. *Current Opinion in Neurobiology, 14*(2), 259–263.

Janata, P., Birk, J. L., Van Horn, J. D., Leman, M., Tillmann, B., & Bharucha, J. J. (2002). The cortical topography of tonal structures underlying Western music. *Science, 298*(5601), 2167–2170.

Jansen, E., & Povel, D. J. (2004). The processing of chords in tonal melodic sequences. *Journal of New Music Research, 33*(1), 31–48.

Jeannerod, M. (1994). The representing brain: Neural correlates of motor intention and imagery. *Behavioral and Brain Sciences, 17*(2), 187–202.

Jeannerod, M. (2002). *La Nature de l'esprit: Sciences cognitives et cerveau*. Paris: Jacob.

Jeannerod, M. (2003). The mechanism of self-recognition in humans. *Behavioural Brain Research, 142*(1–2), 1–15.

Johannsen, G. (Ed.). (2002). *Human Supervision and Control in Engineering and Music*. Special issue of *Journal of New Music Research*, vol. 31. Lisse, The Netherlands: Swets & Zeitlinger.

Johannsen, G. (Ed.). (2004). *Engineering and Music: Supervisory Control and Auditory Communication*. Special issue of *Proceedings of the IEEE*, 92.

Jourdain, R. (1997). *Music, the Brain, and Ecstasy: How Music Captures Our Imagination*. New York: Morrow.

Juslin, P. N. (1997). Emotional communication in music performance: A functionalist perspective and some data. *Music Perception, 14*(4), 383–418.

Juslin, P. N. (2001a). A Brunswikian approach to emotional communication in music performance. In K. R. Hammond & T. R. Stewart (Eds.), *The Essential Brunswik: Beginnings, Explications, Applications* (pp. 426–430). New York: Oxford University Press.

Juslin, P. N. (2001b). Communicating emotion in music performance: A review and a theoretical framework. In P. N. Juslin & J. A. Sloboda (Eds.), *Music and Emotion: Theory and Research*. New York: Oxford University Press.

Juslin, P. N., Friberg, A., & Bresin, R. (2002). Toward a computational model of expression in performance: The GERM model. *Musicae Scientiae*, 63–122. Special issue 2001–2002.

Juslin, P. N. & Laukka, P. (2003). Communication of emotions in vocal expression and music performance: Different channels, same code? *Psychological Bulletin, 129*(5), 770–814.

Juslin, P. N., & Sloboda, J. A. (Eds.). (2001). *Music and Emotion: Theory and Research*. New York: Oxford University Press.

Kant, I. (1790/1948). *Kritik der Urteilskraft* (6th printing of 1924 ed.). Leipzig: F. Meiner.

Kapur, A., Essl, G., Davidson, P., & Cook, P. R. (2003). The electronic tabla controller. *Journal of New Music Research, 32*(4), 351–359.

Karjalainen, M., Mäki-Patola, T., Kanerva, A., Huovilainen, A., & Jänis, P. (2004). Virtual air guitar. In *Proceedings of the 117th Audio Engineering Society Convention*. New York: AES.

Karjalainen, M., Tolonen, T., Välimäki, V., Erkut, C., Laurson, M., & Hiipakka, J. (2001). An overview of new techniques and effects in model-based sound synthesis. *Journal of New Music Research, 30*(3), 203–212.

Kinsbourne, M. (2002). The role of imitation in body ownership and mental growth. In A. N. Meltzoff & W. Prinz (Eds.), *The Imitative Mind: Development, Evolution, and Brain Basis* (pp. 311–327). Cambridge: Cambridge University Press.

Kirlik, A., & Maruyama, S. (2004). Human–technology interaction and music perception and performance: Toward the robust design of sociotechnical systems. *Proceedings of the IEEE, 92*(4), 616–631.

Kivy, P. (1980). *The Corded Shell: Reflections on Musical Expression*. Princeton, NJ: Princeton University Press.

Kivy, P. (2001). *New Essays on Musical Understanding*. Oxford: Clarendon Press.

Klapuri, A. P. (2003). Multiple fundamental frequency estimation based on harmonicity and spectral smoothness. *IEEE Transactions on Speech and Audio Processing*, *11*(6), 804–816.

Klapuri, A. P. (2004). Automatic music transcription as we know it today. *Journal of New Music Research*, *33*(3), 269–282.

Klapuri, A., & Davy, M. (2006). *Signal Processing Methods for Music Transcription*. New York: Springer.

Knuf, L., Aschersleben, G., & Prinz, W. (2001). An analysis of ideomotor action. *Journal of Experimental Psychology: General*, *130*(4), 779–798.

Kohler, E., Keysers, C., Umilta, M. A., Fogassi, L., Gallese, V., & Rizzolatti, G. (2002). Hearing sounds, understanding actions: Action representation in mirror neurons. *Science*, *297*(5582), 846–848.

Kohonen, T. (1995). *Self-Organizing Maps*. Berlin: Springer.

Kristeva, R., Chakarov, V., Schulte-Monting, E., & Spreer, J. (2003). Activation of cortical areas in music execution and imagining: A high-resolution EEG study. *Neuroimage*, *20*(3), 1872–1883.

Krumhansl, C. L. (1990). *Cognitive Foundations of Musical Pitch*. New York: Oxford University Press.

Krumhansl, C. L., & Kessler, E. J. (1982). Tracing the dynamic changes in perceived tonal organization in a spatial representation of musical keys. *Psychological Review*, *89*(4), 334–368.

Krumhansl, C. L., & Schenk, D. L. (1997). Can dancers reflect the structural and expressive qualities of music? A perceptual experiment on Balanchine's choreography of Mozart's Divertimento No. 15. *Musicae Scientiae*, *1*, 63–85.

Kuhl, P. K., & Meltzoff, A. N. (1996). Infant vocalizations in response to speech: Vocal imitation and developmental change. *Journal of the Acoustical Society of America*, *100*(4), 2425–2438.

Kurth, E. (1913/1973). *Die Voraussetzungen der theoretischen Harmonik und der tonalen Darstellungssysteme*. Munich: Musikverlag Emil Katzbichler.

Kusek, D., & Leonhard, G. (2005). *The Future of Music: Manifesto for the Digital Music Revolution*, S. G. Lindsay (Ed.). Boston: Berklee Press.

Laban, R., & Lawrence, F. C. (1947). *Effort*. London: Macdonald & Evans.

Lacourse, E., Claes, M., & Villeneuve, M. (2001). Heavy metal music and adolescent suicidal risk. *Journal of Youth and Adolescence*, *30*(3), 321–332.

Lakin, J. L., Jefferis, V. E., Cheng, C. M., & Chartrand, T. L. (2003). The chameleon effect as social glue: Evidence for the evolutionary significance of nonconscious mimicry. *Journal of Nonverbal Behavior*, *27*(3), 145–162.

Langheim, F. J. P., Callicott, J. H., Mattay, V. S., Duyn, J. H., & Weinberger, D. R. (2002). Cortical systems associated with covert music rehearsal. *Neuroimage*, *16*(4), 901–908.

Langner, G. (1997). Temporal processing of pitch in the auditory system. *Journal of New Music Research*, 26(2), 116–132.

Langner, G., Albert, M., & Briede, T. (2002). Temporal and spatial coding of periodicity information in the inferior colliculus of awake chinchilla (*Chinchilla laniger*). *Hearing Research*, 168(1–2), 110–130.

Laske, O. E. (1975). *Introduction to a Generative Theory of Music*. Utrecht: Utrecht State University, Institute of Sonology.

Lehr, A. (1971). *Van paardebel tot speelklok: De geschiedenis van de klokgietkunst in de Lage Landen*. Zaltbommel, The Netherlands: Europese Bibliotheek.

Lehr, A. (2000a). *Geschiedenis van wetenschappelijk onderzoek in de campanologie*. Asten, The Netherlands: Nationaal Beiaardmuseum.

Lehr, A. (2000b). *Het vormen en gieten van klokken in het verleden*. Asten, The Netherlands: Nationaal Beiaardmuseum.

Leman, M. (1989). Symbolic and subsymbolic information processing in models of musical communication and cognition. *Interface—Journal of New Music Research*, *18*, 141–160.

Leman, M. (1990). Emergent properties of tonality functions by self-organization. *Interface—Journal of New Music Research*, *19*, 85–106.

Leman, M. (1991). The ontogenesis of tonal semantics: Results of a computer study. In P. M. Todd & D. G. Loy (Eds.), *Music and Connectionism*. Cambridge, MA: MIT Press.

Leman, M. (1994). Schema-based tone center recognition of musical signals. *Journal of New Music Research*, 23(2), 169–204.

Leman, M. (1995). *Music and Schema Theory: Cognitive Foundations of Systematic Musicology*. Berlin: Springer.

Leman, M. (1999). Naturalistic approaches to musical semiotics and the study of causal musical signification. In I. Zannos (Ed.), *Music and Signs: Semiotic and Cognitive Studies in Music* (pp. 11–38). Bratislava: ASKO Art & Science.

Leman, M. (2000). An auditory model of the role of short-term memory in probe-tone ratings. *Music Perception*, 17(4), 481–509.

Leman, M. (2003). Foundations of musicology as content processing science. *Journal of Music and Meaning*, 1(1), section 3.

Leman, M. (2005). Musical creativity research. In J. C. Kaufman & J. Baer (Eds.), *Creativity Across Domains: Faces of the Muse* (pp. 103–122). Mahwah, NJ: Lawrence Erlbaum.

Leman, M. (Ed.). (1997). *Music, Gestalt, and Computing: Studies in Cognitive and Systematic Musicology*. Berlin: Springer.

Leman, M., & Camurri, A. (2006). Understanding musical expressiveness using interactive multimedia platforms. *Musicae Scientiae*, special issue on *interdisciplinary musicology*, 209–233.

Leman, M., & Carreras, F. (1997). Schema and gestalt: Testing the hypothesis of psychoneural isomorphism by computer simulation. In M. Leman (Ed.), *Music, Gestalt, and Computing: Studies in Cognitive and Systematic Musicology* (pp. 144–168). Berlin: Springer.

Leman, M., & Schneider, A. (1997). Origin and nature of cognitive and systematic musicology: An introduction. In M. Leman (Ed.), *Music, Gestalt, and Computing: Studies in Cognitive and Systematic Musicology* (pp. 13–29). Berlin: Springer.

Leman, M., Desmet, F., Styns, F., van Noorden, L., & Moelants, D. (submitted). Music perception is rooted in action—an experiment on embodied listening and corporeal empathy with music.

Leman, M., Vermeulen, V., De Voogdt, L., Camurri, A., Mazzarino, B., & Volpe, G. (2003). Relationships between musical audio, perceived qualities and motoric responses: A pilot study. In R. Bresin (Ed.), *Proceedings of the Stockholm Music Acoustics Conference, August 6–9, 2003 (SMAC03)* (pp. 631–633). Stockholm: Royal Institute of Technology (KTH).

Leman, M., Vermeulen, V., De Voogdt, L., & Moelants, D. (2004). Using audio features to model the affective response to music. In S. Adachi (Ed.), *Planting the grains and harvesting the ears—Proceedings of the International Symposium on Musical Acoustics 2004, Nara, Japan* (pp. 74–77). Kyoto: Musical Acoustics Research Group, The Acoustical Society of Japan.

Leman, M., Vermeulen, V., De Voogdt, L., Moelants, D., & Lesaffre, M. (2005). Prediction of musical affect using a combination of acoustic structural cues. *Journal of New Music Research*, 34(1), 39–67.

Leman, M., Vermeulen, V., De Voogdt, L., Taelman, J., Moelants, D., & Lesaffre, M. (2004). Correlation of gestural musical audio cues and perceived expressive qualities. In A. Camurri & G. Volpe (Eds.), *Gesture-Based Communication in Human–Computer Interaction. Selected Revised Papers of the 5th International Gesture Workshop (GW2003)*. Berlin: Springer.

Lerdahl, F. (2001). *Tonal Pitch Space*. New York: Oxford University Press.

Lesaffre, M. (2005). Music information retrieval: Conceptual framework, annotation, and user behavior. Ph.D. thesis, Ghent University.

Lesaffre, M., Leman, M., Martens, J.-P., & De Baets, B. (2004). Methodological considerations concerning manual annotation of musical audio in function of algorithm development. In X. Serra & M. Leman (Eds.), *Proceedings of the 5th International Conference on Music Information Retrieval (ISMIR04)*. Barcelona: Universitat Pompeu Fabra.

Lesaffre, M., Leman, M., Tanghe, K., De Baets, B., De Meyer, H., & Martens, J.-P. (2003). User-dependent taxonomy of musical features as a conceptual framework for musical audio-mining technology. In R. Bresin (Ed.), *Stockholm Music Acoustics Conference (SMAC 03)*. Stockholm: KTH.

Lesaffre, M., Moelants, D., & Leman, M. (2004). Spontaneous user behavior in vocal queries for audio-mining. In W. B. Hewlett & E. Selfridge-Field (Eds.), *Music Query: Methods, Models, and User Studies* (pp. 129–146). Cambridge, MA: MIT Press.

Leslie, K. R., Johnson-Frey, S. H., & Grafton, S. T. (2004). Functional imaging of face and hand imitation: Towards a motor theory of empathy. *Neuroimage*, *21*(2), 601–607.

Levitin, D. J., & Cook, P. R. (1996). Memory for musical tempo: Additional evidence that auditory memory is absolute. *Perception & Psychophysics*, *58*(6), 927–935.

Li, H. & Leman, M. (submitted). A gesture-based typology of sliding-tones in *guqin* music.

Liberman, A. M., & Mattingly, I. G. (1985). The motor theory of speech-perception revised. *Cognition*, *21*(1), 1–36.

Liberman, A. M., & Mattingly, I. G. (1989). A specialization for speech-perception. *Science*, *243*(4890), 489–494.

Lindsay, A. (Ed.). (2006). *Audio Mosaicing*, special issue of *Journal of New Music Research*. Abingdon, UK: Taylor & Francis.

Lindsay, P. H., & Norman, D. A. (1977). *Human Information Processing: An Introduction to Psychology* (2nd ed.). New York: Academic Press.

Lipps, T. (1903). *Ästhetik: Psychologie des Schönen und der Kunst*. Hamburg: L. Voss.

Lombard, M., & Ditton, T. (1997). At the heart of it all: The concept of presence. *Journal of Computer-Mediated Communication*, *3*(2).

Longuet-Higgins, H. C. (1987). *Mental Processes: Studies in Cognitive Science*. Cambridge, MA: MIT Press.

Lotze, M., Scheler, G., Tan, H. R. M., Braun, C., & Birbaumer, N. (2003). The musician's brain: Functional imaging of amateurs and professionals during performance and imagery. *Neuroimage*, *20*(3), 1817–1829.

Lowis, M. J. (2002). Music as a trigger for peak experiences among a college staff population. *Creativity Research Journal*, *14*(3–4), 351–359.

Loy, G. (1991). Composing with computers: A survey of some compositional formalisms and music programming languages. In M. V. Mathews & J. R. Pierce (Eds.), *Current Directions in Computer Music Research*. Cambridge, MA: MIT Press.

Loy, G. (2006). *Musimathics. The Mathematical Foundations of Music*. Cambridge, MA: MIT Press.

Machover, T., & Chung, J. (1989). Hyperinstruments: Musically intelligent/interactive performance and creativity systems. In T. Wells & D. Butler (Eds.),

*Proceedings of the 1989 International Computer Music Conference.* San Francisco: Computer Music Association.

Maguire, E. R., & Snipes, J. B. (1994). Reassessing the link between country-music and suicide. *Social Forces, 72*(4), 1239–1243.

Mancini, M., Bresin, R., & Pelachaud, C. (2006). From acoustic cues to an expressive agent. *Gesture in Human–Computer Interaction and Simulation, 3881,* 280–291.

Marr, D. (1982). *Vision: A Computational Investigation into the Human Representation and Processing of Visual Information.* San Francisco: W. H. Freeman.

Martens, G., De Meyer, H., De Baets, B., Leman, M., Lesaffre, M., & Martens, J.-P. (2005). Tree-based versus distance-based key recognition in musical audio. *Soft Computing, 9*(8), 565–574.

Mathews, M. (1969). *The Technology of Computer Music.* Cambridge, MA: MIT Press.

Mathews, M., Pierce, J., & Guttman, N. (1962). Musical sounds from digital computers. *Gravesaver Blätter, 6*(23/24), 119–125.

Mathews, M., Pierce, R., Reeves, A., & Roberts, L. (1988). Theoretical and experimental explorations of the Bohlen-Pierce scale. *Journal of the Acoustical Society of America, 84*(4), 1214–1222.

Mattheson, J. (1739). *Der volkommene Capellmeister.* Hamburg: Verlegts Christian Herold.

Maturana, H. R., & Varela, F. J. (1980). *Autopoiesis and Cognition: The Realization of the Living.* Dordrecht: Reidel.

Maturana, H. R., & Varela, F. J. (1987). *The Tree of Knowledge: The Biological Roots of Human Understanding.* Boston: New Science Library.

Mauss, M. (1936). Les Techniques du corps. *Journal de psychologie, 32*(3–4), 271–293.

McLachlan, N., & Nigjeh, B. K. (2003). The design of bells with harmonic overtones. *Journal of the Acoustical Society of America, 114*(1), 505–511.

Meltzoff, A. N. (2002a). Elements of a developmental theory of imitation. In A. N. Meltzoff & W. Prinz (Eds.), *The Imitative Mind: Development, Evolution, and Brain Bases* (pp. 19–41). Cambridge: Cambridge University Press.

Meltzoff, A. N. (2002b). Imitation as a mechanism of social cognition: Origins of empathy, theory of mind, and the representation of action. In U. Goswami (Ed.), *Blackwell Handbook of Childhood Cognitive Development* (pp. 6–25). Oxford: Blackwell.

Meltzoff, A. N., & Decety, J. (2003). What imitation tells us about social cognition: A rapprochement between developmental psychology and cognitive neuroscience. *Philosophical Transactions of the Royal Society of London, B358*(1431), 491–500.

Meltzoff, A. N., & Moore, M. K. (1997a). Explaining facial imitation: A theoretical model. *Early Development & Parenting*, *6*(3–4), 179–192.

Meltzoff, A. N., & Moore, M. K. (1977b). Imitation of facial and manual gestures by human neonates. *Science*, *198*(4312), 75–78.

Meltzoff, A. N., & Prinz, W. (Eds.). (2002). *The Imitative Mind: Development, Evolution, and Brain Bases*. Cambridge: Cambridge University Press.

Meredith, D., Lemstrom, K., & Wiggins, G. A. (2002). Algorithms for discovering repeated patterns in multidimensional representations of polyphonic music. *Journal of New Music Research*, *31*(4), 321–345.

Meredith, M. A. (2002). On the neuronal basis for multisensory convergence: A brief overview. *Cognitive Brain Research*, *14*(1), 31–40.

Merleau-Ponty, M. (1945). *Phénoménologie de la perception*. Paris: Gallimard.

Merriam, A. P. (1964). *The Anthropology of Music*. Evanston, IL: Northwestern University Press.

Metzinger, T. (2003). *Being No One: The Self-Model Theory of Subjectivity*. Cambridge, MA: MIT Press.

Metzinger, T., & Gallese, V. (2003). The emergence of a shared action ontology: Building blocks for a theory. *Consciousness and Cognition*, *12*(4), 549–571.

Meyer, L. B. (1956). *Emotion and Meaning in Music*. Chicago: University of Chicago Press.

Michon, J. A. (1967). *Timing in Temporal Tracking*. Soesterberg, The Netherlands: Institute for Perception RVO-TNO.

Mitchell, R. W. (2002). Imitation as a perceptual process. In K. Dautenhahn & C. L. Nehaniv (Eds.), *Imitation in Animals and Artifacts* (pp. 441–469). Cambridge, MA: MIT Press.

Mitchell, R. W., & Gallaher, M. C. (2001). Embodying music: Matching music and dance in memory. *Music Perception*, *19*(1), 65–85.

Moelants, D., Styns, F. & Leman, M. (2006). Pitch and tempo precision in the reproduction of familiar songs. In *Proceedings of the tenth International Conference on Music Perception and Cognition*, Bologna.

Moles, A. (1952). *Physique et technique du bruit*. Paris: Dunod.

Moles, A. (1958). *Théorie de l'information et perception esthétique*. Paris: Flammarion.

Monelle, R. (2000). *The Sense of Music: Semiotic Essays*. Princeton, NJ: Princeton University Press.

Müllensiefen, D., & Frieler, K. (2004). Cognitive adequacy in the measurement of melodic similarity: Algorithmic versus human judgments. In W. B. Hewlett & E. Selfridge-Field (Eds.), *Music Query: Methods, Models, and User Studies* (pp. 147–176). Cambridge, MA: MIT Press.

Neda, Z., Ravasz, E., Vicsek, T., Brechet, Y., & Barabasi, A. L. (2000). Physics of the rhythmic applause. *Physical Review*, E61(6), 6987–6992.

Nettheim, N. (1996). How musical rhythm reveals human attitudes: Gustav Becking's theory. *International Review of the Aesthetics and Sociology of Music*, 27(2), 101–122.

Neuhoff, J. G. (Ed.). (2004). *Ecological Psychoacoustics*. Amsterdam: Elsevier Academic Press.

Ng, K. C. (2004). Music via motion: Transdomain mapping of motion and sound for interactive performances. *Proceedings of the IEEE*, 92(4), 645–655.

Niedenthal, P. M., Barsalou, L. W., Winkielman, P., Krauth-Gruber, S., & Ric, F. (2005). Embodiment in attitudes, social perception, and emotion. *Personality and Social Psychology Review*, 9(3), 184–211.

Nielzén, S., & Cesarec, Z. (1982). Emotional experience of music as a function of musical structure. *Psychology of Music*, 10, 7–17.

North, A. C., Hargreaves, D. J., & Hargreaves, J. J. (2004). Uses of music in everyday life. *Music Perception*, 22(1), 41–77.

Oberholzer, F., & Strumpf, K. (2004). *The Effect of File Sharing on Record Sales: An Empirical Analysis*. http://www.unc.edu/~cigar/papers/FileSharing_March2004.pdf.

Pachet, F. (2003). The continuator: Musical interaction with style. *Journal of New Music Research*, 32(3), 333–341.

Packer, R., & Jordan, K. (2001). *Multimedia: From Wagner to Virtual Reality*. New York: Norton.

Palmer, C. (1997). Music performance. *Annual Review of Psychology*, 48, 115–138.

Pampalk, E., Dixon, S., & Widmer, G. (2004). Exploring music collections by browsing different views. *Computer Music Journal*, 28(2), 49–62.

Panksepp, J., & Bernatzky, G. (2002). Emotional sounds and the brain: The neuroaffective foundations of musical appreciation. *Behavioural Processes*, 60(2), 133–155.

Pantev, C., Engelien, A., Candia, V., & Elbert, T. (2001). Representational cortex in musicians: Plastic alterations in response to musical practice. *Biological Foundations of Music*, 930, 300–314.

Paradiso, J. A. (1999). The brain opera technology: New instruments and gestural sensors for musical interaction and performance. *Journal of New Music Research*, 28(2), 130–149.

Paradiso, J. A., & O'Modhrain, S. (Eds.). (2003). *New Interfaces for Musical Performance and Interaction*, special issue of *Journal of New Music Research*, 32. Lisse, The Netherlands: Swets & Zeitlinger.

Parncutt, R. (1994). A perceptual model of pulse salience and metrical accent in musical rhythms. *Music Perception, 11*(4), 409–464.

Patton, P., Boussaid-Belkacem, K., & Anastasio, T. J. (2002). Multimodality in the superior colliculus: An information theoretic analysis. *Cognitive Brain Research, 14*(1), 10–19.

Pauws, S. (2002). CubyHum: A fully operational query by humming system. In M. Fingerhut (Ed.), *International Conference on Music Information Retrieval (ISMIR02)*. Paris: IRCAM.

Pepperberg, I. M. (2002). Allospecific referential speech acquisition in grey parrots (*Psittacus erithacus*): Evidence for multiple levels of avian vocal imitation. In K. Dautenhahn & C. L. Nehaniv (Eds.), *Imitation in Animals and Artifacts* (pp. 109–131). Cambridge, MA: MIT Press.

Pollick, F. E. (2004). The features people use to recognize human movement style. In A. Camurri & G. Volpe (Eds.), *Gesture-Based Communication in Human–Computer Interaction* (pp. 10–19). Berlin: Springer.

Pollick, F. E., Paterson, H. M., Bruderlin, A., & Sanford, A. J. (2001). Perceiving affect from arm movement. *Cognition, 82*(2), B51–B61.

Pressing, J. (1992). *Synthesizer Performance and Real-Time Techniques*. Madison, WI: A-R Editions.

Prinz, W. (2002). Experimental approaches to imitation. In A. N. Meltzoff & W. Prinz (Eds.), *The Imitative Mind: Development, Evolution, and Brain Bases* (pp. 143–162). Cambridge: Cambridge University Press.

Prinz, W., & Hommel, B. (2002). *Common Mechanisms in Perception and Action*. Oxford: Oxford University Press.

Purves, D., & Lotto, R. B. (2003). *Why We See What We Do: An Empirical Theory of Vision*. Sunderland, MA.: Sinauer.

Rameau, J.-P. (1722/1965). *Traité de l'harmonie*. New York: Broude Brothers.

Reinecke, H.-P. (1964). *Experimentelle Beiträge zur Psychologie des musikalischen Hörens*. Hamburg: H. Sikorski.

Repp, B. H. (1993). Music as motion: A synopsis of Alexander Truslit's (1938) *Gestaltung und Bewegung in der Musik*. *Psychology of Music, 12*(1), 48–72.

Repp, B. H. (1998). Obligatory "expectations" of expressive timing induced by perception of musical structure. *Psychological Research-Psychologische Forschung, 61*(1), 33–43.

Repp, B. H., & Knoblich, G. (2004). Perceiving action identity: How pianists recognize their own performances. *Psychological Science, 15*(9), 604–609.

Repp, B. H., & Penel, A. (2004). Rhythmic movement is attracted more strongly to auditory than to visual rhythms. *Psychological Research-Psychologische Forschung, 68*(4), 252–270.

Reuter, C. (1997). Karl Erich Schumann's principles of timbre as a helpful tool in stream segregation research. In M. Leman (Ed.), *Music, Gestalt, and Computing: Studies in Cognitive and Systematic Musicology* (pp. 362–374). Berlin: Springer.

Révész, G. (1944). *Inleiding tot de muziekpsychologie*. Amsterdam: N.V. Noord-Hollandsche Uitgevers Maatschappij.

Reybrouck, M. (2001). Musical imagery between sensory processing and ideo-motor simulation. In R. I. Godøy & H. Jørgensen (Eds.), *Musical Imagery* (pp. 117–135). Lisse, The Netherlands: Swets & Zeitlinger.

Rickard, N. (2004). Intense emotional responses to music: A test of the physiological arousal hypothesis. *Psychology of Music, 32*(4), 371–388.

Rigg, M. G. (1939). What features of a musical phrase have emotional suggestiveness? *Publications of the Social Science Research Council of the Oklahoma Agricultural and Mechanical College, 1*, 1–38.

Risset, J.-C. (1966). Computer study of trumpet tones. Murray Hill, NJ: Bell Laboratories.

Rizzolatti, G., & Arbib, M. A. (1998). Language within our grasp. *Trends in Neurosciences, 21*(5), 188–194.

Rizzolatti, G., Fadiga, L., Fogassi, L., & Gallese, V. (2002). From mirror neurons to imitation: Facts and speculations. In A. N. Meltzoff & W. Prinz (Eds.), *The Imitative Mind: Development, Evolution, and Brain Bases* (pp. 247–266). Cambridge: Cambridge University Press.

Rizzolatti, G., Fadiga, L., Gallese, V., & Fogassi, L. (1996). Premotor cortex and the recognition of motor actions. *Cognitive Brain Research, 3*(2), 131–141.

Rocchesso, D., & Fontana, F. (Eds.). (2003). *The Sounding Object*. Florence: Mondo Estremo.

Rogers, S. J., Hepburn, S. L., Stackhouse, T., & Wehner, E. (2003). Imitation performance in toddlers with autism and those with other developmental disorders. *Journal of Child Psychology and Psychiatry and Allied Disciplines, 44*(5), 763–781.

Rosenblum, L. (2004). Perceiving articulatory events: Lessons for an ecological psychoacoustics. In J. G. Neuhoff (Ed.), *Ecological Psychoacoustics* (pp. 219–248). Amsterdam: Elsevier Academic Press.

Rovan, J., & Hayward, V. (2000). Typology of tactile sounds and their synthesis in gesture-driven computer music performance. In M. Wanderley & M. Battier (Eds.), *Trends in Gestural Control of Music*. Paris: IRCAM.

Rowe, R. (1993). *Interactive Music Systems: Machine Listening and Composing*. Cambridge, MA: MIT Press.

Rumelhart, D. E., & McClelland, J. L. (1986). *Parallel Distributed Processing: Explorations in the Microstructure of Cognition*, 2 vols. Cambridge, MA: MIT press.

Rustad, R. A., Small, J. E., Jobes, D. A., Safer, M. A., & Peterson, R. J. (2003). The impact of rock videos and music with suicidal content on thoughts and attitudes about suicide. *Suicide and Life-Threatening Behavior*, *33*(2), 120–131.

Sabbe, H. (1987a). A logic of coherence and an aesthetic of contingency: European versus American "open structure" music. *Interface—Journal of New Music Research*, *16*(3), 177–186.

Sabbe, H. (Ed.). (1987b). *Open Structure in 20th Century Music*, special issue of *Interface—Journal of New Music Research*, *16*. Lisse, The Netherlands: Swets & Zeitlinger.

Sabbe, H. (1998). *La musique et l'Occident, démocratie et capitalisme (post)industriel: Incidences sur l'investissement esthétique et economique en musique*. Brussels: Mardaga.

Sabbe, H., Apostel, L., & F. Vandamme (Eds.). (1986). *Reason, Emotion and Music: Towards a Common Structure for Arts, Sciences and Philosophies, Based on a Conceptual Framework for the Description of Music*. Ghent: Communication & Cognition.

Salavuo, M. (2006). Open and informal online communities as forums of collaborative musical activities and learning. *British Journal of Music Education*, *23*(3), 253–271.

Schaeffer, P. (1966). *Traité des objets musicaux: Essai interdisciplines*. Paris: Seuil.

Scheel, K. R., & Westefeld, J. S. (1999). Heavy metal music and adolescent suicidality: An empirical investigation. *Adolescence*, *34*(134), 253–273.

Scherer, K. (1978). Personality inference from voice quality: The loud voice of extroversion. *European Journal of Social Psychology*(8), 467–487.

Scherer, K. R., & Zentner, M. R. (2001). The emotional effects of music: Production rules. In P. N. Juslin & J. A. Sloboda (Eds.), *Music and Emotion: Theory and Research* (pp. 361–392). New York: Oxford University Press.

Schlaug, G. (2001). The brain of musicians: A model for functional and structural adaptation. *Biological Foundations of Music*, *930*, 281–299.

Schmidt, L. A., & Trainor, L. J. (2001). Frontal brain electrical activity (EEG) distinguishes valence and intensity of musical emotions. *Cognition & Emotion*, *15*(4), 487–500.

Schneider, A. (1997). *Tonhöhe, skala, klang: Akustische, tonometrische und psychoakustische Studien auf vergleichender Grundlage*. Bonn: Orpheus.

Schoofs, A., Vanasperen, F., Maas, P., & Lehr, A. (1987). A carillon of major-3rd bells: Computation of bell profiles using structural optimization. *Music Perception*, *4*(3), 245–254.

Schwartz, D. A., Howe, C. Q., & Purves, D. (2003). The statistical structure of human speech sounds predicts musical universals. *Journal of Neuroscience*, *23*(18), 7160–7168.

Scruton, R. (1997). *The Aesthetics of Music*. Oxford: Clarendon Press.

Searle, J. R. (1969). *Speech Acts: An Essay in the Philosophy of Language*. London: Cambridge University Press.

Seashore, C. E. (1938). *Psychology of Music*. New York: McGraw-Hill.

Sethares, W. A. (1994). Adaptive tunings for musical scales. *Journal of the Acoustical Society of America*, 96(1), 10–18.

Sethares, W. A. (1998). *Tuning, Timbre, Spectrum, Scale*. New York: Springer.

Sethares, W. A. (2002). Real-time adaptive tunings using Max. *Journal of New Music Research*, 31(4), 347–355.

Shannon, C. E., & Weaver, W. (1949). *The Mathematical Theory of Communication*. Urbana: University of Illinois Press.

Sheridan, T. B. (2004). Musings on music making and listening: Supervisory control and virtual reality. *Proceedings of the IEEE*, 92(4), 601–605.

Singer, T., Seymour, B., O'Doherty, J., Kaube, H., Dolan, R. J., & Frith, C. D. (2004). Empathy for pain involves the affective but not sensory components of pain. *Science*, 303(5661), 1157–1162.

Singer, W. (2001). Consciousness and the binding problem. *Annals of the New York Academy of Sciences*, 929(1), 123–146.

Singer, W. (2002). *Der Beobachter im Gehirn*. Frankfurt am Main: Suhrkamp.

Smith, J. O. (2004). Virtual acoustic musical instruments: Review and update. *Journal of New Music Research*, 33(3), 283–304.

Stack, S. (2000). Blues fans and suicide acceptability. *Death Studies*, 24(3), 223–231.

Stefani, G. (Ed.). (1975). *Actes du 1er Congrès Internationale de Sémiotique Musicale, Beograd, 17–21 oct. 1973*. Pesaro: Centro di Iniziativa Culturale.

Stradling, R. (2002). Musical healing in cultural contexts. *Social History of Medicine*, 15(2), 341–342.

Striano, T., & Tomasello, M. (2001). Infant development: Physical and social cognition. In N. J. Smelser & P. B. Baltes (Eds.), *International Encyclopedia of the Social and Behavioral Sciences*. Amsterdam: Elsevier.

Stumpf, C. (1883–1890). *Tonpsychologie*, 2 vols. Leipzig: Hirzel.

Styns, F., van Noorden, L., Moelants, D., & Leman, M. (in press). Walking on music. *Human Movement Science*.

Sundberg, J. (Ed.). (2000). *Music and Motion*, special issue of *Journal of New Music Research*, vol. 29. Lisse, The Netherlands: Swets & Zeitlinger.

Sundberg, J. (Ed.). (2003). *Research in Music Performance*, special issue of *Journal of New Music Research*, vol. 32. Lisse, The Netherlands: Swets & Zeitlinger.

Sundberg, J., Friberg, A., & Bresin, R. (2003). Attempts to reproduce a pianist's expressive timing with director musices performance rules. *Journal of New Music Research*, 32(3), 317–325.

Tanghe, K., Lesaffre, M., Degroeve, S., Leman, M., De Baets, B., & Martens, J.-P. (2005). Collecting ground truth annotations for drum detection in polyphonic music. In J. D. Reiss & G. A. Wiggins (Eds.), *Proceedings of the Sixth International Conference on Music Information Retrieval (ISMIR05)*. London: Queen Mary, University of London.

Tanghe, K., Degroeve, S., & De Baets, B. (2005). An algorithm for detecting and labeling drum events in polyphonic music. In *Proceedings of the first Music Information Retrieval Evaluation eXchange* (MIREX). London, Queen Mary University London.

Tarabella, L., & Bertini, G. (2004). About the role of mapping in gesture-controlled live computer music. In U. Kock Will (Ed.), *Computer Music Modeling and Retrieval* (pp. 217–224). Berlin: Springer.

Tarasti, E. (1997). The emancipation of the sign: On the corporeal and gestural meanings in music. *Applied Semiotics/Sémiotique Appliquée*, 2(4), 15–26.

Tarasti, E. (2002). *Signs of Music: A Guide to Musical Semiotics*. Berlin: Mouton de Gruyter.

Tarasti, E. (Ed.). (2003). *Musical Semiotics Revisited*. Imatra: International Semiotics Institute.

Terhardt, E. (1984). The concept of musical consonance, a link between music and psychoacoustics. *Music Perception*, 1(3), 276–295.

Thaut, M. H. (2005). *Rhythm, Music, and the Brain: Scientific Foundations and Clinical Applications*. New York: Routledge.

Theraulaz, G., & Spitz, F. (Eds.). (1997). *Auto-organisation et comportement*. Paris: Hermès.

Todd, N. P. M. (1995). The kinematics of musical expression. *Journal of the Acoustical Society of America*, 97(3), 1940–1949.

Todd, N. P. M., & Cody, F. W. (2000). Vestibular responses to loud dance music: A physiological basis of the "rock and roll threshold"? *Journal of the Acoustical Society of America*, 107(1), 496–500.

Todd, N. P. M., Lee, C. S., & O'Boyle, D. J. (2002). A sensorimotor theory of temporal tracking and beat induction. *Psychological Research-Psychologische Forschung*, 66(1), 26–39.

Todd, N. P. M., O'Boyle, D. J., & Lee, C. S. (1999). A sensory-motor theory of rhythm, time perception and beat induction. *Journal of New Music Research*, 28(1), 5–28.

Todd, P. M., & Loy, D. G. (Eds.). (1991). *Music and Connectionism*. Cambridge, MA: MIT Press.

Toiviainen, P., & Krumhansl, C. L. (2003). Measuring and modeling real-time responses to music: The dynamics of tonality induction. *Perception*, *32*(6), 741–766.

Tomasello, M. (1999). *The Cultural Origins of Human Cognition*. Cambridge, MA.: Harvard University Press.

Trevarthen, C. (2004). *Learning About Ourselves from Children: Why a Growing Human Brain Needs Interesting Companions*. http://www.perception-in-action.ed.ac.uk/PDF_s/Colwyn2004.pdf.

Trevarthen, C., Kokkinaki, T., & Fiamenghi, G. A., Jr. (1999). What infants' imitations communicate: With mothers, with fathers, and with peers. In J. Nadel & G. Butterworth (Eds.), *Imitation in Infancy* (pp. 127–185). Cambridge: Cambridge University Press.

Troje, N. F., Westhoff, C., & Lavrov, M. (2005). Person identification from biological motion: Effects of structural and kinematic cues. *Perception & Psychophysics*, *67*(4), 667–675.

Truslit, A. (1938). *Gestaltung und Bewegung in der Musik*. Berlin-Lichterfelde: C. F. Vieweg.

Tzanetakis, G., & Cook, P. (2001). MARSYAS3D: A prototype audio browser-editor using a large scale immersive visual audio display. In J. Hiipakka et al. (Eds.), *Proceedings of the Seventh International Conference on Auditory Display*. Helsinki: Laboratory of Acoustics and Audio Signal Processing and the Telecommunications Software and Multimedia Laboratory. Helsinki University of Technology.

Tzanetakis, G., & Cook, P. (2002). Musical genre classification of audio signals. *IEEE Transactions on Speech and Audio Processing*, *10*(5), 293–302.

Ungvary, T., & Vertegaal, R. (2000). Designing musical cyberinstruments with body and soul in mind. *Journal of New Music Research*, *29*(3), 245–255.

Välimäki, S. (2003). Some reflections on the postmodern project in musicology and its semiotic essence. In E. Tarasti (Ed.), *Musical Semiotics Revisited* (pp. 147–158). Imatra: International Semiotics Institute.

van den Bos, E., & Jeannerod, M. (2002). Sense of body and sense of action both contribute to self-recognition. *Cognition*, *85*(2), 177–187.

van Gulik, R., Vignoli, F., & van de Wetering, H. (2004). Mapping music in the palm of your hand, explore and discover your collection. In X. Serra & M. Leman (Eds.), *Proceedings of the 5th International Conference on Music Information Retrieval (ISMIR04)*. Barcelona: Universitat Pompeu Fabra.

van Noorden, L., & Moelants, D. (1999). Resonance in the perception of musical pulse. *Journal of New Music Research*, *28*(1), 43–66.

Varela, F. J., Thompson, E., & Rosch, E. (1991). *The Embodied Mind: Cognitive Science and Human Experience*. Cambridge, MA: MIT Press.

Veitl, A. (1997). *Politiques de la musique contemporaine: Le compositeur, la "recherche musicale" et l'état en France de 1958 à 1991*. Paris: L'Harmattan.

Vicente, K. J. (2003). Beyond the lens model and direct perception: Toward a broader ecological psychology. *Ecological Psychology, 15*(3), 241–267.

Visalberghi, E., & Fragaszy, D. (2002). "Do monkeys ape?": Ten years after. In K. Dautenhahn & C. L. Nehaniv (Eds.), *Imitation in Animals and Artifacts* (pp. 471–499). Cambridge, MA: MIT Press.

von Helmholtz, H. L. F. (1863/1968). *Die Lehre von den Tonempfindungen als physiologische Grundlage für die Theorie der Musik* (7th ed.). Hildesheim: Olms.

von Uexküll, J. (1909). *Umwelt und Innenwelt der Tiere*. Berlin: Springer.

Wanderley, M., & Battier, M. (Eds.). (2000). *Trends in Gestural Control of Music*. Paris: IRCAM, Centre Pompidou.

Wanderley, M. M., & Depalle, P. (2004). Gestural control of sound synthesis. *Proceedings of the IEEE, 92*(4), 632–644.

Watson, K. B. (1942). The nature and measurement of musical meanings. *Psychological Monographs, 54*, 1–43.

Wedin, L. (1972). Multidimensional study of perceptual-emotional expression in music. *Scandinavian Journal of Psychology, 13*, 241–257.

Wellek, A. (1963). *Musikpsychologie und Musikästhetik: Grundriss der systematischen Musikwissenschaft*. Frankfurt am Main: Akademische Verlagsgesellschaft.

Whitman, B., & Ellis, D. (2004). Automatic record reviews. In X. Serra & M. Leman (Eds.), *Proceedings of the 5th International Conference on Music Information Retrieval (ISMIR-04)* (pp. 470–477). Barcelona: Universitat Pompeu Fabra.

Wicker, B., Keysers, C., Plailly, J., Royet, J. P., Gallese, V., & Rizzolatti, G. (2003). Both of us disgusted in my insula: The common neural basis of seeing and feeling disgust. *Neuron, 40*(3), 655–664.

Widmer, G. (2001). Using AI and machine learning to study expressive music performance: Project survey and first report. *AI Communications, 14*(3), 149–162.

Widmer, G. (2002). Machine discoveries: A few simple, robust local expression principles. *Journal of New Music Research, 31*(1), 37–50.

Widmer, G., & Goebl, W. (2004). Computational models of expressive music performance: The state of the art. *Journal of New Music Research, 33*(3), 203–216.

Widmer, G., & Tobudic, A. (2003). Playing Mozart by analogy: Learning multi-level timing and dynamics strategies. *Journal of New Music Research, 32*(3), 259–268.

Wiering, F., Typke, R., & Veltkamp, R. C. (2004). Transportation distances and their application in music-notation retrieval. In W. B. Hewlett & E. Selfridge-

Field (Eds.), *Music Query, Methods, Models and User Studies* (pp. 113–128). Cambridge, MA.: MIT Press.

Wilson, M., & Knoblich, G. (2005). The case for motor involvement in perceiving conspecifics. *Psychological Bulletin*, *131*(3), 460–473.

Wilson, S. (2003). The effect of music on perceived atmosphere and purchase intentions in a restaurant. *Psychology of Music*, *31*(1), 93–112.

Winckel, F. (1960). *Vues nouvelles sur le monde des sons*. Paris: Dunod.

Winold, H., Thelen, E., & Ulrich, B. D. (1994). Coordination and control in the bow arm movements of highly skilled cellists. *Ecological Psychology*, *6*(1), 1–31.

Wintersgill, P. (1994). Music and melancholia. *Journal of the Royal Society of Medicine*, *87*(12), 764–766.

Xenakis, I. (1963). *Musiques formelles: Nouveaux Principes formels de composition musicale*. Paris: Richard-Masse.

Zangwill, N. (2004). Against emotion: Hanslick was right about music. *British Journal of Aesthetics*, *44*(1), 29–43.

Zanon, P., & De Poli, G. (2003). Estimation of parameters in rule systems for expressive rendering of musical performance. *Computer Music Journal*, *27*(1), 29–46.

# Name Index

# Subject Index